T0322969

Financial Services Advertising:
Law and Regulation

Financial Services Advertising: Law and Regulation

By

Dr Max Barrett,
LL.B., Ph.D., Dip. Arb.,
Dip. Int. Arb., Dip. FSL, Solicitor

Published by
Clarus Press Ltd,
Griffith Campus,
South Circular Road,
Dublin 8.

Typeset by
Datapage International Ltd.,
18 Docklands Innovation Park,
East Wall Road,
Dublin 3.

Printed by
MPG Books Ltd.,
Victoria Square, Bodmin, Cornwall.

ISBN
978-1-905536-17-7

CONTENTS

PREFACE

This book considers the array of law and regulation that makes express provision as to the content of financial advertisements in Ireland.[1] The book also considers the principal voluntary industry code concerned with such advertisements. This law and regulation and voluntary code between them prescribe an abundance of detail that must appear in financial advertisements, as well as making more general provision which impacts on the content of such advertisements.

Given the extent to which the general public is exposed to advertising, one might expect there to be a single statute that would address the difficulties which inappropriate and unregulated advertising presents. Instead there are a number of key laws and regulatory codes that overlap to a greater or lesser extent in the provision they make regarding financial advertisements, namely the Consumer Credit Act, 1995,[2] the Consumer Protection Act 2007,[3] the European Communities (Misleading and Comparative Marketing) Communications Regulations 2007,[4] and the Consumer Protection Code.[5] Testament to the all-pervasive nature of advertising or to the ad hoc manner in which financial advertisements have traditionally been regulated in Ireland, or both, is a further swathe of legislation, from the Betting Act of the early twentieth century to the MiFID legislation of the early twenty-first century, which makes provision that may or may not be of relevance in the context of any one financial advertisement.

One consequence of there being such an abundance of law and regulation on advertising is that there is an abundance of definitions as to what constitutes an advertisement. As a result, when confronted with a measure that makes provision as to an advertisement, it is prudent to determine firstly what that measure means when it refers to an 'advertisement'.

Before proceeding to outline in more detail what this book considers, it is appropriate to mention what it does not consider. As its title suggests, this book is concerned with financial advertisements only. It is not concerned with other forms of advertising or with marketing more generally. It describes, by reference to law, regulation and the principal voluntary industry code what may, must and may not appear in an advertisement for a financial product or service which is to be published or broadcast in Ireland. Though some mention is made, for example, of contract law and the law of torts and the indirect effect which they and other areas or aspects of law may have on the content and substance of financial advertisements, the focus of this

---

[1] The phrase "financial advertisements" is used in this book to refer to advertisements for financial products and/or services, any one such advertisement being referred to as a "financial advertisement".

[2] No 24 of 1995. Unless otherwise indicated, any reference to "Ireland" in this book is a reference to the state of Ireland.

[3] No 19 of 2007.

[4] SI No 774 of 2007.

[5] Financial Regulator, *Consumer Protection Code* (Dublin: 2006).

book is on those laws and other measures which make express provision as to the content and substance thereof.

Chapter 1 of this book considers in detail Parts II and IX of the Consumer Credit Act, 1995. Part II of the Consumer Credit Act is concerned with the advertising and offering of financial accommodation generally. Part IX makes certain provision in respect of advertisements for housing loans. The Consumer Credit Act requires the inclusion of many of the prescribed warnings that are such a familiar feature of financial advertisements. These warnings and other related provision made by the Consumer Credit Act are considered in Chapter 1 along with certain directions on advertising made under section 135(1) of that Act, formerly by the Director of Consumer Affairs and latterly by the Financial Regulator[6].

Chapter 2 considers the Consumer Protection Act 2007. This enactment establishes general parameters within which traders must operate. Part 3 of the Consumer Protection Act prohibits traders from engaging in unfair, misleading, aggressive and prohibited commercial practices. Breach of certain of the provisions of the Consumer Protection Act is a criminal offence. However, the Act also establishes a suite of civil proceedings that can be brought where a trader engages in any commercial practices that are so prohibited and that may prove to be of more practical significance over time.

Chapter 3 considers the European Communities (Misleading and Comparative Marketing) Communications Regulations 2007. The general purpose of these Regulations is to protect traders from misleading marketing communications and prohibited comparative marketing communications. Unlike, for example, the Consumer Credit Act, the principal focus of these Regulations is to protect traders from each other, albeit that this may result in an indirect benefit to consumers generally.

Chapter 4 considers the Consumer Protection Code. As its title suggests, the Code introduces a variety of consumer protection requirements, including numerous requirements concerning financial advertisements. It is the measure responsible for the recent proliferation of the warnings that appear in, or at the end of, financial advertisements. It is, without doubt, the most significant non-legislative measure that impacts upon the advertisement of financial services in Ireland. Breach of the Consumer Protection Code is a 'prescribed contravention' for the purposes of the Central Bank Act, 1942, punishable in the first instance by the Financial Regulator.

Chapter 5 considers Ireland's broadcasting law régime. So much advertising is broadcast on radio and television that any person seeking to publish a financial advertisement must have a knowledge of the broadcasting régime, the provision and

---

[6] The Irish Financial Services Regulatory Authority generally refers to itself, and is referred to in this book, as the 'Financial Regulator'. For an account as to why the Financial Regulator has adopted and uses a shorter name than the full legal name conferred on it by section 33B of the Central Bank Act, 1942 (No 22 of 1942) (as inserted by section 26 of the Central Bank and Financial Services Authority of Ireland Act, 2003 (No 12 of 2003)), see Financial Regulator, *Regulatory Connection* (Dublin: June 2005). In brief, the Financial Regulator considered that its full legal name was proving too unwieldy for everyday usage and was leading to the use of multiple abbreviations and acronyms and consequent confusion. The Financial Regulator therefore determined that it would and should generally be referred to as the 'Financial Regulator', leaving its legal name for use, as and when appropriate, in the legal context.

prohibitions it makes as regards advertising, and the respective rôles of the Broadcasting Commission of Ireland and the Broadcasting Complaints Commission.

Chapters 6 and 7 respectively consider the Broadcasting Commission of Ireland's General Advertising Code[7] and Children's Advertising Code[8]. These Codes establish a wealth of requirements that broadcasters must observe as regards advertising generally and children's advertising particularly.[9] As broadcasters will not intentionally broadcast advertisements that are in breach of these Codes, the Codes effectively add another layer of regulation that advertisers must observe if their advertisements are to be broadcast.

Chapter 8 considers in a summary fashion certain legal measures and aspects of the law that either make express provision as to, or otherwise may impact on, the content and substance of particular financial advertisements.

Chapter 9 considers the Code of Standards for Advertising, Promotional and Direct Marketing in Ireland, as published by the Advertising Standards Authority for Ireland.[10] The Advertising Standards Authority for Ireland was established by the advertising industry as an independent self-regulatory body that seeks to promote the highest standards of advertising, promotional marketing and direct marketing. Unlike the Codes published by the Broadcasting Commission of Ireland, the Code of Standards published by the Advertising Standards Authority is entirely voluntary. However, because all of the principal media outlets in Ireland are members of the Advertising Standards Authority and because they will not deliberately publish or broadcast advertising that breaches the Code of Standards, the requirements of that Code are effectively mandatory for anyone seeking to publish a financial advertisement in an Irish magazine or newspaper or on an Irish radio or television station. The Advertising Standards Authority for Ireland also operates an effective and free-to-use complaints process for consumers aggrieved by particular advertising.

Appendix A contains the consolidated text of the principal provisions of the Consumer Credit Act considered in Chapter 1. Appendix B contains the text of the two directions made to date under s 135(1) of the Consumer Credit Act. Appendices C to F (inclusive) contain check-lists that reduce the Consumer Protection Code and the financial advertisement-related provisions of the Advertising Standards Authority's Code of Standards, the BCI General Advertising Code and the BCI Children's Advertising Code, to a series of questions which, if answered in the affirmative, suggest compliance with the relevant code.

I am grateful to my brother, Dr Gavin Barrett, BL, who first suggested that what was becoming a very long article might usefully be expanded into a book, and who read this book in early draft form and made comments thereon. I am grateful to my

---

[7] Broadcasting Commission of Ireland, *General Advertising Code* (Dublin: 2007).

[8] Broadcasting Commission of Ireland, *Children's Advertising Code* (Dublin: 2005).

[9] Commercial communications that are not governed by the BCI Children's Advertising Code are required to comply with the BCI General Advertising Code (which itself makes certain provision in respect of children). See further: Broadcasting Commission of Ireland, *BCI General Advertising Code Guidance Notes* (Dublin: 2007), 2; and the BCI General Advertising Code, esp. para 3.2.4 thereof.

[10] Advertising Standards Authority for Ireland, *Manual of Advertising Self-Regulation with the Code of Standards for Advertising, Promotional and Direct Marketing in Ireland*, 6th edition, (Dublin: 2007).

parents, Michael and Della Barrett, for their customary support, to my brother, Conor Barrett, for his constant encouragement, to my children, Athena, Petros and Mikhalis for rightly insisting that their father stop working on Sunday afternoons and bring them off instead for walks in Powerscourt Gardens, and to my wife, Agapi, to whom this book is dedicated. The responsibility for any errors contained herein is entirely my own. While it is hoped that this book will be of assistance to persons seeking to publish financial advertisements that are in compliance with the law, regulation and codes considered herein, this book is not a substitute for legal advice which should be sought in relation to any particular issue arising. This book states the law accurately as it stood up to 17 March 2008 although the reader should note that it has been possible to include several legal developments which occurred after this date but before the book went to press.

Dr Max Barrett
Dublin, Saint Patrick's Day 2008

TABLE OF LEGISLATION

Table of Legislation

EUROPEAN DIRECTIVES

IRISH STATUTORY INSTRUMENTS

Table of Legislation

IRISH CODES OF REGULATION

TABLE OF CASES

TABLE OF CASES OF THE ADVERTISING STANDARDS AUTHORITY FOR IRELAND

TABLE OF DECISIONS OF THE
BROADCASTING COMPLAINTS COMMISSION

TABLE OF WARNINGS

Table of Warnings

PART 1
LAW AND REGULATION

Chapter 1

THE CONSUMER CREDIT ACT, 1995[1]

Introduction

Part II of the Consumer Credit Act, 1995 is concerned with the advertising and offering of financial accommodation. Part IX of that Act, which is concerned with housing loans made by mortgage lenders, makes certain incidental provision in respect of advertisements for housing loans amongst other matters. Both Parts, insofar as relevant to the subject-matter of this book, are considered below.[2] Any person minded

[1–01]

---

[1] No 24 of 1995. The Consumer Credit Act has been amended on a number of occasions since its enactment. For ease of reference, a consolidated version of the provisions considered in this Chapter is set out in Appendix A to this book.

[2] The Consumer Credit Act applies generally, unless otherwise provided, to all credit agreements, hire-purchase agreements and consumer-hire agreements to which a consumer is party. (Consumer Credit Act, s 3(1). The meaning of the terms "credit agreement", "hire-purchase agreement", "consumer-hire agreement" and "consumer" are considered hereafter). The Act does not apply to a credit union or to a body the members of which are credit unions and the principal objects of which are the promotion of the credit union movement and the provision of services to credit unions. (Credit Union Act, 1997 (No 15 of 1997), s 184). Nor does it apply to a registered society within the meaning of the Friendly Societies Acts or "(aa) any transaction or proposed transaction conducted in the course of relevant trading operations within the meaning of s 39A (inserted by s 17 of the Finance Act, 1981) of the Finance Act, 1980, or within the meaning of s 39B (inserted by section 30 of the Finance Act, 1987) of the Finance Act, 1980. . .(b) a credit agreement in the form of an authentic act signed before a notary public or a judge. . .(c) any transaction entered into by a pawnbroker in respect of a pledge on which a loan or advance is made or to be made, or anything done with a view to such a transaction being entered into. . .(d) an agreement for the provision on a continuing basis of a service or a utility where the consumer has the right to pay for it, by means of instalment or deferred payments. . .(e) credit granted or made available without payment of interest or any other charge other than by a seller of goods who has invited by advertisement consumers to avail of such credit. . .(f) a credit agreement other than a credit agreement operated by means of a credit

3

to publish a financial advertisement should also be mindful at all times of the prohibition in Part X of the Consumer Credit Act on knowingly, with a view to financial gain, sending to a minor any document inviting the minor to (a) borrow credit, (b) obtain goods on credit or hire, (c) obtain services on credit, or (d) apply for information or advice on borrowing credit or otherwise obtaining credit or hiring goods.[3] Breach of this prohibition is a summary criminal offence.[4]

Some Key Definitions

[1–02]   The Consumer Credit Act uses a number of defined terms which are amplified upon in this book when first encountered. However, there are a number of key definitions which it is useful to highlight before proceeding further, namely the definitions of "advertisement", "consumer", "credit" and "housing loan".

[1–03]   The term "advertisement" is broadly defined in the Act and includes "every form of advertising, whether in a publication, by television or radio, by display of notices, signs, labels, showcards or goods, by distribution of samples, circulars, catalogues, price lists or other material, by exhibition of pictures, models or films, or in any other way, and references to the publishing of advertisements shall be construed accordingly".[5]

[1–04]   The term "consumer" is defined as "(a) a natural person acting outside the person's business, or (b) any person or person of a class, declared to be a consumer in an order made under [s 2(9) of the Consumer Credit Act]".[6] (The term "business" includes a trade or profession).[7]

[1–05]   The term "credit", for the purposes of the 1995 Act, "includes a deferred payment, cash loan or other similar financial accommodation".[8] (The term "cash" includes money in any form[9], and the term "financial accommodation" includes credit and also the letting of goods).[10]

[1–06]   Lastly, the term "housing loan" is defined in s 2(1) of the Consumer Credit Act as "(a) an agreement for the provision of credit to a person on the security of a mortgage of a freehold or leasehold estate or interest in land- (i) for the purpose of enabling the person to have a house constructed on the land as the principal residence of that person or that person's dependants, or (ii) for the purpose of enabling the person to improve a

---

card under which no interest is charged provided the consumer agrees to repay the credit in a single payment, or (g) a credit agreement between an employer and an employee made on terms which are more favourable to the employee than terms offered generally to the public in the normal course of business." (Consumer Credit Act, s 3(2)).

[3] Consumer Credit Act, 1995, s 139.
[4] Consumer Credit Act, 1995, s 12(1)(j).
[5] Consumer Credit Act, 1995, s 2(1).
[6] Consumer Credit Act, 1995, s 2(1). S 2(9) of the Consumer Credit Act empowers the Minister for Finance, by means of order notified in *Iris Oifigiúil*, to declare any specified person or any person of a specified class of persons to be a consumer for the purposes of the Act.
[7] Consumer Credit Act, 1995, s 2(1).
[8] *ibid.*
[9] *ibid.*
[10] *ibid.*

house that is already used as the principal residence of that person or that person's dependants, or (iii) for the purpose of enabling the person to buy a house that is already constructed on the land for use as the principal residence of that person or that person's dependants, or (b) an agreement for refinancing credit provided to a person for a purpose specified in paragraph (a)(i), (ii) or (iii), or (c) an agreement for the provision of credit to a person on the security of a mortgage of a freehold or leasehold estate or interest in land on which a house is constructed where the house is to be used, or to continue to be used, as the principal residence of the person or the person's dependants, or (d) an agreement for the provision of credit to a person on the security of a mortgage of a freehold or leasehold estate or interest in land on which a house is, or is to be, constructed where the person to whom the credit is provided is a consumer".[11]

Part II of the Consumer Credit Act

Part II of the Consumer Credit Act, 1995 is concerned with advertisements published or displayed for the purpose of a business carried on by the advertiser and indicating a willingness to: provide or to arrange for the provision of credit to a consumer; enter into a hire-purchase or consumer-hire agreement for the letting of goods by the advertiser to a consumer[12]; or arrange the letting of goods under a hire-purchase or consumer-hire agreement by another person to a consumer.[13] **[1–07]**

---

[11] The term "house" is defined in s 2(1) of the 1995 Act as including "any building or part of a building used or suitable for use as a dwelling and any out-office, yard, garden or other land appurtenant thereto or usually enjoyed therewith" and the term "mortgage" is defined as including a charge. Under s 3(3)(a) of the 1995 Act, the provisions of the 1995 Act may, by statutory instrument, be applied to housing loans advanced by a local authority. Under s 3(3)(b) of the 1995 Act, "[a] loan, not secured by mortgage, made by a local authority for the purposes of carrying out improvement works (within the meaning of s 1 of the Housing (Miscellaneous Provisions Act, 1979) to a house shall be regarded as a housing loan (within the meaning of this Act) for the purposes of this Act."

[12] The term "hire purchase agreement" is defined in s 2(1) of the Consumer Credit Act, 1995 as meaning "an agreement for the bailment of goods under which the hirer may buy the goods or under which the property in the goods will, if the terms of the agreement are complied with, pass to the hirer in return for periodical payments; and where by virtue of two or more agreements, none of which by itself constitutes a hire-purchase agreement, there is a bailment of goods and either the hirer may buy the goods, or the property therein will, if the terms of the agreements are complied with, pass to the hirer, the agreements shall be treated for the purpose of this Act as a single agreement made at the time when the last agreement was made." The term "hirer" is defined in s 2(1) as meaning "a consumer who takes, intends to take or has taken from an owner under a hire-purchase agreement or a consumer-hire agreement in return for periodical payments. A "consumer-hire agreement", again per s 2(1), is "an agreement of more than three months duration for the bailment of goods to a hirer under which the property in the goods remains with the owner." The key distinctions between the two forms of agreement are that there is no minimum duration specified for 'hire purchase agreements' and title passes under a 'hire purchase agreement' but not under a 'consumer hire agreement'.

[13] Per s 20(1) of the Consumer Credit Act, 1995. Under s 20(2) of the Consumer Credit Act, Part II of that Act does not apply to any advertisement published or displayed by a society referred to in s 3(2)(a) of the Act, *viz.* "(i) a society which is registered as a credit union under the Industrial and Provident Societies Acts, 1893 to 1978, by virtue of the Credit Union Act, 1966...[and] (ii) any registered society within the meaning of the Friendly Societies Acts...".

Credit advertisements

[1–08]   Section 21 of the Consumer Credit Act, 1995 is concerned with credit advertisements generally. It requires of any "advertisement in which a person offers to provide or arrange for the provision of credit" that such advertisement, if mentioning an interest rate or making any claim in relation to the cost of credit, contain a clear and prominent statement of the APR, using a representative example if no other means is practicable (provided it is indicated that this is only a representative example).[14] No other rate of interest may be included in the advertisement.[15] "APR" is the "annual percentage rate of charge, being the total cost of credit[16] to the consumer, expressed as an annual percentage of the amount of credit granted and calculated in accordance with s 9 [of the 1995 Act]".[17]

[1–09]   The effect of s 21(1) is to ensure that all credit advertisements published by, amongst others, financial product and service providers refer to a standardised interest rate (the APR), thus enabling consumers to make direct comparisons between the interest charges published by different financial product and service providers in their respective advertisements.

[1–10]   To counter any temptation that might arise among advertisers to 'bury' the APR within a credit advertisement to which s 21(1) of the Consumer Credit Act refers, s 21(2) requires that any statement of the APR in such an advertisement be afforded no less prominence than a statement relating to "(a) any period over which payment is to be made, (b) the amount of any advance payment or the fact that no advance payment is required, and (c) the amount, number or frequency of any other payments or charges (other than the cash price of the goods or services) or of any repayments."

[1–11]   Sub-sections (3), (4), (5) and (6) of s 21 make brief but important provision in relation to credit advertisements. Between them they require that: where credit offered is

---

The Credit Union Act, 1966 was repealed by s 5(1)(a) of the Credit Union Act, 1997, and any society which prior to the commencement of s 5(3) of the 1997 Act, was registered as a credit union under the Industrial and Provident Societies Acts, 1893 to 1978, was thereafter deemed to be registered as a credit union under the 1997 Act. (Pursuant to Regulation 2 of the Credit Union Act, 1997 (Commencement) Order, 1997 (SI No 403 of 1997), s 5(3) was commenced with effect from 1 October 1997). As mentioned elsewhere, by virtue of s 184 of the 1997 Act, the Consumer Credit Act does not apply to a credit union or to a body the members of which are credit unions and the principal objects of which are the promotion of the credit union movement and the provision of services to credit unions. (The term "credit union" when used in the 1997 Act means a credit union registered under, or deemed by s 5(3) of the 1997 Act to be registered under, the 1997 Act. (Per Credit Union Act, 1997, s 2(1))).

[14] Consumer Credit Act, 1995, s 21(1). The heading to s 21 is "Credit advertisements" and this phrase is used in this Chapter as a short-hand reference to advertisements to which s 21 refers.

[15] Consumer Credit Act, 1995, s 21(1).

[16] The term "total cost of credit" is defined in s 2(1) of the Consumer Credit Act, 1995, as meaning "the total cost of credit to the consumer being all the costs, comprising interest, collection and all other charges, which the consumer has to pay for the credit exclusive of any sum payable as a penalty or as compensation or damages for breach of the agreement." The term "agreement" is defined, again in s 2(1), as meaning an agreement to which the 1995 Act applies.

[17] Consumer Credit Act, 1995, s 2(1).

subject to the payment of charges other than the repayment of capital and interest on the sums borrowed, such conditions must be specified in the related credit advertisement[18]; a credit advertisement must state if security is required (or is required in specific circumstances) in relation to any credit offered[19]; and where an advertisement refers to the availability of credit and the credit is subject to restrictions, those restrictions must be clearly indicated in the advertisement.[20] It is not an offence to provide credit at a lower rate than that advertised.[21]

Advertising financial accommodation relating to goods or services

Section 22 of the Consumer Credit Act, 1995, is concerned with advertisements which refer to the availability of a financial accommodation in relation to the acquisition of goods or the provision of a service. It requires that all such advertisements include, where applicable, a statement of: "(a) the nature of the financial accommodation, (b) the cash price of the goods or service, (c) the APR and the total cost of credit or the hire-purchase price, (d) the number and amount of instalments, (e) the duration of the intervals between instalment payments, (f) the number of any instalments which have to be paid before delivery of the goods, and (g) details of any deposit payable." **[1–12]**

Advertising of consumer-hire agreements

It will be recalled that a consumer-hire agreement is "an agreement of more than three months duration for the bailment of goods to a hirer under which the property in the goods remains with the owner."[22] Under s 23 of the 1995 Act "[a]n advertisement in which a person offers to arrange the letting of goods under a consumer-hire agreement or indicates the availability of such a letting" must include a statement to the effect that the agreement is for letting, hiring or leasing only and that the goods remain the property of the owner.[23] This statement must be afforded no less prominence than any statement of the sum of the amount payable by the hirer.[24] In the case of a visual advertisement, such statement must be enclosed by a boxed boundary line.[25] Where any figures relating to the amount payable by a hirer under a consumer-hire agreement are indicated in an advertisement to which s 23(1) applies, those figures must: (i) be clearly displayed and fully inclusive of all amounts payable, including taxes[26]; and (ii) indicate (if it is the case) that the figures quoted indicate the amount payable for part of the agreement only.[27] **[1–13]**

Comparative advertising

Under s 24 of the Consumer Credit Act, 1995, where an advertisement purports to compare the level of repayments or cost under one or more forms of financial **[1–14]**

---

[18] Consumer Credit Act, 1995, s 21(3). This requirement does not apply to advertisements relating to housing loans. (Consumer Credit Act, 1995, s 21(3)).
[19] Consumer Credit Act, 1995, s 21(4).
[20] Consumer Credit Act, 1995, s 21(6).
[21] Consumer Credit Act, 1995, s 21(5).
[22] Consumer Credit Act, 1995, s 2(1).
[23] Consumer Credit Act, 1995, s 23(1).
[24] Consumer Credit Act, 1995, s 23(1)(i).
[25] Consumer Credit Act, 1995, s 23(1)(ii).
[26] Consumer Credit Act, 1995, s 23(2).
[27] Consumer Credit Act, 1995, s 23(3).

accommodation, the advertisement must contain the relevant terms of each of the forms of financial accommodation to which the advertisement refers.

Cost-free credit

[1–15]   Section 25 of the Consumer Credit Act, 1995, prohibits any advertisement from describing credit as being without interest or charge "if the availability of the credit is dependent on the consumer concluding with the creditor or any other person a maintenance contract (for any goods involved) or an insurance contract or on any other condition, compliance with which would, or would be likely in the future to, involve the consumer in any cost additional to that payable if the goods were bought for cash".[28] In short, for credit to be advertised as free, it must be completely free. It is perhaps worth noting in this regard the guidance given by the Financial Regulator to the financial sector in a letter of 12 June 2007 entitled "Review of Advertising Issues". Though the letter is concerned with the requirements of the Consumer Protection Code, the opinion expressed by the Financial Regulator in that letter under the heading "Terms such as 'free'" is nonetheless of interest in that it suggests the degree of care that a financial product or service provider needs to apply in the context of s 25. Thus, per the Financial Regulator, "[C]are should be taken when using such terms. ... The Financial Regulator considers that an unqualified description of a service as 'free' is misleading in instances where only certain fees are disapplied (for example, bank accounts where transaction and maintenance fees are not applied but other charges may apply). As another example, a service should not be advertised as 'free' if charges apply where certain criteria, such as maintenance of a minimum balance, annual turnover or minimum number of transactions, have not been met."[29]

Part IX of the Consumer Credit Act

[1–16]   Part IX of the 1995 Act makes certain incidental provision that impacts on advertisements for housing loans. The provisions of Part IX do not operate separately from the provisions considered hitherto in that an advertisement which advertises credit for a housing loan will be subject both to those provisions considered elsewhere above and also to those provisions of Part IX considered hereafter.

Housing loans

[1–17]   Under s 128(1) of the Consumer Credit Act, 1995, a mortgage agent[30] must ensure that any information document, any application form for a housing loan, and any document approving a housing loan include the following notice:

---

[28] It will be recalled that the term "cash", when used in the 1995 Act, includes money in any form. (Consumer Credit Act, 1995, s 2(1)).

[29] Letter of 12 June 2007 to the financial sector from the Financial Regulator entitled "Review of Advertising Issues", 1. As of 21 April 2008, the text of this letter was available on-line at www.financialregulator.ie/frame_main.asp?pg =%2Findustry%2Fin%5Fbci% 5Fintr%2Easp&nv =%2Findustry%2Fin_nav.asp.

[30] The term "mortgage agent" is defined in s 115(2) of the 1995 Act to mean any or all of "(a) a mortgage lender, (b) a mortgage intermediary, (c) an insurer, or (d) an insurance intermediary". Each of these categories of person is itself further defined. Thus the term: "mortgage lender" is defined (in s 2(1) of the 1995 Act) as "a person who carries on a business

> **WARNING: YOUR HOME IS AT RISK IF YOU DO NOT KEEP UP PAYMENTS ON A MORTGAGE OR ANY OTHER LOAN SECURED ON IT.**

The term "information document" employed in s 128(1) of the Consumer Credit Act, 1995 and various other of the provisions referred to hereafter means "any document, leaflet, notice, circular, pamphlet, brochure, film, video or facsimile issued to the general public or to certain persons (whether solicited or not) for the purpose of giving information in relation to housing loans"[31] and thus will generally extend to written advertisements, though would not extend, for example, to radio advertisements.   [1–18]

Under s 128(2) of the Consumer Credit Act, a mortgage agent must ensure, where the interest rate for a housing loan is variable, that any information document, application or document approving such loan include the following further notice, after the notice required under s 128(1):   [1–19]

> **THE PAYMENT RATES ON THIS HOUSING LOAN MAY BE ADJUSTED BY THE LENDER FROM TIME TO TIME.**

Section 132 of the Consumer Credit Act requires that where a fee is payable by an applicant for a housing loan in respect of any of a number of specified matters, the mortgage agent must ensure that a statement of reasonable prominence that such fee is payable (and specifying the amount of the fee or how it is determined) and the circumstances in which it may be refunded, if such is the case, be included in or attached to any information document issued by or on behalf of the mortgage agent which refers to such loan, any application form issued for the purposes of applying for such loan,[32] and any document sent to the applicant approving the loan, in relation to the matters specified at (b), (c), (d) and (e) hereafter. The specified matters in respect of which the fact that there is a fee payable will give rise to the foregoing obligations are any of the following: (a) the making, accepting or administering of an application for a loan, (b) the valuation of the security for the loan, (c) legal services in connection   [1–20]

---

that consists of or includes making housing loans"; "mortgage intermediary" is defined (in s 2(1)) as "a person (other than a mortgage lender or credit institution) who, in return for a commission or some other form of consideration — (a) arranges, or offers to arrange, for a mortgage lender to provide a consumer with a housing loan, or (b) introduces a consumer to an intermediary who arranges, or offers to arrange, for a mortgage lender to provide the consumer with such a loan"; "insurer" is defined (in s 115(2) of the Consumer Credit Act) as bearing "the meaning assigned to it by the Insurance Act, 1989"; and "insurance intermediary" is defined (again in s 115(2)) as meaning "an insurance agent or insurance broker within the meaning of the Insurance Act, 1989". The meaning of the term "housing loan" has been considered elsewhere in the main text above. It is outside the scope of this book to enter into a consideration of the Insurance Acts and Regulations.

[31] Consumer Credit Act, 1995, s 115(2).

[32] Where application is other than by application form, the statement must issue to the applicant within 10 days of receipt of the application. (Consumer Credit Act, 1995, s 132).

with the loan, (d) services provided by a mortgage agent in relation to the loan, and (e) non-acceptance of an offer or approval of a loan.[33]

[1–21] Under s 133(1) of the Consumer Credit Act, 1995, a mortgage agent must ensure that any information document which refers or relates to an endowment loan,[34] any application form issued to a person for the purpose of applying for such a loan, and any document approving such a loan, contain in a prominent position the following notice:

> **WARNING: THERE IS NO GUARANTEE THAT THE PROCEEDS OF THE INSURANCE POLICY WILL BE SUFFICIENT TO REPAY THE LOAN IN FULL WHEN IT BECOMES DUE FOR REPAYMENT.[35]**

[1–22] Section 133(3) of the Consumer Credit Act provides, amongst other matters, that the requirements of s 133(1) do not apply where: the insurer underwriting the endowment loan insurance policy guarantees that the proceeds of the policy at the initial premium will be sufficient to repay the loan in full when it becomes due for repayment; or the mortgage lender undertakes to accept such proceeds in full and final settlement of the loan debt. Section 133(5) of the Consumer Credit Act provides that where the possibility exists that early surrender of an endowment loan insurance policy may result in a return to the consumer that would amount to less than such a consumer has paid by way of premia and other charges, any document as is referred to in s 133(1) must contain a statement referring to this possibility.

[1–23] Under s 134(1) of the 1995 Act, where it is a mortgage lender's policy to charge interest in respect of arrears on all or certain housing loans, the mortgage lender must ensure that, amongst other matters, "any information document relating to ... such a loan ... shall state the amount of the increase in interest and other charges which a borrower may become liable to pay in respect of such arrears."[36]

Criminal offences

[1–24] Under s 26(1) of the Consumer Credit Act, a person must not display or publish or cause to be displayed or published an advertisement to which Part II of the Consumer Credit Act, 1995 applies but which is not in compliance with Part II.[37] Breach of this

---

[33] Consumer Credit Act, 1995, s 132.

[34] The term "endowment loan" is defined in s 115(2) of the Consumer Credit Act as meaning "a housing loan which is to be repaid out of the proceeds of an insurance policy on its maturity, other than a policy providing mortgage protection insurance only."

[35] When application for an endowment loan is made, other than by way of application form, the applicant must, within 10 days of receipt of the application, be supplied by the mortgage agent with a notice that accords with s 133(1). (Consumer Credit Act, 1995, s 133(2)).

[36] The same statement, per s 134(1), must also appear in any "application form for, or document approving, such a loan and any communication in relation to arrears of payments due on such a loan".

[37] For the purposes of s 26, an advertisement that is displayed is treated as being published on every day that it is displayed. (Consumer Credit Act, 1995, s 26(3)).

prohibition is a summary criminal offence.[38] However, there is a significant exemption for any person whose business it is to publish or arrange for the publication of advertisements: in any proceedings arising in respect of an offence under s 26(1) it is a defence for any such person (so long as they are not the provider of the relevant credit) "to show that he received the advertisement in question for publication in the ordinary course of business and did not know and had no reason to suspect that its publication would constitute a contravention of [s 26(1)]."[39] So, oddly perhaps, the less publishers know about the law concerning credit advertisements, the better placed they will be, at least in the event of any prosecution arising pursuant to s 26 of the Consumer Credit Act. This is perhaps an unusual exemption to afford persons who provide the fora within which offending advertising appears. Insofar as financial accommodation provided through a credit intermediary[40] is concerned, where the provider of that financial accommodation has devised any part of an advertisement or supplied, or been requested to supply, information in relation to such advertisement but is not the advertiser, the provider of the financial accommodation is responsible for ensuring that the advertisement complies with the requirements of Part II of the Consumer Credit Act.[41] Breach of this provision is a criminal offence.[42] However, in any related criminal proceedings it is a defence for the accused provider to show that the advertisement which led to the prosecution "was displayed or published without his consent or connivance or that he made reasonable efforts to ensure that it complied with [Part II] ... or to prevent its publication."[43] As for Part IX of the Consumer Credit Act, 1995, breach of, amongst other provisions, ss 128, 133(1) or (2), 134 or 135(3) is a summary offence.[44] Where an offence under the Consumer Credit Act is committed by a body corporate or by a person acting on behalf of a body corporate and is proved to have been so committed with the consent, connivance or approval of, or to have been facilitated by any neglect on the part of any director, manager, secretary or any other officer of such body or a person who was purporting to act in

---

[38] Consumer Credit Act, 1995, s 12(1)(c).

[39] Consumer Credit Act, 1995, s 26(2).

[40] i.e. "a person, other than a credit institution or a mortgage lender, who in the course of his business arranges or offers to arrange for a consumer the provision of credit or the letting of goods in return for a commission, payment or consideration of any kind from the provider of the credit or the owner, as the case may be". (Consumer Credit Act, 1995, s 2(1)). A "credit institution" is defined in s 2(1) as "(a) the holder of a licence granted under section 9 of the Central Bank Act, 1971, (b) a body licensed to carry on banking under regulations made under the European Communities Act, 1972, (c) a building society incorporated or deemed to be incorporated under s 10 of the Building Societies Act, 1989, (d) a society licensed to carry on the business of a trustee savings bank under s 10 of the Trustee Savings Bank Act, 1989, (e) such person or class of persons as may be prescribed by the Bank [*i.e.* the Central Bank and Financial Services Authority of Ireland] for the purposes of this Act", as well as a long list of named entities, provided in all instances that the APR charged by any person coming within the foregoing categories in respect of any credit granted to a consumer is less than 23 per cent.

[41] Consumer Credit Act, 1995, s 27(1).

[42] Consumer Credit Act, 1995, s 12(1)(c).

[43] Consumer Credit Act, 1995, s 27(2).

[44] Consumer Credit Act, 1995, s 12(1)(i).

any such capacity, such person shall also be guilty of an offence and may be proceeded against and punished as if such person were guilty of the first-mentioned offence.[45]

Directions under s 135 of the Consumer Credit Act, 1995

[1–25]   Under s 135(1) of the Consumer Credit Act, as amended, the Central Bank and Financial Services Authority of Ireland may, if it considers it expedient to do so, give a direction to any mortgage agent regarding the matter and form of any advertisement or information document that is published or displayed by or on behalf of such mortgage agent in relation to a housing loan. Such a direction may direct that an advertisement or information document be withdrawn.[46] Without prejudice to the generality of the foregoing, the following directions may also be issued under s 135: a direction prohibiting the issue by a mortgage agent of advertisements or information documents of specified description; a direction requiring a mortgage agent to modify, in a specified manner, advertisements or information documents of a specified description; a direction prohibiting the issue by a mortgage agent of any advertisements or information documents which are, or are substantially, repetitions of a specified advertisement or information document; a direction requiring a mortgage agent to withdraw any specified advertisement or information document or any advertisement or information document of a specified description; and a direction requiring a mortgage agent to include specified information in any advertisement or information document to be published by that mortgage agent or on its behalf or in any statement to the public made by it or on its behalf.[47] Any mortgage agent who is the subject of a direction made under s 135(1) must comply with same. At the time of writing, two directions of general application have been made thus far under s 135(1).[48] These are considered below.

(1) Direction effective 24 March 1997

[1–26]   The first direction made under s 135(1) of the Consumer Credit Act took effect from 24 March 1997. It was published under the auspices of the Director of Consumer Affairs who, at the time the direction was published, was the person competent to issue such directions. The complete text of the direction appears in Appendix B of this book. The direction requires that all printed advertisements for "residential mortgage credit"[49] in newspapers, magazines or other direct printed advertisements and on the internet must include the following information: (i) the maximum percentage of the value of the property which will normally be advanced to a borrower and an indication as to whether other criteria apply; (ii) the maximum loan to income proportion that will normally be provided and an indication of whether other criteria apply; (iii) the cost per month of a typical €100,000, 20-year variable rate mortgage (and the additional cost per month of a 1 per cent rise — presumably a 1 per cent per annum rise — in the rate of interest applied); and a health warning stating "the [*sic*]

---

[45] Consumer Credit Act, 1995, s 12(3).
[46] Consumer Credit Act, 1995, s 135(1).
[47] Consumer Credit Act, 1995, s 135(3).
[48] Consumer Credit Act, 1995, s 135(2).
[49] The term "residential mortgage credit" is not defined in the direction or in the Consumer Credit Act, 1995. However, the terms "mortgage" and "credit" are defined in the 1995 Act. The definitions of these terms have been considered elsewhere above.

cost of your monthly repayments may increase — if you do not keep up your repayments you may lose your home." The direction further provides that, with effect from 24 March 1997, a statement must be made in all radio, television and billboard advertisements for residential mortgage credit that "Lending terms and conditions will apply." It is perhaps open to question whether there is any consumer who would not appreciate, even without such a warning, that lending terms and conditions invariably apply to the provision of residential mortgage credit. The direction concludes with a reminder that it is an offence to include any misleading information in advertisements and a warning that the Director of Consumer Affairs would be checking the veracity of statements in advertisements and for compliance with the terms of his direction.

(2) Direction effective 1 January 2007

The second direction made under s 135(1) of the Consumer Credit Act took effect from 1 January 2007 and is concerned with debt consolidation housing loans. The text of this direction appears in Appendix B of this book. The direction states itself to be without prejudice to, and not to provide any derogation from, any provision of the 1995 Act or other law applicable to such advertisement. It requires that certain information be displayed in all advertisements and information documents that promote "debt consolidation housing loans" and which are displayed by or on behalf of a mortgage agent.[50] The required information is as follows: (a) where sample debt consolidation figures are quoted, the difference between the total cost of credit of the consolidated mortgage and the total cost of credit of the individual debts that are the subject of consolidation; (b) monthly repayment amounts where any repayment amounts are displayed and the repayment frequency will be monthly (weekly equivalents can be displayed but cannot be more prominent than the monthly amounts displayed); (c) the repayment term on which sample repayments are based, if sample repayments are displayed (no such repayment term quoted may exceed 20 years; moreover, it must be afforded the same prominence as the sample repayments); and (d) the following warning prominently, in a box, in bold type and in a font larger than the 'normal' font size used throughout the advertisement or information document[51]:

[1–27]

> **Warning: This new loan may take longer to pay off than your previous loans. This means you pay more than if you paid over a shorter term.**

In addition, the direction provides that: any examples of existing debts must be based upon generally prevailing interest rates at the time an advertisement or information document is published; and interest-only housing loans must not be advertised as being suitable for debt consolidation purposes.

---

[50] The term "debt consolidation housing loans" is not defined in the direction or in the Consumer Credit Act, 1995. However, the term "housing loan" is defined in the Consumer Credit Act. (The definition of this term has been considered elsewhere above).

[51] It is not clear what constitutes the "normal' font size used in advertisement, whether, for example, it is the average of the largest and smallest font sizes used in the advertisement or the average of the font sizes used in the main or entire text of the advertisement.

Chapter 2

THE CONSUMER PROTECTION ACT 2007[1]

Introduction

Part 3 (ss 41 to 63) of the Consumer Protection Act 2007 is concerned with unfair,   **[2–01]**
misleading, aggressive and prohibited commercial practices. It is of relevance to the
financial services sector and to financial product and service providers minded to
publish advertisements.[2] Section 41(1) of the Consumer Protection Act 2007 prohibits
a trader[3] from engaging in an unfair commercial practice. Section 42 (1) prohibits a
trader from engaging in a misleading commercial practice. Section 52 prohibits
a trader from engaging in an aggressive commercial practice. Section 55(1) prohibits
traders from engaging in any defined prohibited commercial practices. What
constitutes an unfair, misleading, aggressive or prohibited commercial practice is
considered further below.

Unfair commercial practices

A commercial practice is unfair if it satisfies two tests prescribed in s 41(2) of the   **[2–02]**
Consumer Protection Act 2007. The first test is that it is contrary to the requirements
of professional diligence, i.e. the general principle of good faith in the trader's field of
activity and/or the standard of skill and care that such trader may reasonably be
expected to exercise in respect of consumers.[4] The second test is that the commercial

---

[1] No 19 of 2007. As of 21 April 2008, the text of the Consumer Protection Act was available on-line at www.oireachtas.ie/documents/bills28/acts/2007/a1907.pdf. At the time of writing, a Bill (the Consumer Protection (Amendment) Bill 2008) has been introduced before Seanad Éireann that seeks to eliminate a difficulty with s 83(1) of the 2007 Act and expressly empower the District Court to exercise jurisdiction in relation to indictable cases brought under the Act.

[2] An "advertisement" for the purposes of the Consumer Protection Act 2007 is defined as including "any form of advertising or marketing". (Consumer Protection Act 2007, s 2(1)).

[3] The term "trader", when used in the 2007 Act, refers to a person who is acting for purposes related to that person's trade, business or profession and also a person acting on behalf of such person. (Consumer Protection Act 2007, s 2(1)).

[4] Consumer Protection Act 2007, s 41(2)(a). For the purposes of the Consumer Protection Act, the term "'consumer' means a natural person (whether in the State or not) who is acting for purposes unrelated to the person's trade, business or profession". (Consumer Protection Act 2007, s 2(1)).

15

practice would be likely to: cause appreciable impairment of the average consumer's ability to make an informed choice in relation to the product concerned; and cause the "average consumer" to make a "transactional decision" that the average consumer would not otherwise make.[5]

[2–03] The term "average consumer" when employed in the Consumer Protection Act 2007 bears the meaning assigned to it in the Unfair Commercial Practices Directive (i.e. the Directive that the 2007 Act seeks in part to implement)[6] "and when applied in relation to a particular commercial practice[7] or product of a trader (a) if the commercial practice or product is directed at a particular group of consumers, the expression shall be read as 'the average member of that group'; and (b) if the commercial practice or the product is a practice or product that would be likely to materially distort the economic behaviour only of a clearly identifiable group of consumers[8] whom the

---

[5] Consumer Protection Act 2007, s 41(2)(b).

[6] Directive No 2005/29/EC of the European Parliament and of the Council of 11 May 2005 (OJ No L149, 11 June 2005, 22) concerning unfair business-to-consumer commercial practices in the internal market and amending Council Directive 84/450/EEC, Directives 97/7/EC, 98/27/EC and 2002/65/EC of the European Parliament and of the Council and Regulation No 2006/2004 of the European Parliament and of the Council.

[7] The term "'commercial practice' means any conduct (whether an act or omission), course of conduct or representation by the trader in relation to a consumer transaction, including any such conduct or representation made or engaged in before, during or after the consumer transaction". The term "'representation' includes — (a) any oral, written, visual, descriptive or other representation by a trader, including any commercial communication, marketing or advertising, and (b) any term or form of a contract, notice or other document used or relied on by a trader in connection with a consumer transaction". The term "'consumer transaction' means a promotion or supply of a product to a consumer". The term "'product' means goods or services" The term "'goods or services' means goods or services or both". The term "'goods' means real or personal property of any nature or description and includes — (a) ships, aircraft or other vehicles, (b) animals, (c) minerals, trees or crops, whether on, under or attached to land or not, (d) gas, electricity or water, (e) computer software, (f) tickets or like evidence of a right to be in attendance at a particular place at a particular time or times or a right of transportation, (g) any voucher, coupon or other document or thing intended to be used as a substitute for money in the payment, in whole or in part, for a product or otherwise exchanged for a product, and (h) any description of interest (present or future, vested or contingent) or obligation arising out of or incidental to goods". The term "'services' means any service or facility provided for gain or reward or otherwise than free of charge, including, without limitation — (a) services or facilities for — (i) banking, insurance, grants, loans, credit or financing ... and (c) any rights, benefits, privileges, obligations or facilities that are, or are to be provided, granted or conferred in the course of services, but does not include services provided under a contract of employment". All of the foregoing definitions are contained in the Consumer Protection Act 2007, s 2(1).

[8] By virtue of s 2(3) of the Consumer Protection Act, a word or expression that is used in the Act and also used in the Unfair Commercial Practices Directive "shall have the same meaning as it has in the Directive". Article 2(c) of the Unfair Commercial Practices Directive defines the phrase "to materially distort the economic behaviour of consumers" to mean "using a commercial practice to appreciably impair the consumer's ability to make an informed decision, thereby causing the consumer to take a transactional decision that he would not have taken otherwise".

trader could reasonably be expected to foresee as being particularly vulnerable because of their mental or physical infirmity, age or credulity, the expression shall be read as 'the average member of that vulnerable group.'"[9]

The term "transactional decision" means "in relation to a consumer transaction, any decision by the consumer concerning whether, how or on what terms to do, or refrain from doing any of the following: (a) purchase the product; (b) make payment in whole or in part for the product; (c) retain or return the product after its purchase; (d) dispose of the product; (e) exercise a contractual right in relation to the product".[10]   **[2–04]**

In determining whether a commercial practice is unfair under s 41(2) of the Consumer Protection Act 2007, the commercial practice falls to be considered in its factual context, taking account of all its features and the circumstances.[11] Though it would be possible for a financial advertisement to put a trader in breach of the prohibition on unfair commercial practices, it seems generally unlikely that a regulated entity would engage in advertising that would place it in breach of s 41. Offhand, financial advertisements by their nature seem more likely to place a trader in breach of the prohibition in s 42(1) on engaging in a misleading commercial practice.   **[2–05]**

Misleading commercial practices

According to s 43(1) and (2) of the Consumer Protection Act, there are two kinds of misleading commercial practice. Thus a commercial practice is misleading if: it includes the provision of false information in relation to any one or more prescribed matters and that information would be likely to cause the average consumer to make a transactional decision that the average consumer would not otherwise make[12]; it would be likely to cause the average consumer to be deceived or misled in relation to   **[2–06]**

---

[9] Consumer Protection Act 2007, s 2(2). The reference to the "average consumer" appears in the eighteenth recital of the Unfair Commercial Practices Directive where it is stated that "It is appropriate to protect all consumers from unfair commercial practices; however the Court of Justice has found it necessary in adjudicating on advertising cases since the enactment of Directive 84/450/EEC to examine the effect on a notional, typical consumer. In line with the principle of proportionality, and to permit the effective application of the protections contained in it, this Directive takes as a benchmark the average consumer, who is reasonably well-informed and reasonably observant and circumspect, taking into account social, cultural and linguistic factors, as interpreted by the Court of Justice, but also contains provisions aimed at preventing the exploitation of consumers whose characteristics make them particularly vulnerable to unfair commercial practices. Where a commercial practice is specifically aimed at a particular group of consumers, such as children, it is desirable that the impact of the commercial practice be assessed from the perspective of the average member of that group. It is therefore appropriate to include in the list of practices which are in all circumstances unfair a provision which, without imposing an outright ban on advertising directed at children, protects them from direct exhortations to purchase. The average consumer test is not a statistical test. National courts and authorities will have to exercise their own faculty of judgement, having regard to the case-law of the Court of Justice, to determine the typical reaction of the average consumer in a given case."

[10] Consumer Protection Act 2007, s 2(1).

[11] Consumer Protection Act 2007, s 41(3).

[12] Consumer Protection Act, s 43(1).

any one or more specified matters and to make a transactional decision that the consumer would not otherwise make.[13]

[2–07]   Among the specified matters referred to in the preceding paragraph and which may be relevant in the context of financial advertising are: the existence or nature of a product[14]; the main characteristics of a product[15]; the price of the product, the manner in which that price is calculated or the existence or nature of a specific price advantage[16]; the nature, attributes or rights of the trader[17]; and the legal rights of a consumer (whether contractual or otherwise) or matters respecting when, how or in what circumstances those rights may be exercised.[18] In determining whether a commercial practice within the meaning of s 43(1) or (2) is misleading, the commercial practice falls to be considered in its factual context, taking account of all its features and the circumstances.[19]

---

[13] Consumer Protection Act 2007, s 43(2).

[14] Consumer Protection Act 2007, s 43(3)(a).

[15] Consumer Protection Act 2007, s 43(3)(b).

[16] Consumer Protection Act 2007, s 43(3)(c).

[17] Consumer Protection Act 2007, s 43(3)(f).

[18] Consumer Protection Act 2007, s 43(3)(j). The following are all of the matters prescribed by s 43(3) of the 2007 Act for the purposes of s 43(1) and (2), not all of which are relevant in the context of financial advertising: "a) the existence or nature of a product; (b) the main characteristics of a product, including, without limitation, any of the following: (i) its geographical origin or commercial origin; (ii) its availability, including, without limitation, its availability at a particular time or place or at a particular price; (iii) its quantity, weight or volume; (iv) its benefits or fitness for purpose; (v) the results to be expected from it; (vi) the risks it presents to consumers; (vii) its usage or prior history; (viii) its composition, ingredients, components or accessories; (ix) the specifications of the product, including, without limitation, the grade, standard, style, status or model of the product; (x) the after-supply customer assistance available to consumers in relation to the product; (xi) the handling of consumer complaints in relation to the product; (xii) the method or date of (I) the product's delivery, supply or provision, or (II) in the case of goods, the product's manufacture; (xiii) the results and material features of tests or checks carried out on the product; (xiv) in relation to a service, its execution or performance; (c) the price of the product, the manner in which that price is calculated or the existence or nature of a specific price advantage; (d) the need for any part, replacement, servicing or repair in relation to the product; (e) the existence, extent or nature of any approval or sponsorship (direct or indirect) of the product by others; (f) the nature, attributes or rights of the trader, including, without limitation, the following: (i) the trader's identity, qualifications, assets or status; (ii) the trader's affiliation or connection with others; (iii) the existence, extent or nature of- (I) any industrial, commercial or intellectual property rights the trader may have, or (II) any award, distinction, approval or sponsorship (direct or indirect) the trader has or has received; (g) the extent of the trader's commitments; (h) the trader's motives for the commercial practice; (i) the nature of the trader's supply process; (j) the legal rights of a consumer (whether contractual or otherwise) or matters respecting when, how or in what circumstances those rights may be exercised." The term "supply", when used in the 2007 Act "in relation to the supply of goods or services to a consumer, includes- (a) sell, lease, take by way of mortgage or other security, assign, award by chance or otherwise effect a disposition of, (b) offer or agree to supply or expose or display for supply". (Consumer Protection Act 2007, s 2(1)).

[19] Consumer Protection Act 2007, s 43(5).

A number of provisions in s 43 are of particular interest in the context of advertising. **[2–08]**
First, if an alleged misleading commercial practice involves the provision of
information, it is not a defence in any proceeding against a trader for engaging in
that misleading commercial practice to show that the information is factually
correct.[20] Second, without prejudice to the general provision that the determination
whether a particular commercial practice is misleading falls to be considered in its
factual context, taking account of all its features and the circumstances, (i) if a
commercial practice involves a representation or creates an impression (in advertising,
marketing or otherwise) that a product was previously offered at a different price or at
a particular price, consideration must be given to whether the product was offered
openly and in good faith at that price and at the same place for a reasonable time
before the relevant representation was made[21]; and (ii) if the commercial practice
involves a representation or creates an impression (in advertising, marketing or
otherwise) that a product is being offered by a trader at or below a price recommended
by the manufacturer, producer or supplier of the product (other than the trader),
consideration must be given to whether that recommended price was recommended in
good faith.[22]

As if to confirm that a trader who publishes an advertisement is more likely to fall **[2–09]**
afoul of the misleading commercial practice provisions of the Consumer Protection
Act 2007 than the unfair commercial practice provisions, s 44 of the Consumer
Protection Act 2007 makes specific provision as regards misleading competitors or
causing product confusion through marketing or advertising. Thus s 44(1) provides
that "[a] commercial practice involving marketing or advertising is misleading if it
would be likely to cause the average consumer (a) to confuse (i) a competitor's product
with the trader's product, or (ii) a competitor's trade name, trade mark or some other
distinguishing feature or mark with that of the trader, and (b) to make a transactional
decision that the average consumer would not otherwise make." Section 44(2)
provides that in determining whether a commercial practice is misleading (in this
instance under s 44(1)) the commercial practice must be considered in its factual
context, taking account of all its features and the circumstances.

Section 45 of the Consumer Protection Act 2007 Act makes provision in respect of **[2–10]**
codes of practice. Thus under s 45(1) a commercial practice is misleading if "(a) it
involves a representation that the trader abides, or is bound by a code of practice, (b)
the representation referred to in ... (a) would be likely to cause the average consumer
to make a transactional decision that the average consumer would not otherwise
make, and (c) the trader fails to comply with a firm commitment in that code of
practice."[23] Section 45(2) provides that in determining whether a commercial practice
is misleading (in this instance under s 45(1)) the commercial practice must be
considered in its factual context, taking account of all its features and the
circumstances. The term "code of practice" is defined in s 2(1) of the Consumer

---

[20] Consumer Protection Act 2007, s 43(4).

[21] Consumer Protection Act 2007, s 43(6)(a).

[22] Consumer Protection Act 2007, s 43(6)(b).

[23] The term "firm commitment" means a commitment that is not merely aspirational but is
capable of being verified. (Consumer Protection Act 2007, s 45(3)).

Protection Act 2007 as meaning "any code, agreement or set of rules or standards that is not imposed by or under an enactment but purports to govern or define commercial practices of one or more traders (whether generally or in respect of a particular trade, business or professional sector or one or more commercial practices) who agree, commit or undertake to abide or be bound by such rules or standards." Thus s 45 would not apply to the Consumer Protection Code (adopted under, amongst other provisions, s 33S(6) of the Central Bank Act, 1942) or either of the two advertising codes published by the Broadcasting Commission of Ireland pursuant to s 19(1) of the Broadcasting Act, 2001,[24] and considered hereafter. However, it would apply, for example to the "Code of Standards for Advertising, Promotional and Direct Marketing in Ireland", as published by the Advertising Standards Authority for Ireland, also considered hereafter, as that is a code of practice which is not imposed by or under an enactment and which purports to govern or define commercial practices of one or more traders as regards a commercial practice (advertising and promotional and direct marketing). Under s 89 of the Consumer Protection Act, a code of practice is expressly stated to be admissible in evidence in court proceedings "and, if any provision of the code is relevant to a question arising in those proceedings, the provision may be taken into account in determining that question."[25]

[2–11] Section 46 of the Consumer Protection Act 2007 is concerned with misleading commercial practices involving the withholding, omission or concealment of material information. Though regulated financial product and service providers may perhaps be unlikely to deliberately withhold, omit or conceal material information, s 46 gives them a further statutory incentive not to do so. Section 46(1) provides that a commercial practice is misleading where a trader omits or conceals "material information" (i.e. material information that the average consumer would need, in the context, to make an informed transactional decision)[26] and such practice would be likely to cause the average consumer to make a transactional decision that the average consumer would not otherwise make. Section 46(2) provides that a commercial practice is misleading if a trader: provides the "material information" referred to in s 46(1) in a manner that is unclear, unintelligible, ambiguous or untimely or, alternatively, fails to identify the commercial intent of the practice (where such intent is not apparent from the context)[27]; and such practice would be likely to cause the average consumer to make a transactional decision that the average consumer would not otherwise make.[28]

[2–12] Of particular relevance in the context of advertising is s 46(3) of the Consumer Protection Act 2007 which provides that where a commercial practice is or includes an "invitation to purchase", each of certain matters referred to in s 46(3)(a)-(f)

---

[24] No 4 of 2001.

[25] s 88 of the Consumer Protection Act establishes a process whereby an 'industry' code of practice may be submitted to the National Consumer Agency for its review or approval. However, any code of practice, whether approved under s 88 or not, may be admitted and relied upon in court proceedings in accordance with s 89 of the Consumer Protection Act.

[26] Consumer Protection Act 2007, s 46(1).

[27] Consumer Protection Act 2007, s 46(2)(a)(i) and (ii).

[28] Consumer Protection Act 2007, s 46(2)(b).

constitutes "material information" for the purposes of s 46 (unless already apparent to the consumer in the context of the commercial practice). The matters referred to include but are not limited to: the main characteristics of the product (to the extent appropriate to the medium and product), certain trader details, the price of the product (or, in certain instances, the manner in which price is to be calculated), certain defined charges, the handling of consumer complaints, and (if applicable) the legal rights of the consumer to withdraw from or cancel the consumer transaction.[29] The term "invitation to purchase" is defined in s 2(1) of the Consumer Protection Act 2007 as meaning "a representation by the trader in a consumer transaction that (a) indicates characteristics of the product and includes its price; and (b) enables the consumer to purchase the product".[30] Clearly not all financial advertisements will constitute an "invitation to purchase" within the meaning of s 2(1) of the 2007 Act, but some will.

Section 46(5) provides that in determining whether a commercial practice is misleading (in this instance under s 46) the commercial practice must be considered in its factual context, taking account of all its features and the circumstances, including in this instance "(a) the space or time available in any communications medium used, and (b) any measures taken by the trader to make the material information available to consumers by other means." The implicit acknowledgment in s 46(5) that the space available, e.g. in a newspaper advertisement, simply may not permit a comprehensive reference to all the 'material information' referred to elsewhere in s 46 is an appropriate acknowledgment of the space constraints presented in practice by the medium of advertising.

[2–13]

---

[29] Per s 46(3) of the Consumer Protection Act "If a commercial practice is or includes an invitation to purchase, each of the following constitutes material information for the purposes of this section, unless already apparent to the consumer in the context of the commercial practice: (a) the main characteristics of the product, to an extent appropriate to the medium and the product; (b) the geographical address of the trader, the identity of the trader (such as his or her trading name) and, if the trader is acting in a consumer transaction as an agent of another trader, the geographical address and the identity of that other trader; (c) the price of the product (inclusive of taxes) or, if the nature of the product is such that the price cannot reasonably be calculated in advance, the manner in which the price is calculated; (d) any freight, delivery or postal charges that apply in relation to the product or, if such charges cannot reasonably be calculated in advance, a statement of the fact that such charges will apply and be payable by the consumer; (e) the handling of consumer complaints in relation to the product or the arrangement for payment, delivery or performance, if such handling or arrangement does not meet or accord with- (i) the standard of skill and care that the trader may reasonably be expected to exercise in respect of consumers, or (ii) the general principle of good faith in the trader's field of activity; (f) if applicable, the legal rights of a consumer (whether contractual or otherwise) to withdraw from or cancel the consumer transaction." Per s 46(4) of the 2007 Act, the 'material information' referred to in s 46(3) is in addition to any other information that a trader is required by law to provide to a consumer.

[30] Per s 2(1) of the Consumer Protection Act 2007: the term "consumer transaction" means "a promotion or supply of a product to a consumer"; and the term "consumer" means "a natural person (whether in ... [Ireland] or not) who is acting for purposes unrelated to the person's trade, business or profession".

[2–14] Section 50 of the Consumer Protection Act 2007, amongst other matters, empowers the Minister for Enterprise, Trade and Employment to make consumer information regulations "if the Minister considers it to be in the interest of consumers that advertisements for a product, or a class or type of product, contain or refer to any information relating to those products (or do both those things)",[31] which regulations may, amongst other matters, be made for different classes or types of products or traders or advertisements.[32] It is an offence for: a trader to supply a product in breach of a regulation made under s 50[33]; a trader to publish (or cause to be published) an advertisement that fails to comply with any such regulation.[34]

Aggressive commercial practices

[2–15] A commercial practice is aggressive "if by harassment, coercion or undue influence[35] it would be likely to (a) cause significant impairment of the average consumer's freedom of choice or conduct in relation to the product concerned, and (b) cause the average consumer to make a transactional decision that the average consumer would not otherwise take".[36] A trader who engages in any such practice is guilty of a criminal offence.[37] Though it seems technically possible that an advertisement would in and of itself place a trader in breach of the prohibition on engaging in aggressive commercial practices, it is very difficult to conceive of a practical instance in which this would arise. For this reason the provisions in the Consumer Protection Act 2007 concerning aggressive commercial practices are not considered further herein.

Prohibited commercial practices

[2–16] Section 55(1) and (3) of the Consumer Protection Act 2007 identify numerous prohibited commercial practices. Those practices that may be of interest in the context of financial advertisements are listed hereafter, with those that seem less likely to be of interest being listed in the footnotes below. Before proceeding, it is perhaps worth recalling that the term "product" when employed in the Consumer Protection Act embraces both goods and services, and that the term "services" means any service or facility "provided for gain or reward or otherwise than free of charge, including, without limitation — (a) services or facilities for — (i) banking, insurance, grants, loans, credits or financing ...".[38] Thus the term "product" embraces the typical product range of a typical financial product or service provider. The prohibited commercial practices that seem of most relevance in the context of financial advertisements are:

---

[31] Consumer Protection Act 2007, s 50(2).
[32] Consumer Protection Act 2007, s 50(3).
[33] Consumer Protection Act 2007, s 51(1).
[34] Consumer Protection Act 2007, s 51(2).
[35] The term "undue influence" when used in s 53 "means exploiting a position of power in relation to a consumer so as to apply pressure (without necessarily using or threatening to use physical force) in a way that significantly limits the consumer's ability to make an informed choice in relation to the trader's product." (Consumer Protection Act 2007, s 53(4)).
[36] Consumer Protection Act 2007, s 53.
[37] Consumer Protection Act 2007, s 54.
[38] *Cf.* Consumer Protection Act 2007, s 2(1).

- a representation that a trader has an approval, authorisation or endorsement that such trader does not have, or making such a representation when such trader is not in compliance with that approval, authorisation or endorsement[39];
- a representation that a trader is signatory to a code of practice, if such trader is not[40];
- a representation that a product has an approval, authorisation or endorsement that it does not have, or making such a representation when the trader making such representation is not in compliance with that approval, authorisation or endorsement[41];
- a representation that supply of a product is legal, if it is not, or creating such an impression[42];
- a representation that describes a product as 'gratis', 'free', 'without charge' or anything similar, if a consumer has to pay anything other than the necessary and reasonable cost of responding to the representation and collecting the product or having it delivered[43];
- a representation that a commercial practice of a trader has an approval, authorisation or endorsement that it does not have, or making such a representation when such trader is not in compliance with the approval, authorisation or endorsement[44];
- a representation that a code of practice has an approval or other endorsement that it does not have[45];
- displaying a quality, standard or trust mark or symbol, or having some equivalent type of mark or symbol, without having obtained necessary authorisation to do so[46];
- making an invitation to purchase a product without disclosing the existence of any reasonable grounds a trader may have for believing that such trader will not be able to supply, or procure another trader to supply, the product or an equivalent product at the price specified in the invitation, or to do so for a reasonable period of time or in reasonable quantities, having regard to the scale of any marketing or advertising of the product and the price specified (bait advertising)[47];
- making an invitation to purchase a product and then (with the intention of promoting a different product — a practice known as 'bait and switch') demonstrating a defective sample of the product or refusing to show or display the product to a consumer, take an order from a consumer for the product, or deliver the product to such consumer within a reasonable period of time[48];

---

[39] Consumer Protection Act 2007, s 55(1)(a).
[40] Consumer Protection Act 2007, s 55(1)(b).
[41] Consumer Protection Act 2007, s 55(1)(d).
[42] Consumer Protection Act, s 55(1)(f).
[43] Consumer Protection Act 2007, s 55(1)(h).
[44] Consumer Protection Act 2007, s 55(1)(i).
[45] Consumer Protection Act 2007, s 55(1)(j).
[46] Consumer Protection Act 2007, s 55(1)(k).
[47] Consumer Protection Act 2007, s 55(1)(l).
[48] Consumer Protection Act 2007, s 55(1)(m).

- making a false representation that a product is available only for a limited time, or on particular terms for a limited time, in order to elicit an immediate decision from a consumer, depriving such consumer of sufficient opportunity or time to make an informed choice in relation to the trader's product[49];
- subject to s 55(2) of the 2007 Act, providing after-supply service to a consumer in a language that is not an official language of the EEA Member State in which the trader is located, nor the language in which the trader and such consumer communicated prior to the agreement to supply[50];
- making a representation or creating an impression that a right given to consumers under an enactment is a distinctive feature of a trader's promotion or supply[51];
- using editorial content in the media to promote a product (if a trader has paid for that promotion) if it is not made clear that the promotion is a paid promotion, whether in the content itself or in any oral, written, visual or descriptive representation in the promotion[52];
- making a representation to a consumer that is inaccurate to a material degree in respect of market conditions, or in respect of the possibility of finding a product, with the intention of inducing such consumer to purchase a product at conditions less favourable than normal market conditions[53];
- operating, running or promoting a competition or prize promotion without awarding the prizes described or reasonable equivalents[54];
- making a representation or creating an impression that a consumer has won or will win a prize or other equivalent benefit if there is no prize or equivalent benefit, or in claiming the prize, such consumer has to make a payment or incur a loss[55];
- making a representation or creating an impression that a trader is not acting for purposes related to such trader's trade, business or profession, when such trader is so acting, or is acting as a consumer, when such trader is not[56];
- making a representation or creating an impression that a consumer cannot leave the premises until a contract is formed[57];

---

[49] Consumer Protection Act 2007, s 55(1)(n).

[50] Consumer Protection Act 2007, s 55(1)(o). Section 55(2) of the Consumer Protection Act 2007 provides that s 55(1)(o) does not apply where "(a) prior to the agreement to supply, the trader clearly discloses to the consumer the language or languages in which the after-supply service is available; [or] (b) the primary language in which the trader and consumer communicated prior to the agreement to supply is the official language of the [EEA Member State] ... in which the trader is located but is not the official language of the ... [EEA Member State] of the consumer." It is not entirely clear whether, in referring to the EEA Member State "of the consumer", the 2007 Act means to refer to the State of which the consumer is a citizen and/or the State in which such consumer is situate and/or resident and/or domiciled at or after the time the relevant agreement is concluded.

[51] Consumer Protection Act 2007, s 55(1)(p).

[52] Consumer Protection Act 2007, s 55(1)(q).

[53] Consumer Protection Act 2007, s 55(1)(t).

[54] Consumer Protection Act 2007, s 55(1)(u).

[55] Consumer Protection Act 2007, s 55(1)(v).

[56] Consumer Protection Act 2007, s 55(1)(a).

[57] Consumer Protection Act 2007, s 55(3)(a).

third of three standardised interest rates that have been considered thus far in this book. The first of these is 'APR' the "annual percentage rate of charge, being the total cost of credit to the consumer, expressed as an annual percentage of the amount of credit granted and calculated in accordance with section 9 [of the Consumer Credit Act, 1995]".[115] It will be recalled that, s 21(1) of the Consumer Credit Act requires of any "advertisement in which a person offers to provide or arrange for the provision of credit" that such advertisement, if mentioning an interest rate or making any claim in relation to the cost of credit, contain a clear and prominent statement of the APR, using a representative example if no other means is practicable (provided it is indicated that this is only a representative example).[116] No other rate of interest may be included in the advertisement.[117] The second standardised interest rate is the 'compound annual rate', a term commonly abbreviated in advertisements to 'CAR', being the equivalent annual rate of interest, payable at the end of the year on a deposit.[118] When used in the context of the Consumer Protection Code, the term 'CAR' is employed in the context of tracker bonds only.[119] Again, while a credit institution must include the CAR in any tracker bond advertisement, it is not confined to quoting the CAR only, a fact which creates a certain potential for confusion, prompting the suspicion that consumers would be better protected and better informed if the only interest rate that could be quoted in tracker bond advertisements was the 'CAR'.

Past performance

The Consumer Protection Code requires that any information about the past performance of an advertised product or service must: be based on a similar product (or, presumably, a service, where appropriate) to that being advertised; not be selected so that the success or otherwise of the advertised product or service is exaggerated or disguised; state the source of the information; be based on actual performance; state the period chosen (which period must be related to the term of the product advertised, with the longest term available being included where the term is open-ended); include the most recent period; indicate, where applicable, details of transaction costs, interest and tax that have been taken into account; and state the basis on which performance is quoted (where applicable).[120]

[4–44]

Position or holding in product

Where a regulated entity has a position or holding in a product (not a service) that it advertises, it must include a statement to this effect in the relevant advertisement.[121]

[4–45]

---

[115] Consumer Credit Act, 1995, s 2(1).
[116] Consumer Credit Act, 1995, s 21(1).
[117] *ibid.*
[118] Consumer Protection Code, 4.
[119] See the Consumer Protection Code Clarifications under the heading "Interest Rates quoted in Advertisements". (There are generally no page numbers in the Consumer Protection Code Clarifications).
[120] Consumer Protection Code, 37 *et seq.*, Chapter 7, para 27.
[121] Consumer Protection Code, 38, Chapter 7, para 29.

Simulated performance

[4–46]   Information about the simulated performance of an advertised product or service (or of a regulated entity) is required to: be based on a relevant simulated performance; not be selected so that the success or otherwise of the advertised product or service or the regulated entity is exaggerated or disguised, as appropriate; state the source; and indicate whether and to what extent transaction costs, interest and tax have been taken into account.[122]

Guaranteed and partially guaranteed investments

[4–47]   There is a general prohibition on any advertisement describing a product or investment (but not, it seems, services) to be guaranteed or partially guaranteed unless: there is a legally enforceable third-party guarantee in place in respect of the consumer's claim under the guarantee; the relevant regulated entity has made (and can show itself to have made) an assessment of the value of the guarantee; the advertisement provides sufficient detail about the guarantor and guarantee to enable a consumer to make a fair assessment about the value of the guarantee; and in instances where the guarantee is from a connected party, the advertisement states this.[123]

Taxation

[4–48]   Where an advertisement contains a reference to the impact of tax, it must: state the assumed rate of tax; state, where applicable, that the tax reliefs are the current tax reliefs and that the value of same apply to the consumer, the provider of the advertised product or service or its provider, as appropriate; state, where applicable, that the matters referred to affect only certain consumers with certain liabilities and identify the affected class(es) of consumer and the type of liabilities concerned; state who is responsible for obtaining the advertised tax benefits; not describe an advertised product or service as being free from income tax without stating with equal prominence, where applicable, that the income is payable from a product on which income tax has already been paid (and likewise as regards capital tax).[124] This level of detail is perhaps sufficient to deter regulated entities from generally referring to taxation in their advertisements.

Date of return

[4–49]   Where the return on an advertised product/service is not set until a particular date (e.g. the applicable maturity date), this must be stated clearly.[125]

Withdrawal

[4–50]   Where a planned withdrawal from capital is offered in lieu of an income equivalent, the effect of such withdrawal must be clearly explained by a regulated entity in any advertisement for the relevant product.[126] Where a product is not readily realisable,

---

[122] Consumer Protection Code, 38, Chapter 7, para 30.

[123] Consumer Protection Code, 38, Chapter 7, para 32.

[124] Consumer Protection Code, 38 *et seq.*, Chapter 7, para 33.

[125] Consumer Protection Code, 39, Chapter 7, para 35.

[126] Consumer Protection Code, 39, Chapter 7, para 37.

the advertisement for same must state that it may be difficult for consumers to sell or exit the product and/or obtain information about its value or the extent of the risks to which it is exposed.[127] An advertisement for a product that cannot be encashed prior to maturity (or which incurs an early redemption charge) must state this clearly.[128]

Charges

If a product is subject to front-end loading (i.e. greater charges earlier in the term of the product), any related advertisement must state that: deductions for charges and expenses are disproportionately loaded in the early period and do not arise uniformly throughout the term of the product; if the consumer withdraws early this front-end loading will impact on the amount of money that such consumer receives back; and, where applicable, that a consumer may not get back her initial investment sum.[129]

[4–51]

In addition to the foregoing, Chapter 7 of the Consumer Protection Code introduces five new warnings that must be introduced into advertisements for savings and investment products. As with all warnings prescribed by the Consumer Protection Code, these warnings must be boxed and in bold font of a size larger than the font size used throughout the document.[130] The five warnings are as follows:

[4–52]

i. where an advertisement contains information on past performance, the following warning must appear[131]:

> **Warning: Past performance is not a reliable guide to future performance.**

ii. where an advertisement contains information on simulated performance, the following warning must appear[132]:

> **Warning: These figures are estimates only. They are not a reliable guide to the future performance of this investment.**

iii. where the product (but not, it seems, a service) that is the subject of an advertisement can fluctuate in price or value, the following warning must appear[133]:

> **Warning: The value of your investment may go down as well as up.**

---

127 Consumer Protection Code, 39, Chapter 7, para 39.
128 Consumer Protection Code, 40, Chapter 7, para 40.
129 Consumer Protection Code, 40, Chapter 7, para 41.
130 Consumer Protection Code, 11, Chapter 2, para 6.
131 Consumer Protection Code, 38, Chapter 7, para 28.
132 Consumer Protection Code, 38, Chapter 7, para 31.
133 Consumer Protection Code, 39, Chapter 7, para 34.

iv. where a product the subject of an advertisement is described as being likely to yield income or as being suitable for a consumer particularly seeking income and where such income can fluctuate, the following warning must appear[134]:

> **Warning: The income you get from this investment may go down as well as up.**

v. where an advertised product or service is denominated or priced in foreign currency or its value may be affected by foreign exchange rate changes, the following warning must appear[135]:

> **Warning: This [product/service] may be affected by changes in currency exchange rates.**

[134] Consumer Protection Code, 39, Chapter 7, para 36.
[135] Consumer Protection Code, 39, Chapter 7, para 38.

Chapter 5

BROADCASTING LEGISLATION

Introduction

Although Irish broadcasting legislation is not directed at financial product and service [5–01] providers, it is nonetheless of practical interest to such product and service providers in that such legislation determines whether and when broadcast advertising by such provider will be permitted. This Chapter gives an overview of Ireland's broadcasting legislation. Chapters 6 and 7 respectively consider certain advertising codes issued pursuant to such legislation, specifically the BCI General Advertising Code and the BCI Children's Advertising Code.

Establishment of Radio Telefís Éireann

Section 3 of the Broadcasting Authority Act, 1960[1] established an Authority initially [5–02] known as 'Radio Éireann'[2]—now Radio Telefís Éireann (or 'RTÉ')[3]—the organisational mandate of which has recently been amended so that it: is required to establish and maintain a national television and sound broadcasting service; is required to establish, maintain and operate one or more multiplexes[4]; and may establish and

---

[1] No 10 of 1960.

[2] Broadcasting Authority Act, 1960, s 3(1).

[3] The change in name was effected by s 3 of the Broadcasting Authority (Amendment) Act, 1966 (No 7 of 1966).

[4] The term "multiplex" means "an electronic system which combines programme material and related and other data in a digital form and the transmission of that material and data so combined by means of wireless telegraphy directly or indirectly for reception by the general public". (Broadcasting (Amendment) Act 2007 (No 15 of 2007), s 2). The term "programme material" means "audio-visual material or audio material and includes advertisements and material which, when transmitted, will constitute a direct offer to the public for the sale or supply to them of goods or other property (whether real or personal) or services". (Broadcasting (Amendment) Act 2007, s 2).

maintain broadcasting services of a local, community or regional character.[5] The national television and broadcasting service provided by RTÉ is required to have the character of a public, free-to-air service and to be made available to the whole community on the island of Ireland.[6] Under the Broadcasting (Amendment) Act 2007, RTÉ is also obliged to maintain television and sound broadcasting services which are to be made available, insofar as RTÉ considers reasonably practicable, to Irish communities outside the entire island of Ireland.[7] RTÉ must endeavour to ensure that the programme schedules of these extra-terrestrial television and sound broadcasting services are, insofar as reasonably practicable, representative of the programme schedule of the national television and sound broadcasting services.[8] As with the television and sound broadcasting services that RTÉ is required to establish and maintain, the extra-territorial service is required to have the character of a public service.[9]

Broadcasting Advertisements

[5–03] Section 20 of the 1960 Act empowers RTÉ, among other matters, to broadcast advertisements, to fix, cancel and vary charges and conditions for such broadcasts, and to reject, in whole or in part, any advertisement presented for broadcast.[10] An "advertisement" is defined in s 20(8) of the 1960 Act as "including references to advertising matter in sponsored programmes, that is to say, programmes supplied for advertising purposes by or on behalf of an advertiser". In 2001, this definition of advertisement was extended to include references to "teleshopping material",[11] i.e. "material which, when transmitted, will constitute a direct offer to the public for the sale or supply to them of goods or other property (whether real or personal) or services."[12]

Maximum Advertising Times

[5–04] In the case of a broadcasting service provided by RTÉ (not being a broadcasting service which consists of programme material supplied by it pursuant to a contract entered into under the Broadcasting Act, 2001) the total daily times and maximum hourly period for broadcasting advertisements and teleshopping material as fixed by RTÉ is subject to ministerial approval.[13] The same arrangement applies in respect of

---

[5] Broadcasting (Amendment) Act 2007, s 3(1)(a).

[6] Broadcasting Act, 2001 (No 4 of 2001), s 28(1).

[7] Broadcasting Authority Act, 1960, s 16(1A), as inserted by the Broadcasting (Amendment) Act 2007, s 3(1)(b).

[8] Broadcasting Authority Act, 1960, s 16(1C), as inserted by the Broadcasting (Amendment) Act 2007, s 3(1)(b).

[9] Broadcasting Authority Act, 1960, s 16(1B), as inserted by the Broadcasting (Amendment) Act 2007, s 3(1)(b).

[10] Broadcasting Authority Act, 1960, s 20. The Act further provides that RTÉ may provide for different circumstances and for additional special charges to be made in special cases. (Cf. the Broadcasting Authority Act, 1960, ss 20(1) and (7)).

[11] Broadcasting Act, 2001, s 31(1).

[12] Broadcasting Act, 2001, ss 31(2) and (3) and 19(18).

[13] Broadcasting Act, 2001, s 31(1).

Teilifís na Gaeilge.[14] Section 19(3) of the 2001 Act empowers the Broadcasting Commission of Ireland to make rules as regards the maximum total daily and hourly times allowed for the transmission of advertisements and teleshopping material on a broadcasting service or sound broadcasting service and also to make different rules with regard to different classes of broadcasting service or sound broadcasting service.

The Broadcasting Complaints Commission

Section 4 of the Broadcasting Authority (Amendment) Act, 1976,[15] inserted new   **[5–05]**
sections 18A to 18C into the 1960 Act. Section 18A established a body known as the Broadcasting Complaints Commission which, under s 18B, had power, amongst other matters, to investigate and decide complaints that a particular advertisement contravened an advertising code drawn up by RTÉ.[16] Sections 18A to 18C were subsequently repealed by the Broadcasting Act, 2001[17] but the Broadcasting Complaints Commission was continued in being.[18] The rôle of the Broadcasting Complaints Commission is considered further in the context of the 2001 Act below.

Independent Radio and Television

Section 4(1) of the Radio and Television Act, 1988[19], provided for the licensing of   **[5–06]**
commercial broadcasting stations by a body originally known as The Independent Radio and Television Commission[20] and now known as the Broadcasting Commission of Ireland[21]. The 1988 Act makes provision for advertising by independent broadcasting and television services. Section 10(1) of the 1988 Act provides that programmes broadcast in a sound broadcasting service pursuant to any sound broadcasting service may have advertisements inserted into them. Section 10(2) requires the Broadcasting Commission of Ireland to draw up, from time to time, a code of standards and practice in advertising and every sound broadcaster must comply with same. Section 10(4) prescribes maximum daily and hourly advertising times.[22] Section 10(6) requires the Broadcasting Commission of Ireland to ensure that sound broadcasters comply with s 10(2), (3) (considered below) and (4). Section 10(5) effectively replicates the definition of "advertisement" contained in s 20(8) of the 1960 Act. Section 11 of the 1988 Act requires sound broadcasting contractors to give due and adequate consideration to non-frivolous, non-vexatious complaints made by members of the public and (while a sound broadcasting contractor) to maintain due

---

[14] Broadcasting Act, 2001, s 49.

[15] No 37 of 1976.

[16] See s 18B(1)(e) of the Broadcasting Authority Act, 1960 (now repealed) as inserted by the Broadcasting Authority (Amendment) Act, 1976, s 4.

[17] Broadcasting Act, 2001, s 3 and First Schedule.

[18] Broadcasting Act, 2001, s 22(1).

[19] No 20 of 1988.

[20] Radio and Television Act, 1988, s 3(1).

[21] Broadcasting Act, 2001, s 10.

[22] These time limits are treated seriously and The Independent Radio and Television Commission (now the Broadcasting Commission of Ireland) has, for example, terminated the broadcasting contract of a radio station which broadcast programmes that were, in effect, advertising promotions for certain businesses. See further in this regard *Radio Limerick One Limited* v. *The Independent Radio and Television Commission* [1997] 2 ILRM 1.

and proper records of all such complaints and any reply thereto or action consequent upon same, such records to be available for inspection on demand by the Broadcasting Commission of Ireland.[23]

'Pirate' Broadcasts

[5–07]   Section 3(1) of the Broadcasting and Wireless Telegraphy Act, 1988,[24] requires that a broadcast not be made from any premises or vehicle in Ireland unless it is made pursuant to and in accordance with a licence from the Commission for Communications Regulation.[25] Section 5 of the 1988 Act prohibits the doing of certain acts relating to material broadcast in contravention of s 3. These acts include advertising by means of a broadcast done in breach of s 3(1) of the 1988 Act, inviting another to so advertise, or making an advertisement with the intent that it may comprise, or be included in, a broadcast to be so made.[26] In proceedings for an offence under s 5, a court may treat a defendant as having advertised by means of a prohibited broadcast if it is proved that: a broadcast was made in contravention of s 3(1); the broadcast was partly or wholly comprised of an advertisement; there is a reference in the advertisement which the court considers is a reference to the defendant; and there is produced in court anything which (by reason of something printed thereon or on a label attached thereto) purports to relate to the subject-matter of the advertisement, and there is something printed thereon or a label attached thereto which the court considers is likely to be taken as an indication that the defendant prepares, manufactures, assembles, imports, provides, supplies, promotes, organises or is otherwise connected with the provision of the goods, service, accommodation, facility, entertainment or other event, or other thing, to which the advertisement relates.[27]

Broadcasting Act, 2001

[5–08]   In 2001, Ireland's existing broadcasting code was overhauled by means of the Broadcasting Act of that year. This enactment established a legal framework for digital terrestrial television in Ireland. It conferred additional functions on The Independent Radio and Television Commission,[28] which was re-named the 'Broadcasting Commission of Ireland'.[29] It modified the functions of the Broadcasting Complaints Commission,[30] and it established a new body, 'Teilifís na Gaeilge'[31], that is responsible for the operation of Ireland's predominantly Irish-language television station, TG4.[32] Under s 19 of the 2001 Act, the Broadcasting Commission of Ireland has responsibility (subject to ministerial direction) to adopt codes of practice

---

[23] Radio and Television Act, 1988, ss 11(1) and (2).
[24] No 19 of 1988.
[25] Prior to the enactment of the Communications (Regulation) Amendment Act 2007 (No 22 of 2007), s 4(2) and Schedule (Part 6), a ministerial licence was required.
[26] Broadcasting and Wireless Telegraphy Act, 1988, s 5(2)(f).
[27] Broadcasting and Wireless Telegraphy Act, 1988, s 5(4).
[28] See s 11 of the Broadcasting Act, 2001.
[29] Broadcasting Act, 2001, s 10.
[30] Broadcasting Act, 2001, Part III.
[31] Broadcasting Act, 2001, s 44.
[32] Broadcasting Act, 2001, s 45.

concerning such matters as advertising and the protection of children in the broadcasting field.[33] Pursuant to s 19, the Broadcasting Commission has now adopted a General Advertising Code and a Children's Advertising Code, considered in Chapters 6 and 7 hereof. Under s 19(3) of the 2001 Act, the Commission also has responsibility for setting the total daily times and maximum hourly periods for the transmission of advertisements[34] and teleshopping material[35] on a broadcasting or sound broadcasting service. Section 21(1) of the 2001 Act requires that the Broadcasting Commission, amongst other matters, enforce any code or rules prepared or made under the 2001 Act. This is without prejudice to the role of the Broadcasting Complaints Commission which, notwithstanding the repeal by the 2001 Act[36] of s 18A of the 1960 Act-the provision that established the Broadcasting Complaints Commission-remains extant.[37]

Advertising on Teilifís na Gaeilge

Section 20(1), (2) and (4) of the 1960 Act are expressly applied by the 2001 Act to Teilifís na Gaeilge.[38] Thus Teilifís na Gaeilge may, amongst other matters, broadcast advertisements, fix conditions for such broadcasts, and reject, in whole or in part, any advertisement presented for broadcast.[39] In addition Teilifís na Gaeilge is prohibited from accepting any advertisement which is directed towards any religious or political end or has any relation to an industrial dispute.[40]   **[5–09]**

Complaints to the Broadcasting Complaints Commission

Under s 24(2) of the 2001 Act, the Broadcasting Complaints Commission may investigate and decide upon (amongst other matters) a complaint that a broadcaster has breached a code adopted under (amongst other matters) s 19(1)(a) or (c) of the 2001 Act, which includes any purported breach of the BCI General Advertising and Children's Advertising Codes. The Commission does not have the power to investigate and decide upon a complaint which, in its opinion is frivolous or vexatious.[41] Nor, save in instances where the Commission considers that special reasons apply, which reasons must be stated by the Commission in its later decision, does the Commission have power to investigate and decide upon a withdrawn complaint.[42]   **[5–10]**

---

[33] Broadcasting Act, 2001, s 19(1).

[34] The term "advertisement" is not defined in the Broadcasting Act, 2001. However, s 1(3) of the 2001 Act provides that that Act and the Broadcasting Authority Acts, 1960 to 1993, shall be construed together as one and thus the definition of "advertisement" in s 20(8) of the Broadcasting Authority Act, 1960 applies.

[35] The term "teleshopping material" when used in s 19 of the Broadcasting Act, 2001, means "material which, when transmitted, will constitute a direct offer to the public for the sale or supply to them of goods or other property (whether real or personal) or services. (Broadcasting Act, 2001, s 19(18)).

[36] Section 3 and First Schedule.

[37] *Per* Broadcasting Act, 2001, s 22(2).

[38] Broadcasting Act, 2001, s 50(1).

[39] Broadcasting Authority Act, 1960, s 20.

[40] Broadcasting Act, 2001, s 50(2).

[41] Broadcasting Act, 2001, s 24(14).

[42] *ibid.*

[5–11] A complaint under s 24(2) must be in writing and must be made to the Broadcasting Complaints Commission within a 30-day timeframe.[43] The moment from which that 30-day timeframe commences varies. Thus if the complaint relates to one broadcast, the 30 days run from the date of the broadcast.[44] If the complaint relates to two or more unrelated broadcasts, the 30 days run from the date of the earlier (or earliest) such broadcast.[45] If the complaint relates to two or more related broadcasts of which at least two are made on different dates, the 30 days run from the later (or latest) of those dates.[46] Where the Broadcasting Complaints Commission proposes to investigate a complaint made under s 24 of the 2001 Act, the Commission must afford the broadcaster to whom the complaint relates an opportunity to comment on the complaint.[47]

[5–12] Where a complaint is made to the Broadcasting Complaints Commission it is possible that (a) a person employed by the broadcaster concerned, or (b) (if the making of any programme, the subject of a complaint, was commissioned by the broadcaster concerned) the person commissioned to make that programme, may request the Broadcasting Complaints Commission, for reasons specified by such person, to afford that person the opportunity to comment on the complaint.[48] If so, the Broadcasting Complaints Commission must, after having considered the reasons specified, afford such person that opportunity.[49] However, before affording this opportunity, the Broadcasting Complaints Commission must be satisfied that the complaint made may adversely affect either (i) an interest of a person referred to at (a) above (being an interest that the Broadcasting Complaints Commission considers relevant to the person's employment by the broadcaster concerned), or (ii) the prospects of the person referred to at (b) obtaining further commissions in respect of programmes from the broadcaster concerned.[50]

[5–13] Where the Broadcasting Complaints Commission proposes to consider a complaint referred to in s 24(2)(e) of the 2001 Act[51], the Broadcasting Complaints Commission must afford the relevant advertiser an opportunity to make submissions to the Broadcasting Complaints Commission in relation to the relevant advertisement.[52] As

---

[43] Broadcasting Act, 2001, s 24(3).

[44] Broadcasting Act, 2001, s 24(3)(a)(i).

[45] Broadcasting Act, 2001, s 24(3)(a)(ii).

[46] Broadcasting Act, 2001, s 24(3)(b).

[47] Broadcasting Act, 2001, s 24(4). The broadcaster to whom the complaint relates is referred to in the 2001 Act (and hereafter in this book) as "the broadcaster concerned".

[48] Broadcasting Act, 2001, s 24(5).

[49] *ibid.*

[50] *ibid.*

[51] i.e. "a complaint that on occasion specified in the complaint a broadcaster failed to comply with a provision of a code under para (b) or (c) of s 19(1) [of the Broadcasting Act, 2001] or of a code under s 4 of the Broadcasting Act, 1990, continued in force under s 19(17) [of the Broadcasting Act, 2001]". Both the General Advertising Code (adopted by the Broadcasting Commission of Ireland pursuant to s 19(1)(b) of the 2001 Act) and the Children's Advertising Code (adopted pursuant to s 19(1)(c) of the Broadcasting Act, 2001) are codes to which this definition refers.

[52] Broadcasting Act, 2001, s 24(6).

soon as may be after deciding a complaint, the Broadcasting Complaints Commission must send a statement in writing of its decision to: (i) the person who made the complaint; (ii) the broadcaster concerned; and (iii) in instances where the broadcast which prompts a complaint is made on a broadcasting service which is not a free-to-air service provided by RTÉ or Teilifis na Gaeilge, the Broadcasting Commission of Ireland.[53]

Where the Broadcasting Complaints Commission decides a complaint concerning, **[5–14]** amongst other matters, a breach of the BCI General Advertising Code or the BCI Children's Advertising Codes, the Commission must, as soon as possible after its decision, send a statement in writing of its decision to the person with whom the broadcaster concerned agreed to broadcast the relevant advertisement (assuming such person is not the complainant).[54] Any consideration by the Broadcasting Complaints Commission of a complaint made under s 24 must be carried out by the Commission in private.[55] However, unless the Commission considers it inappropriate to do so, it is required to publish particulars of its decision on a complaint as soon as may be after making its decision and in such manner as it considers suitable.[56] If the Commission considers that publication of these particulars should be, or include publication, by the broadcaster concerned, then the broadcaster must publish the particulars in such manner as is agreed between the Commission and the broadcaster concerned.[57] Without prejudice to the foregoing, the broadcaster concerned must (unless the Commission considers it inappropriate) broadcast every decision by the Commission in which the Commission finds wholly or partly in favour of the complainant, including (in the case of a complaint that in a broadcast by a broadcaster an assertion was made of inaccurate facts or information in relation to a person which constituted an attack on that person's honour or reputation) any correction of inaccurate facts or information relating to the person concerned, at a time and in a manner corresponding to that in which the broadcast complained of took place.[58]

The Broadcasting Complaints Commission has no power to award costs or expenses **[5–15]** in any proceedings under s 24.[59] (The expenses incurred by the Commission in performing its functions are generally defrayed by the Broadcasting Commission of Ireland pursuant to s 23 of the 2001 Act). A person may not act as a member of the Broadcasting Complaints Commission in relation to a matter in which s/he has a material financial or other beneficial interest.[60]

---

[53] Broadcasting Act, 2001, s 24(7).
[54] Broadcasting Act, 2001, s 24(8).
[55] Broadcasting Act, 2001, s 24(9).
[56] Broadcasting Act, 2001, s 24(10).
[57] *ibid.*
[58] Broadcasting Act, 2001, s 24(11).
[59] Broadcasting Act, 2001, s 24(12).
[60] Broadcasting Act, 2001, s 24(13).

Religion, Politics and Industrial Disputes

[5–16]   Section 20(4) of the 1960 Act prohibits RTÉ from accepting any advertisement directed towards a religious or political end or which has any relation to an industrial dispute.[61] Section 10(3) of the Radio and Television Act, 1988, contains a similar prohibition in respect of independent sound broadcasters and s 50(2) of the 2001 Act applies s 20(4) of the 1960 Act to Teilifís na Gaeilge. The 2001 Act further provides that nothing in s 20(4) of the 1960 Act or s 10(3) of the 1988 Act (including either of those sections as applied by the 2001 Act) shall be construed as preventing a notice of the fact that: (i) a particular religious newspaper, magazine or periodical is available for sale or supply; (ii) any event or ceremony associated with a particular religion will take place, provided that the contents of the notice do not address the issue of the merits or otherwise of adhering to any religious faith or belief or of becoming a member of any religion or religious organisation.[62]

[5–17]   Section 20(4) of the 1960 Act was invoked by the Broadcasting Complaints Commission when adjudicating, in July 2005, on a complaint concerning a radio advertisement on two radio stations (RTÉ One and Today FM) by the then interim National Consumer Agency.[63] The advertisement encouraged listeners to participate in a consultative process regarding the then proposed revocation of certain legislation. The Broadcasting Complaints Commission decided that a consultation process regarding legislation is a political matter.[64] Moreover, in this instance, the listener was not only invited to participate in the consultative process (and so influence a political decision) but was also encouraged to access the National Consumer Agency's web-site or place a telephone call with it and thereby access information on the stance that the National Consumer Agency had adopted regarding the proposed revocation of the legislation. As a result, the Commission concluded, the advertisement was directed towards a political end and so prohibited under s 20(4) of the 1960 Act. The Commission therefore upheld the complaint made.

[5–18]   The constitutionality of, and rationale for, s 10(3) of the 1988 Act has been considered by the Superior Courts in *Murphy v The Independent Radio and Television Commission and The Attorney General,*[65] and again in *Colgan v The Independent Radio and Television Commission, Ireland and The Attorney General.*[66]

[5–19]   In the *Murphy* case, the applicant was a pastor attached to the Irish Faith Centre, a bible-based Christian ministry. In the High Court the applicant had unsuccessfully challenged a decision of The Independent Radio and Television Commission to refuse permission to 98FM (an independent radio station) to broadcast an advertisement concerning a presentation on the purported resurrection of Jesus Christ. On appealing this decision to the Supreme Court, the sole argument eventually made by the

---

[61] Broadcasting Authority Act, 1960, s 20(4).
[62] Broadcasting Act, 2001, s 65.
[63] Broadcasting Complaints Commission Decisions No 134/05 and 144/05.
[64] In arriving at this conclusion, the Broadcasting Complaints Commission had regard to the decision of the High Court in the *Colgan* case, considered latter in the main text above.
[65] [1999] 1 IR 12.
[66] [2000] 2 IR 490.

applicant was that s 10(3) was unconstitutional in that it violated the guarantees of freedom of religion contained in Article 44.2.1° and 3° of the Constitution, violated the guarantees of free speech and free expression in Article 40.6 of the Constitution, and violated the principle of proportionality in its total prohibition on the broadcasting of any advertisement "directed towards any religious end". All three arguments were rejected in a unanimous decision of the Supreme Court delivered by Barrington J. In the course of delivering judgment, Barrington J. considered the purpose of the prohibition contained in s 10(3), stating that:

> "It seems to the [Supreme] Court important to stress that there are three kinds of advertisements which are totally banned. These are:-
>
> 1. advertisements directed towards any religious end,
> 2. advertisements directed towards any political end,
> 3. advertisements which have any relation to an industrial dispute.
>
> One can best glean the policy of the Act of 1988 by looking at the three kinds of prohibited advertisement collectively. One might get a false impression by singling out one kind of banned advertisement and ignoring the others. All three kinds of banned advertisement relate to matters which would have proved extremely divisive in Irish society in the past. The Oireachtas was entitled to take the view that the citizens would resent having advertisements touching on these topics broadcast into their homes and that such advertisements, if permitted, might lead to unrest. Moreover the Oireachtas may well have thought that in relation to matters of such sensitivity, rich men should not be able to buy access to the airwaves to the detriment of their poorer rivals."[67]

Insofar as the arguments advanced under Articles 44.2.1° and 3° and 40.6 were concerned, Barrington J concluded that as both the right of freedom of expression and the right of freedom of communication are personal rights they can both, in certain circumstances, be limited in the interests of the common good. This brought Barrington J to the issue of proportionality, more particularly whether the limitation imposed by s 10(3) upon the various constitutional rights under consideration was proportionate to the purpose which the Oireachtas wished to achieve thereby. In this regard, the learned judge stated that:

> "In the present case the limitation placed on the various constitutional rights is minimalist. The applicant has the right to advance his views in speech or by writing or by holding assemblies or associating with persons of like mind to himself. He has no lesser right than any other citizen to appear on radio or television. The only restriction placed upon his activities is that he cannot advance his views by a paid advertisement on radio or television....Counsel for the applicant argued that it would have been possible to have had-instead of a blanket ban on religious advertising-a more selective administrative system whereby inoffensive religious advertisements would be permitted and religious advertise-ments likely to cause offence, banned. No doubt this is true. But the Oireachtas may well have decided that it would be inappropriate to involve agents of the State in deciding which advertisements, in this sensitive area would be likely to cause offence and which not. In any event, once the Statute is broadly within the area of the competence of the

---

[67] [1999] 1 IR 12 at 22.

Oireachtas and the Oireachtas has respected the principle of proportionality, it is not foe this Court to interfere simply because it might have made a different decision."[68]

[5–20] The Supreme Court concluded that the prohibition on religious advertising contained in s 10(3) of the 1988 Act: is rationally connected to the objective of the Act; is not arbitrary, unfair or based on irrational considerations; appears to impair the various constitutional rights considered as little as possible; affects those rights in a manner proportionate to the objective of the Act.

[5–21] Whereas the *Murphy* case involved an advertisement directed towards a religious end, the *Colgan* case was concerned with an advertisement directed towards a political end, specifically an advertisement on abortion which a pro-life association known as 'Youth Defence' had sought to broadcast and which The Independent Radio and Television Commission had directed certain independent radio stations not to broadcast on the basis that the advertisement was political in nature. The applicant, a member of 'Youth Defence', sought unsuccessfully to have the decision of The Independent Radio and Television Commission quashed and challenged (unsuccessfully) the constitutionality of s 10(3) of the 1988 Act. In the course of delivering judgment, O'Sullivan J considered what s 10(3) means by the phrase "political end". In this regard, O'Sullivan J concluded as follows:

> "In the absence of a statutory definition of 'political end', I consider that an advertisement has a political end within the meaning of section 10(3) if it is directed towards furthering the interests of a particular political party or towards procuring changes in the laws of this country or, I would add, countering suggested changes in those laws, or towards procuring changes in the laws of a foreign country or countering suggested changes in those laws or procuring a reversal of government policy or of particular decisions of governmental authorities in this country or, I would add, countering suggested reversals thereof or procuring a reversal of governmental policy or of particular decisions of governmental authorities in a foreign country or countering suggested reversals thereof."[69]

The applicant contended that the advertisement was simply an anti-abortion advertisement, that its purpose was to dissuade Irish mothers, primarily young Irish mothers, from going abroad for abortions. The applicant contended that the advertisement was not intended to procure either a constitutional referendum on the issue of abortion or a change in the law pertaining to abortion, both of which the applicant had accepted in evidence as being objectives of 'Youth Defence'. O'Sullivan J considered that the advertisement at issue was so closely bound up with the political objectives of 'Youth Defence' that "it would be unrealistic and artificial to shut one's eyes to these objectives and construe the advertisement out of context and severed from its background".[70] Accordingly, O'Sullivan J concluded that the advertisement at issue did have a political end and that The Independent Radio and Television Commission had been correct in prohibiting it.[71]

---

[68] *ibid.* at 26 *et seq.*
[69] [2000] 2 IR 490 at 504.
[70] *ibid.* at 507.
[71] *ibid.*

Insofar as the constitutionality of s 10(3) was concerned, O'Sullivan J's judgment is [5–22] largely concerned with the issue of whether he was bound by the decision of the Supreme Court in the *Murphy* case, or whether the decision of the Supreme Court in the *Murphy* case could be distinguished by reference to the facts of that case. In this regard, counsel for the applicant submitted that religious advertisements could be distinguished from political advertisements on the basis that religious advertisements are more sensitive. O'Sullivan J rejected the contention that the *Murphy* decision could be distinguished in terms of the different sensitivity of religious and political advertisements. He considered himself bound by the Supreme Court decision that the impairment of constitutional rights effected by s 10(3) is minimalist and proportionate. O'Sullivan J also rejected the contention that in light of the positive guarantee afforded the right to life of the unborn in Article 40.3.3 of the Constitution, an advertisement with the political end of vindicating such a right must itself be exempted from any general prohibition on advertisements with a political end (even assuming such a general prohibition to be constitutional).

Broadcasting Bill 2008[72]

On 22 May 2008, a Broadcasting Bill was initiated before Seanad Éireann. The Bill, if [5–23] enacted, will establish a new broadcasting content regulator to be known as the Broadcasting Authority of Ireland (BAI). This new authority will discharge the existing functions of the (to be dissolved) Broadcasting Commission of Ireland and Broadcasting Complaints Commission. It will also undertake certain additional functions, notably as regards the oversight of public funding to public service broadcasters. Enforcement of, and investigations regarding compliance with, broadcasting codes and rules will become the responsibility of a committee of the BAI to be known as the Compliance Committee. In its initial form the Bill anticipates that the BAI will be funded principally by means of a levy on the broadcasting sector.

---

[72] No 29 of 2008.

Chapter 6

THE BCI GENERAL ADVERTISING CODE[1]

Introduction

Pursuant to s 19(1)(b) of the Broadcasting Act, 2001,[2] the Broadcasting Commission of Ireland (or 'BCI') has published a General Advertising Code which came into effect on 10 April 2007.[3] The BCI General Advertising Code is directed at broadcasters. However, it is of practical significance for financial product or service providers in that its provisions will be applied by affected broadcasters in Ireland to any radio or television advertising that such providers may seek to broadcast. The title of the BCI General Advertising Code is something of a misnomer as many of its provisions apply to all 'commercial communications', a term which is included but not limited to

[6–01]

---

[1] Broadcasting Commission of Ireland, *General Advertising Code* (Dublin: 2007). The General Advertising Code is published in the English and Irish languages and the comment on, and quotes from, the BCI Code in this text are concerned with, and drawn from, the English-language version. As of 21 April 2008, the text of the BCI General Advertising Code was available on-line at www.bci.ie/documents/BCI_gen_ad_code_mar_07.pdf.

[2] No 4 of 2001.

[3] BCI General Advertising Code, 3.

'advertising', whereas other of its provisions apply to advertising only.[4] Consistent with the principle of home state supervision established under the 'Television without Frontiers' Directive[5], whereby television stations are obliged to conform with the rules laid down in the jurisdiction in which they are licensed, prominent foreign television broadcasters such as the BBC, Channel 4, ITV and Sky TV, are not required to comply with the terms of the BCI General Advertising Code, even where they broadcast advertisements that are specifically aimed at the Irish market.

The BCI Guidance Notes

[6–02] In addition to publishing the BCI General Advertising Code, the Broadcasting Commission has published a useful set of non-binding guidance notes on the Code. These guidance notes also took effect on 10 April 2007.[6] The guidance notes are intended to assist broadcasters and the general public in their interpretation (and broadcasters in their application) of the Code. Somewhat unusually perhaps, given that the Broadcasting Commission of Ireland published both the General Advertising Code and the related Guidance Notes, the Broadcasting Commission disclaims all liability for any guidance given in the Guidance Notes, reserves the right to review and revise any guidance provided, requires broadcasters to "make their own independent assessment after taking their own advice" and after making appropriate inquiries and undertaking appropriate research.[7]

Applicability of BCI General Advertising Code

[6–03] All broadcasters licensed in Ireland and/or those who make use of a frequency or satellite capacity or link-up in Ireland must comply with the General Advertising Code. In practical terms this means that the Code applies to RTÉ radio and television, TG4 and the various community, local, national and regional radio and television services licensed under the Radio and Television Act, 1988[8] and/or the Broadcasting Act, 2001.[9]

Compliance with BCI General Advertising Code

[6–04] Compliance with the Code is a matter for broadcasters.[10] They are required to ensure that their staff are familiar with the provisions of the Code.[11] Compliance with the Code is policed and assessed by the Broadcasting Commission of Ireland by reference

---

[4] The meaning of the terms 'commercial communication' and 'advertising' (and various other terms employed in the BCI General Advertising Code) are considered later in the main text above.

[5] Council Directive 89/552/EEC of 3 October 1989 on the co-ordination of certain provisions laid down by law, regulation or administrative action in Member States concerning the pursuit of television broadcasting activities (OJ No L298, 17 October 1989, 23), as amended.

[6] Broadcasting Commission of Ireland, *BCI General Advertising Code Guidance Notes* (Dublin: 2007).

[7] BCI Guidance Notes, 2. Notwithstanding this disclaimer, it would of course be difficult, if not impossible, for the Broadcasting Commission to resile from any interpretation of the BCI General Advertising Code contained in the BCI Guidance Notes.

[8] No 20 of 1988.

[9] BCI General Advertising Code, 2.

[10] *ibid.*

[11] *ibid.*

to applicable statutory provisions, the General Advertising Code, and the practices and policies of the Broadcasting Commission.[12] Complaints in respect of the Code fall to be adjudicated upon by the Broadcasting Complaints Commission.[13]

Copy Clearance and Guidance

The Broadcasting Commission does not provide a 'copy clearance' (or pre-broadcast [6–05] vetting) service in respect of commercial communications to advertisers, broadcasters or the general public. Such a service is available from broadcasters and other entities.[14] The Broadcasting Commission is satisfied to provide non-binding general guidance on the General Advertising Code.[15] Some limited provision as regards the provision of such guidance is set out in the General Advertising Code itself, the BCI Guidance Notes amplifying further on when, how and on what basis the Broadcasting Commission is willing to provide such guidance.[16]

Objectives of the BCI General Advertising Code

The BCI General Advertising Code states itself to have five principal objectives: (i) to [6–06] ensure that the general public can be confident that commercial communications are legal, honest, truthful and decent; (ii) to ensure that the editorial integrity of broadcasts are not impinged upon by commercial communications; (iii) to provide clear guidance to broadcasters on the standards to which commercial communications must adhere; (iv) to provide guidance to the general public on the standards which they can expect in commercial communications on broadcasting services; and (v) to

---

[12] BCI Guidance Notes, 3.

[13] BCI General Advertising Code, 2.

[14] BCI Guidance Notes, 3.

[15] BCI General Advertising Code, 2. While such guidance may not be binding on those to whom it is issued, the extent to which (if at all) the Broadcasting Commission could itself seek to resile from any such guidance that it gives, is open to question.

[16] Thus, per the BCI Guidance Notes, at 4: "When requested, the BCI is happy to provide general guidance for broadcasters, advertisers and the public regarding the provisions of [the]...Code. However, the BCI only provides more specific guidance in relation to atypical commercial communications when such requests are accompanied by supporting documentation, such as a script. In the interest of clarity, the guidelines for those seeking advice in relation to such material are as follows:- 1. Requests for advice must be submitted in writing or email and include the complete text and, where relevant, audio/video copy of the commercial communication in question. 2. The submission should clearly state the section/s of the Code, which the broadcaster believes are relevant, and set out the reasons why it believes the commercial communication in question complies with the Code. Queries which are submitted without a text or comment will not be considered. 3. The BCI is mindful of the short timeframes under which broadcasters operate and will endeavour to provide an initial response to the query as soon as possible. However, broadcasters should note that this could take up to two working days or longer if the query is especially complex. Failure to provide a script and/ or comment will delay this process. 4. The BCI response will set out the BCI's view in relation to the submission but interested parties will be invited to make follow-up submissions within an agreed timeframe. Following this the BCI will take a final view on the matter. 5. While a commercial communication is under consideration, broadcasters will normally be requested to refrain from airing the communication. 6. These procedures come into effect from 10th April 2007. 7. Scripts can be sent by post or emailed to codes@bci.ie."

provide broadcasters with a comprehensive, yet simple and flexible code that does not impede in an unwarranted manner on their right to communicate commercial messages.[17] The BCI Guidance Notes summarise the objectives of the Code as being "primarily to recognise the right of the public to honest, legal, truthful and decent commercial communications and to inform them that broadcasters are required to recognise this right."[18] The BCI Guidance Notes suggest that the Code also highlights the need for a common understanding between broadcasters and the general public about the standards expected of commercial communications.

Advertising Defined

[6–07]   The BCI General Advertising Code contains the most comprehensive definition of advertising of all the measures considered in this text. It defines the general term "advertising".[19] It also defines the terms "misleading advertising",[20] "comparative advertising",[21] "surreptitious advertising",[22] "subliminal advertising",[23] "virtual advertising",[24] "interactive advertising"[25] and "split-screen

---

[17] BCI General Advertising Code, 3.

[18] BCI Guidance Notes, 5.

[19] "Advertising" is defined as "[a]ny form of announcement broadcast in return for payment or for similar consideration or broadcast for self-promotional purposes by a public or private undertaking in connection with a trade, business, craft or profession in order to promote the supply of products or services, including immovable property, activities, rights and obligations, in return for payment." (BCI General Advertising Code, 3).

[20] "Misleading advertising" is defined as "[a]dvertising which contains any element of spoken or visual presentation which misleads or is likely to mislead, either directly or by implication, by act or omission, with regard to the merits of the product or service advertised or its suitability for the purpose recommended and which, by reason of its misleading nature, is likely to prejudice the interests of individuals or a competitor." (BCI General Advertising Code, 4).

[21] "Comparative advertising" is defined as "[a]dvertising that contains explicit or implicit identification of a competitor or products or services offered by a competitor." (BCI General Advertising Code, 4).

[22] "Surreptitious advertising" is defined as "[t]he representation in words or pictures of products, services, the name, the trade mark or the activities of a producer of products or a provider of services in programmes when such representation is intended to serve advertising and might mislead the public as to its nature, Such representation is deemed to be intentional if it is done in return for payment or similar consideration." (BCI General Advertising Code, 4).

[23] "Subliminal advertising" is defined as meaning "[a]dvertising that includes any technical device which, by using images of very brief duration or by any other means, exploits the possibility of conveying a message to, or otherwise influencing the minds of, members of an audience without their being aware or fully aware of what has been done." (BCI General Advertising Code, 4).

[24] "Virtual advertising" is defined as "[a]n advertising technique which allows broadcasters to electronically insert virtual advertising messages or sponsorship announcements into a television programme by altering the broadcast signal itself." (BCI General Advertising Code, 4).

[25] "Interactive advertising" is defined as "[a]n advertising technique which allows the viewer to interact with television by actively choosing the advertising content to which s/he wishes to be exposed for so long as s/he wants. Interactive advertising allows the viewer to provide information directly to the broadcaster/advertiser by means of a return path, and/or participate in an interactive environment which is separate from the broadcast content." (BCI General Advertising Code, 4).

advertising".[26] Although the various terms, as defined, are sometimes capitalised, this capitalised form is not used consistently throughout the text of the BCI General Advertising Code (and in this text are used in whatever form is appropriate, depending on where they appear).

Having defined "advertising" and the various forms thereof, the Code then identifies [6–08] certain announcements that do not constitute advertising, namely: "[i] informational announcements about upcoming programmes on broadcast services[27]....[ii] free-of-charge air time given to any registered charity for it to make an appeal....[iii] public service announcements (such as public safety and health announcements) that are not broadcast for payment or similar consideration....[iv] certain information announcements of forthcoming concerts, recitals or performances[28]....[v] announcements of outside broadcasting events or of non-broadcast events organised in whole or in part by the broadcaster if the public are allowed entry free of charge[29].

The fact that a particular announcement does not constitute "advertising" within the [6–09] meaning of the BCI General Advertising Code does not mean that such announcement therefore falls outside the scope of the Code. It is required to comply with those provisions of the BCI General Advertising Code that are concerned with commercial

---

[26] "Split-screen advertising" is defined as meaning "[a]n advertising technique which allows the simultaneous presentation of editorial content and commercial information on the same screen, divided into two or more parts." (BCI General Advertising Code, 4).

[27] Such informational announcements may include the date and time of transmission of the named programmes and include 'trailers' and/or a brief description of the content of such programmes. However, they may not contain advertising content; if they do, they will constitute advertising. (BCI General Advertising Code, 5).

[28] I.e. "forthcoming concerts, recitals or performances, whether intended for broadcast or not, given by the National Symphony Orchestra, the RTÉ Concert Orchestra, and other RTÉ performing groups or of any other comparable groups which are employed by or under contract to RTÉ or employed by or under contract to a sound broadcasting contractor or a television broadcasting contractor licensed in the State." (BCI General Advertising Code, 5). Persons hearing or watching such announcements would perhaps be surprised to learn that they do not constitute "advertising" for the purposes of the BCI General Advertising Code. The BCI Guidance Notes indicate that the exclusion, from the definition of "advertising", of announcements concerned with the foregoing, applies whether the public is granted free entry, or is required to pay a fee, to view the performance. (BCI Guidance Notes, 7).

[29] The BCI General Advertising Code further provides in respect of such announcements that "[i] The broadcaster may credit the sponsor providing the facilities, for example the commercial outlet providing the facilities for the outside broadcast, at the beginning and/or end of the programme and at prudent intervals during the programme on an informational basis....[ii] In the case of non-broadcast events jointly sponsored by the broadcaster and one or more commercial concern, the broadcaster may credit the joint sponsor(s) in broadcast announcements.....[iii] In both of these cases, sponsorship acknowldgements shall comply with the sponsorship rules contained in this code." (BCI General Advertising Code, 5). The BCI Guidance Notes confirm that the exclusion from the definition of "advertising" of announcements coming within category [v], as mentioned in the main text above, only applies where the public are admitted to the relevant event free of charge and does not "extend to paid events including those where the broadcaster has made a contra deal for tickets or other similar commercial promotional arrangements". (BCI Guidance Notes, 8).

communications but not with those provisions concerned exclusively with "advertising".[30] The Guidance Notes mention in the context of announcements which are excluded from the definition of "advertising" that such announcements may not contain references to products or services which are prohibited under Section 9 of the BCI General Advertising Code or otherwise under Irish or European legislation.[31]

Some Other Key Terms Defined

[6–10]   In addition to defining the term "advertising" and various species of advertising, the BCI General Advertising Code also defines a limited number of other terms, namely "commercial communication", "child"/"children", "sponsorship", "teleshopping", and "product placement". A "commercial communication" is defined as "[a]ny form of announcement on radio and television coming within the recognised character [presumably the popularly recognised character] of advertising, sponsorship and teleshopping and any other form of commercial communication."[32] The terms "child" and "children" are defined as referring to persons under 18 years of age.[33] (The Code does not indicate whether it means in this definition to refer to people who have not yet commenced, or who have not yet completed, their eighteenth year). "Sponsorship" is defined as "[a]ny contribution made by a public or private undertaking not engaged in television and/or radio broadcasting activities or in the production of audio visual works, to the financing of television and/or radio programmes with a view to promoting its name, its trademark, its image, its activities, its products or its services."[34] "Teleshopping" is defined as "[a] direct offer broadcast to the public with a view to the sale, purchase, rental or supply of products or the provision of services, including immovable property, rights and obligations, in return for payment."[35] Lastly, the term "product placement" is defined as "[t]he inclusion of, or a reference to, a product or service within a programme in return for payment or similar consideration to the programme maker or broadcaster for the specific purpose of promoting that product or service."[36]

General Principles and Rules Applying to All Commercial Communications

[6–11]   In the BCI General Advertising Code, four classes of principle are addressed under the above heading: those concerned with protecting the individual and society; those concerned with protecting human dignity and preventing both harm and serious or widespread offence; those concerned with 'transparency' (in effect, that a commercial arrangement within programming must be identifiable and identified as such); and those identifying the basis on which commercial communications will be assessed by the Broadcasting Commission of Ireland. As the heading suggests, these general

---

[30] BCI Guidance Notes, 7.

[31] *ibid.* The commercial communications proscribed by Section 9 of the BCI General Advertising Code are considered later in the main text .

[32] BCI General Advertising Code, 3.

[33] *ibid.*

[34] *ibid.*

[35] *ibid.*

[36] BCI General Advertising Code, 4.

principles apply to all commercial communications, including advertisements, a point emphasised in the BCI Guidance Notes[37].

Protecting the Individual and Society

The BCI General Advertising Code requires that all commercial communications: (i) be prepared with a sense of responsibility to the individual and to society and not prejudice the interests of either[38]; (ii) be legal, honest, decent and truthful[39]; (iii) comply with all applicable Irish and European legislation[40]; (iv) not contain any spoken or visual presentation which is likely to (or does) mislead "either directly or by implication, by act or omission" as regards the merits of the product or service being promoted or its suitability for the recommended purposes[41]; (v) not contain inaccurate or misleading claims, illustrations, representations or statements (whether direct or implied)[42]; (vi) not omit relevant information in such manner as to mislead or be likely to mislead[43]; (vii) avoid disclaimers and asterisked or footnoted information that contradicts more prominent aspects of the message (such disclaimers and asterisked or footnoted information to be located and presented in such manner as to be clearly audible and/or visible)[44]; (viii) where required to carry a tag-line or on-screen message, do so in a way that is clearly audible and/or visible.[45] The BCI Guidance Notes state, with regard to the foregoing, that broadcasters must devise mechanisms whereby they may satisfy themselves that such matters as the claims and details made in a commercial communication are legal, decent, honest and truthful.[46]

[6–12]

The requirement that commercial communications be legal, honest, decent and truthful and also that they not prejudice human dignity or cause harm or serious or widespread offence was the subject of a complaint concerning a financial

[6–13]

---

[37] BCI Guidance Notes, 8.

[38] BCI General Advertising Code, 6, para 3.1.

[39] *ibid.*

[40] BCI General Advertising Code, 6, para 3.1.1.

[41] BCI General Advertising Code, 6, para 3.1.2.

[42] BCI General Advertising Code, 6, para 3.1.3.

[43] BCI General Advertising Code, 6, para 3.1.4. The Code adds that this particular requirement means that all the pertinent details of an offer must be stated in a clear and understandable manner.

[44] BCI General Advertising Code, 6, para 3.1.5. The BCI Guidance Notes state in this regard that broadcasters should take steps to ensure that the main offer in a commercial communication (or other significant information) is not contained in the 'footnoted' text only. (BCI Guidance Notes, 9).

[45] BCI General Advertising Code, 6, para 3.1.6. The BCI Guidance Notes state in this regard that "It is not the BCI's general practice to describe standards in respect of the placement and size of on-screen taglines or other information. However, in the interests of best practice, where practicable, broadcasters should consider using plain language which is easily understood by listeners and viewers. In terms of on-screen messages, broadcasters should be mindful of the varying abilities of the public in terms of their physical and educational ability to read on-screen text. Broadcasters should also take into consideration the time required to read the specific text and matters of readability such as the contrast between the text and background picture onto which it is placed." (BCI Guidance Notes, 10).

[46] BCI Guidance Notes, 8.

advertisement that was considered by the Broadcasting Complaints Commission in August 2007.[47] The advertisement complained of was for Halifax/Royal Bank of Scotland. It involved a conversation between a couple where a woman threatened to leave her partner because she had been made a "better offer". Instead of fighting to retain her, the man responded "Go ahead", to which the woman retorted "You're such a banker". At this point in the advertisement it became apparent that the conversation was not between a couple but between a woman and her banker and that the woman was talking about changing banks. The complainant alleged that the line "You're such a banker" was in fact an ironic reference to a rhyming slang word that he found gratuitous and offensive.

[6–14]   RTÉ indicated that the Copy Clearance Committee within RTÉ had been of the view that the term banker was a reference to bankers, no more, and was consistent with previous usage of the word in previous advertisements by Halifax/Royal Bank of Scotland. The advertiser gave a similar response, stating that the complainant's claim that the woman in the advertisement had engaged in an ironic reference to an offensive slang word was "imaginative but incorrect"[48] and that the word 'banker' had been used in its literal sense to refer to a person who owns or manages a bank. In its decision, the Broadcasting Complaints Commission concluded that: the advertisement was for a banking product; the man in the advertisement was a banker and was addressed by the woman as such; the tone throughout the advertisement was mild and light-hearted; and "given the tone and the product being promoted...the use of the word banker could not be considered unacceptable".[49] The Commission therefore rejected the complaint made.

[6–15]   The General Advertising Code also states that broadcasters must be mindful of the potential for sound effects to alarm and/or distract listeners and viewers.[50] In this regard, the BCI General Advertising Code states that: particular care should be taken when including sound effects such as horns, ringing phones, screeching tyres and sirens in commercial communications (and must not include them at the beginning of a commercial communication).[51] Insofar as comparative advertising is concerned, commercial communications containing direct or implied comparisons with other products or services are permitted under the BCI General Advertising Code "provided they objectively compare products or services meeting the same needs or intended for the same purpose."[52] However, the Code requires that: points of comparison be based on substantiable facts; and the subject-matter of the comparison must not be chosen in such way as to confer an artificial or unfair advantage to a product/service provider.[53]

---

[47] Broadcasting Complaints Commission Decision No 226/07.
[48] Broadcasting Complaints Commission Decision No 226/07, 1.
[49] Broadcasting Complaints Commission Decision No 226/07, 2.
[50] BCI General Advertising Code, 6, para 3.1.7.
[51] *ibid*. The Guidance Notes explain that the reason for proscribing such sound effects at the start of a commercial communication is to avoid creating potentially hazardous distractions and so cause confusion to a consumer.
[52] BCI General Advertising Code, 6, para 3.1.8.
[53] *ibid*.

The requirement that commercial communications be prepared with a sense of responsibility to the individual and society and not prejudice the interests of either (and also that commercial communications be appropriately scheduled) was the subject of a complaint concerning a financial advertisement that was adjudicated upon by the Broadcasting Complaints Commission in August 2007.[54] The advertisement complained of was for Bank of Ireland and contained a number of fictional monsters, including 'Dave Bogeyman' who lived under a child's bed and was hoping to find a new place to live. The complainant complained that the advertisement was frightening for children and queried the use of a child in an advertisement seeking adult custom. **[6–16]**

RTÉ (which had broadcast the advertisement) indicated that its own Copy Clearance Committee had imposed restrictions on the airing-time of the advertisement, which RTÉ had complied with. The advertisers indicated, amongst other matters, that: they always sought to avoid contravening the advertising codes applicable to them; they had exercised care during the production process of the relevant advertising campaign; the 'bogeyman' was part of children's folklore; they had presented the 'bogeyman' as having the typical concerns of ordinary consumers, e.g. money and mortgage concerns; 'Dave Bogeyman' had been modelled on the tarsier monkey, "a very cute, tiny, wide-eyed furry creature"[55], and that he was innocuous and charming by comparison to what children regularly encountered on television, computer games and in the cinema; and that airing-time restrictions imposed by RTÉ had been complied with. **[6–17]**

In its decision, the Broadcasting Complaints Commission concluded that: the only aspect of the characters depicted that may initially have been scary was their eyes; the tone and tenor of the advertisement was gentle with no scary music or menacing voices employed; the use of a child's voice and a child's bedroom coupled with the scary eyes meant the advertisement was inappropriate for broadcast in or around children's broadcasting (but that the broadcaster had curtailed its scheduling and broadcasting of the advertisement appropriately); and the complainant had viewed the advertisement on RTÉ 1 during programming aimed at adults and the content of the advertisement was appropriate for broadcast at that time and to the target audience. The Commission therefore rejected the complaint made. **[6–18]**

The issue as to whether a particular financial advertisement was misleading was considered by the Broadcasting Complaints Commission in October 2003.[56] The facts were straightforward. An advertisement on RTÉ radio for AA motor insurance stated that eligibility was subject to a three-year no-claims or accident-free motoring record. However, when the complainant rang AA Insurance, he was advised by an automatic answering machine/screening service that a four-year accident-free requirement applied. On speaking to a sales assistant, he was advised that a five-year accident-free requirement applied. When he subsequently received quotation documentation from AA Insurance, the complainant was again advised that a four-year no-claims **[6–19]**

---

[54] Broadcasting Complaints Commission Decision No 236/07.
[55] Broadcasting Complaints Commission Decision No 236/07, 2.
[56] Broadcasting Complaints Commission Decision No 136/03.

bonus applied along with a requirement that he obtain a letter from his previous insurer regarding his previous no-claims bonus history. The complainant claimed that the automatic advice received, the advice from the sales assistant and the later written quotation were all inconsistent with the advertisement as broadcast. AA Insurance indicated that the advertisement had been factually correct when broadcast and continued to be correct, that the telephone system and the sales assistant had been incorrect and remedial action had been taken in this regard. RTÉ indicated that in light of the foregoing it intended to continue the broadcast as it was factually true and correct. The Broadcasting Complaints Commission decided that the advertisement had been misleading and upheld the complaint made.

Offence, Harm and Human Dignity

[6–20]   The BCI General Advertising Code requires that commercial communications: not prejudice human dignity or cause harm or serious or widespread offence[57]; not support or condone discrimination against any person or section of the community[58]; not be offensive to religious or political beliefs[59]; not encourage behaviour prejudicial to environmental protection or to health and safety[60]; and be appropriately scheduled with regard to broadcast time, channel/service and programme type, the nature of the product or service being promoted and the likely audience composition.[61]

[6–21]   With regard to the last point above, the Guidance Notes indicate that the General Advertising Code seeks to address the role that context plays in determining the level of harm/offence that can be caused by an inappropriate commercial communication.[62] The Guidance Notes further indicate that it is these contextual factors that will be taken into account when the Broadcasting Commission of Ireland or the Broadcasting Complaints Commission are assessing compliance/complaints.[63] The contextual factors, per the Guidance Notes, may provide a reasonable justification for the content and scheduling of commercial communications but are also intended to guide broadcasters on how to avoid causing undue offence or harm.[64]

[6–22]   Provision is made under the heading 'Offence, Harm and Human Dignity' in respect of the protection of children. However, this provision only applies to those commercial communications that do not come within the scope of the BCI Children's Advertising Code.[65] The BCI General Advertising Code propounds the general precept that commercial communications must not cause moral or physical detriment to

---

[57] BCI General Advertising Code, 6, para 3.2.
[58] The Code makes particular mention in this regard of discrimination on the basis of age, gender, marital status, membership of the Traveller community, family status, sexual orientation, disability, race or religion. (BCI General Advertising Code, para 3.2.1)
[59] BCI General Advertising Code, 6, para 3.2.2.
[60] *ibid.*
[61] BCI General Advertising Code, 6, para 3.2.3.
[62] BCI Guidance Notes, 11.
[63] *ibid.*
[64] *ibid.*
[65] BCI General Advertising Code, 7, para 3.2.4.

children.[66] More particularly it requires that commercial communications "[i] not directly exhort children to buy a product or a service by exploiting their inexperience or credulity...[ii] not directly encourage children to persuade their parents or others to purchase the goods or services being advertised...[iii] not exploit the special trust children place in parents, teachers or other persons...[iv] not unreasonably show children in dangerous situations."[67]

Turning to portrayals of, and references to, living persons, the BCI General Advertising Code provides that individual living persons must not, without their permission, normally be portrayed, or referred to, in commercial communications.[68] The Code does not expressly refer to 'prior' permission, though clearly it would be, at the least, imprudent to proceed otherwise. The BCI General Advertising Code allows accurate and inoffensive references to living persons in commercial communications for books, films, magazines, newspapers, ratio and television programmes and the like, that feature such persons.[69] The Guidance Notes state of the provisions in respect of individual living persons that they are intended both to protect their dignity and also to respect their commercial rights.[70] The Guidance Notes suggest that the practical import of the provision made in this regard is that any reference to an individual which takes the form of a caricature or impersonation is prohibited, unless done with that individual's approval.[71] The Guidance Notes further state in this regard that broadcasters should "secure or request" documentation proving that such approval has been given. The phrase "secure or request" suggests that a broadcaster could, after requesting but before securing such proof, proceed to broadcast a commercial communication that portrays or refers to a living person. However, such a broadcaster would thereby be exposing itself to, at the least, a heightened risk of breaching the BCI General Advertising Code in this regard.

[6–23]

The BCI General Advertising Code requires that commercial communications not be calculated to induce unwarranted fear in a listener or viewer.[72] The Guidance Notes state that this rule is intended to ensure that any "appeal to fear" in a commercial communication is justifiable in the context of the activity, product or service promoted in the relevant commercial communication.[73] By way of example, it suggests that images calculated to induce a reasonable fear of the consequences of dangerous driving may be appropriate in a commercial communication in respect of what the Guidance Notes describe as "drink driving".[74]

[6–24]

---

[66] *ibid.*
[67] *ibid.*
[68] BCI General Advertising Code, 7. para 3.2.5.
[69] *ibid.*
[70] BCI Guidance Notes, 12.
[71] *ibid.*
[72] BCI General Advertising Code, 7. para 3.2.6.
[73] BCI Guidance Notes, 13.
[74] *ibid.*

Transparency

[6–25] The BCI General Advertising Code requires that commercial communications operate on a principle of transparency.[75] By this the Code means that any commercial arrangement within programming must be identifiable as such and the listener or viewer (as appropriate) must be made aware of such arrangement.[76]

[6–26] Having established this general principle, the BCI General Advertising Code proceeds to make certain related provision, namely that: (i) presenters and other 'on-air' personnel must not advertise or endorse products or services during editorial content[77]; (ii) advertisers or sponsors must not exercise any editorial influence over the conduct of programmes[78]; and (iii) commercial communications must not include the words 'guarantee', 'guaranteed', 'warranty' or 'warranted' unless a legal guarantee or warranty (as appropriate) is available to the broadcaster and the purchaser.[79] In particular, as regards this latter point, the BCI General Advertising Code prohibits any commercial communication from containing a direct or implied reference that purports to diminish or remove a purchaser's common law or statutory legal rights.[80]

[6–27] Continuing with matters of transparency, the BCI General Advertising Code makes provision in respect of testimonials, 'free' products and services, the use of news presenters in commercial communications and product placements.

---

[75] BCI General Advertising Code, 7, para 3.3.

[76] *ibid.*

[77] BCI General Advertising Code, 7, para 3.3.1. The BCI Guidance Notes indicate that under this rule broadcasters also have a responsibility to ensure that guests do not promote their products or services on air. (BCI Guidance Notes, 14). It is perhaps open to query just how far this rule is taken in practice, e.g. with chat shows where many of the guests are invited to appear ostensibly because they are well-known to the public but happen coincidentally to have published a book or released a sound recording that they are seeking to promote. The BCI Guidance Notes further provide that broadcasters should take particular care in the context of 'on-air' competitions. In this regard the BCI Guidance Notes state that "It has been the BCI's experience that descriptions of competition prizes and the mechanisms used to enter the competition may lead to advertising content and product or service endorsement taking place during competition announcements. In this respect, broadcasters should ensure that competitions comply with the rules under the heading of sponsorship…including rules in respect of competitions." (BCI Guidance Notes, 14).

[78] BCI General Advertising Code, 7, para 3.3.2. The Guidance Notes stress the importance of this rule in the context of outside broadcasts that are sponsored by a commercial venture. Apart from acknowledging the sponsor (in line with the sponsorship rules considered later in the main text above), such broadcasts are required (per the BCI Guidance Notes) not to include content which describes the sponsor's goods/products in such manner as to constitute advertising. "Content which breaches the sponsorship rules are likely to constitute advertising and will count towards advertising minuteage." (BCI Guidance Notes, 14).

[79] BCI General Advertising Code, 7, para. 3.3.3 The BCI Guidance Notes state that "This rule is intended to prevent the casual use of the term 'guarantee' during commercial communications" but presumably it is intended to prevent casual usage of all the terms referred to. (BCI Guidance Notes, 14).

[80] BCI General Advertising Code, 8, para 3.3.3.

The issue as to whether a particular financial advertisement blurred the distinction **[6–28]** between programming and a commercial communication was at issue in a complaint considered by the Broadcasting Complaints Commission in May 2005.[81] This was a complaint brought by RTÉ which claimed that it was applying this aspect of the BCI General Advertising Code more rigorously than other broadcasters and sought clarity as to the Broadcasting Complaints Commission's thinking in this regard. At issue was an advertisement broadcast by Newstalk 106 (a radio station) which featured two well-known RTÉ sports commentators talking about, and hence promoting, a particular insurance company. Newstalk 106 responded that: the advertisement featured two well-known personalities promoting a particular insurer and its products; it (Newstalk) assumed that the two men were contractually free to so act; and the complaint was motivated by the mistaken belief that the sporting broadcasters should only be heard on RTÉ. The advertiser gave a detailed response. It contested the suggestion that the commercial represented an attempt by them to blur the distinction between advertising and programming. It maintained that the advertisement followed an established and well-known marketing technique of having a pastiche of conversation between two well-known individuals and queried why it would have followed such a well-known technique (and included a telephone number for the insurance company) if it was seeking to confuse advertising and programming. It maintained that it was unaware of any confusion that had been caused to the general public by the advertisement in question. It maintained that anyone who listened up to the half-way point of the commercial (i.e. 21 seconds into a 40-second commercial) would have been in no doubt that they were listening to a commercial and not a programme. Lastly, it pointed to the fact that the format of the advertisement continued to be adhered to in a number of advertisements current at the time of the response. If RTÉ was looking for amplification by the Broadcasting Complaints Commission as to its thinking in this area, it was likely disappointed. The Commission rejected the complaint made and expressed the view that Newstalk 106 had not breached the advertising codes and that a listener could easily discern the advertisement complained of to be an advertisement.

Testimonials

The BCI General Advertising Code states that commercial communications may **[6–29]** make use of testimonials but such testimonials must be genuine, relevant and contemporary and relate to the person giving the testimonial (with documentary evidence of testimonials being available to the relevant broadcaster).[82] The BCI Guidance Notes define a testimonial as "a statement given by an individual reflecting their genuine views about the product or service promoted."[83] The Guidance Notes further state in this regard that the use of a male or female actor to give an incorrect impression of a testimonial is likely to be classified as misleading and in breach of the BCI General Advertising Code.[84] To avoid such difficulty, the BCI Guidance Notes

---

[81] Broadcasting Complaints Commission Decision No 101/05.
[82] BCI General Advertising Code, 8, para 3.3.4.
[83] BCI Guidance Notes, 15.
[84] *ibid.*

advise broadcasters to make clear that the person in a purported testimonial is in fact an actor, so ensuring audience awareness that the testimonial is not genuine.[85]

'Free' products or services

[6–30] The BCI General Advertising Code requires that commercial communications not describe products or services as 'free' unless the products or services are supplied to the recipient of same at no cost or no extra cost, apart from the actual cost of post or carriage.[86] The BCI Guidance Notes add that a trial may be described as 'free', notwithstanding that the customer has to pay for the costs of returning the goods, provided this cost is made clear in the relevant communication.[87]

News presenters

[6–31] The BCI General Advertising Code states that commercial communications must not feature persons who regularly present news programmes, though an exception is made in the case of commercial communications making charity appeals for registered charities or public service campaigns for e.g. education, health, or safety.[88] The BCI Guidance Notes amplifies on what constitutes a 'news programme' stating that the term means "main news bulletins, including extended news bulletins e.g. TV 3 News, RTÉ Six One News, Today FM Lunchtime News. It does not prohibit presenters of current affairs programmes or of weather, entertainment, traffic news items, etc., being featured in commercial communications."[89]

Product placement

[6–32] Under the BCI General Advertising Code, product placement is prohibited.[90] The term "product placement" is defined in the BCI General Advertising Code as "[t]he inclusion of, or a reference to, a product or service within a programme in return for payment or similar consideration to the programme maker or broadcaster for the specific purpose of promoting that product or service".[91] Incidental references to products/services within a programme are permitted where their inclusion is justified editorially but broadcasters are required to ensure that their inclusion does not afford undue prominence to the product/service during the programme.[92] Insofar as television is concerned, the BCI General Advertising Code provides that "the inclusion of products in a programme acquired from outside Ireland and films

---

[85] *ibid.* The Guidance Notes also mention certain testimonials by professionals, stating that "Rule 8.2.2 [of the BCI Code] prohibits testimonials by health professionals or by persons who, because of their celebrity, could encourage the use of medicines, medical treatments, products and services and/or cosmetic treatments and services. In addition, this rule prohibits testimonials which give the impression of professional advice or recommendation made by persons who appear in the commercial communication and who are presented whether actually or by implication, as being qualified to give such advice or recommendation." (BCI Guidance Notes, 15).

[86] BCI General Advertising Code, 8, para 3.3.5.

[87] BCI Guidance Notes, 15.

[88] BCI General Advertising Code, 8, para 3.3.6.

[89] BCI Guidance Notes, 15.

[90] BCI General Advertising Code, 8, para 3.3.7.

[91] BCI General Advertising Code, 4.

[92] BCI General Advertising Code, 8, para 3.3.7.

made for cinema are not considered product placement provided that no broadcaster regulated in the State and involved in the broadcast of that programme or film directly benefits from the arrangement." So, for example, a product placement of an international 'brand' in a United States television programme/cinema film imported into Ireland is permissible provided that no broadcaster regulated in Ireland and involved in the broadcast of the said television programme/cinema film directly benefits from the arrangement. The Guidance Notes explain that the difficulty with product placement is that it is deemed to be a form of surreptitious advertising and so prohibited by the BCI General Advertising Code.[93]

The principle of transparency is echoed in later provisions of the BCI General Advertising Code such as those concerned with the separation requirements in advertising, the prohibitions on product placement and on subliminal and surreptitious advertising, and the sponsorship rules, all considered below.

[6–33]

Assessment

The BCI General Advertising Code states that commercial communications will be assessed by reference to the principles and rules of the Code.[94] The principles contained in the BCI General Advertising Code are stated to be "indivisible", i.e. all commercial communications must conform to all the principles. In this regard the BCI General Advertising Code notes that broadcasters need to be mindful of all the provisions of the Code because any one commercial communication may be governed by more than one such provision.[95] The BCI General Advertising Code further states that commercial communications shall be assessed "in whole" (i.e. in their entirety) and in context against the principles and rules contained in the Code and in light of the following contextual factors: time of broadcast; type of programme; channel/service type; nature of the product or service; and the likely composition of the audience listening to (or watching) the programme.[96] Lastly in this regard, the BCI Code notes that it is intended to be applied in spirit as well as in the letter. The Guidance Notes add that the foregoing provisions regarding assessments will be used by the Broadcasting Complaints Commission when assessing complaints by members of the general public.[97]

[6–34]

General Rules Pertaining to All Advertising

The general rules pertaining to all advertising are almost entirely concerned with the maximum time limits for, and the maximum duration of, intervals between advertisements, as well as such matters as the types of programming into which advertising maybe inserted, the signalling and sound level of advertising breaks and the prohibition of isolated advertising in television broadcasts.[98] These rules are more properly the subject of a text on broadcasting law than a text on advertising law (as they do not impact on the content of financial advertisements) and are not considered here. Perhaps

[6–35]

---

[93] Per para 4.9 of the BCI General Advertising Code.
[94] BCI General Advertising Code, 8, para 3.4.
[95] *ibid.*
[96] BCI General Advertising Code, 8, para 3.4.1.
[97] BCI Guidance Notes, 16.
[98] BCI General Advertising Code, 9, paras. 4.1 to 4.10 (inclusive).

the matter of greatest interest to persons considering publishing an advertisement is the prohibition on misleading, subliminal or surreptitious advertising.[99]

Split-Screen, Virtual and Interactive Advertising and Teleshopping[100]

[6–36] The BCI General Advertising Code provides that general principles and rules applicable to all commercial communications (and, as relevant, the general rules pertaining to all advertising) apply to split-screen, virtual and interactive advertising.[101] The subject of interactive advertising may be of some interest to persons intending to publish advertisements for financial services. It will be recalled that interactive advertising is defined in the BCI General Advertising Code as "[a]n advertising technique which allows the viewer to interact with television by actively choosing the advertising content to which s/he wishes to be exposed for as long as s/he wants. Interactive advertising allows the viewer to provide information directly to the broadcaster/advertiser by means of a return path, and/or participate in an interactive environment which is separate from the broadcast content."[102]

[6–37] The BCI General Advertising Code requires that: interactive advertising not bring the viewer directly/immediately to advertised products or services, with viewers being warned that they are about to access an area not governed by the BCI General Advertising Code (to be done via an interim screen on which a click must be entered before accessing the interactive content).[103] Lastly, the BCI General Advertising Code provides that interactive advertising must not immediately/directly bring a viewer to commercial communications for products/services prohibited under the BCI Code.[104]

[6–38] The term "[t]eleshopping" is defined in the BCI General Advertising Code as "[a] direct offer broadcast to the public with a view to the sale, purchase, rental or supply of products or the provision of services, including immovable property, rights and obligations in return for payment."[105] It is not typical in Ireland for teleshopping to be concerned with financial services. Consequently the provisions of the BCI General Advertising Code pertaining to same are not considered here.

Sponsorship

[6–39] The term "sponsorship", for the purposes of the BCI General Advertising Code, means "[a]ny contribution made by a public or private undertaking not engaged in television and/or radio broadcasting activities or in the production of audio visual works, to the financing of television and/or radio programmes with a view to

---

[99] BCI General Advertising Code, 9, para 4.9.

[100] BCI General Advertising Code, 9, paras. 5 and 6

[101] BCI General Advertising Code, 9, para 5.1.1. Certain further provision is made by the BCI General Advertising Code (at paras. 5.1.2. to 5.1.4) regarding when, and what type of, split-screen advertising is permitted (and when it is not permitted). This further provision does not impact on the substance of financial advertisements and is not considered further in this text.

[102] BCI General Advertising Code, 4, para 2.

[103] BCI General Advertising Code, 10, para 5.3.2.

[104] BCI General Advertising Code, 10, para 5.3.3.

[105] BCI General Advertising Code, 4, para 2.

promoting its name, its trademark, its image, its activities, its products or its services."[106] The BCI Code states that such "sponsorship" may occur through the provision of direct funding by a sponsor or through investment-in-kind through the provision of facilities or services or the supply of products and services (including prizes).[107] Sponsorship *per se* does not constitute advertising for the purposes of the General Advertising Code.[108] On-air acknowledgments of sponsors and references to their products or services are permitted (provided those references do not in themselves constitute advertising).[109] Such acknowledgements (or announcements) must not make promotional references to the products and/or services of the sponsor which contain advertising copy, product attributes, descriptions, endorsements, or a call to action; generic branding slogans are allowed; and prices may only be quoted "where their inclusion is required by statute".[110]

The effect of all of this in practice, per the Guidance Notes, is that a programme may **[6–40]** now be sponsored, for example, by the 'Ford Focus' or by 'Eircom Broadband' whereas previous to the publication of the General Advertising Code such sponsorship acknowledgements would have constituted advertising.[111] Certain constraints are imposed. Thus: programme material must not be sponsored by one or more sponsors involved in the manufacture, provision or supply of a service that the Code does not allow to be advertised[112], e.g. cigarette manufacturers; programmes may not be sponsored where the prospective sponsor's products or services are not permitted to appeal to the typical audience for that programme[113] (e.g. alcohol advertising during children's programmes); programmes may not be sponsored where it is not permissible to advertise during such programme[114]; news, current affairs and religious programmes must not be sponsored on television[115]; and news programmes must not be sponsored on the radio.[116] According to the BCI Guidance Notes, "News programmes are defined as main news bulletins, including extended news bulletins e.g. TV 3 News, RTÉ Six One News, Today FM Lunchtime News etc. It does not prohibit sponsorship of weather, entertainment, traffic news items, current affairs or religious programmes on radio." Presumably in its reference to "religious programmes" and the potential for sponsorship of same, the Guidance Notes mean to draw a distinction between "religious programmes" and a "religious service". As advertising must not be inserted into the broadcast of a "religious service"[117], the broadcast of a radio or television religious service cannot be sponsored as the Code

---

[106] BCI General Advertising Code, 3, para 2.
[107] BCI General Advertising Code, 11, para 7.1.
[108] BCI General Advertising Code, 11, para 7.2.
[109] BCI Guidance Notes, 22.
[110] BCI General Advertising Code, 11, para 7.2 and BCI Guidance Notes, 22.
[111] BCI Guidance Notes, 22.
[112] BCI General Advertising Code, 11, para 7.3.
[113] BCI General Advertising Code, 11, para 7.4.
[114] *ibid.* Para 4.5 of the BCI General Advertising Code (at 9) provides that "Advertising shall not be inserted in any religious service".
[115] BCI General Advertising Code, 11, para 7.5.
[116] BCI General Advertising Code, 11, para 7.6.
[117] Per BCI General Advertising Code, 9, para 4.5.

states that a programme must not be sponsored, amongst other circumstances, where it is not permitted to advertise during that programme. In addition, the BCI General Code expressly provides that there cannot be sponsorship of a "religious programme" on television.[118]

Competitions[119]

[6–41] As a general rule, competitions must comply with the rules regarding sponsorship considered above.[120] Recognising that competition announcements need to contain some reference to the prizes on offer, the BCI General Advertising Code allows such announcements to contain short factual references to same but such references "shall not contain advertising copy, endorsements, attributes or a call to action".[121] The mechanism whereby an individual may participate in a competition (e.g. the 'how to enter and win' section) must not itself contain advertising content.[122] The Guidance Notes elaborate on this last provision, stating that a question should not promote the attributes of a sponsor's product or service and the 'mechanism to enter' must not include/require a call to purchase a sponsor's product/service as a means of entering a competition.[123]

Rules Pertaining to Specific Products and Services

[6–42] In addition to the foregoing rules, the BCI General Advertising Code introduces a variety of rules specific to certain products and services, including financial products and services, betting services and premium-rate telecommunication services. Each of these categories of product and/or service may be, or is, relevant in the context of advertising financial services in Ireland and is considered hereafter.

Financial Services and Products

[6–43] The BCI General Advertising Code contains only two rules under this heading. First, that commercial communications for financial products and services be presented in terms that do not mislead (by exaggeration, omission or in any other way).[124] Second, that such commercial communications comply with all other applicable laws, regulations and (presumably mandatory) rules, and codes of practice.[125] The requirements made under this heading are intended to apply to all financial products and services, including regulated credit arrangements, hire purchase, leasing, loans (including mortgages), savings, investments insurance, and financial services and products.[126]

---

[118] BCI General Advertising Code, 11, para 7.6.

[119] For a brief summary of the law generally applicable, and the self-regulation potentially applicable, to the operation of lotteries, see the chapter on Ireland by Barrett, G. and D. Voigt in Micklitz. H.W. and J. Kessler, eds., *Marketing Practices Regulation and Consumer Protection in the EC Member States and the US* (Baden-Baden: 2002) at 186ff.

[120] BCI General Advertising Code, 11, para 7.7.

[121] *ibid.*

[122] *ibid.*

[123] BCI Guidance Notes, 24.

[124] BCI General Advertising Code, 15, para 8.7.1.

[125] BCI General Advertising Code, 15, para 8.7.2.

[126] BCI Guidance Notes, 34.

Betting Services

Commercial communications which "seek to promote services to those who want to [6-44] bet" are permitted under the BCI General Advertising Code.[127] Although neither the BCI General Advertising Code nor the BCI Guidance Notes make express reference to spread-betting, such services would seem to be governed by the rules established under this heading. Commercial communications which seek to promote services to those who want to bet: (i) may contain the address of the service provider and factual descriptions of the services it provides[128]; (ii) must not contain anything which could be deemed an encouragement to bet,[129] including free bets as prizes in competitions[130]; and (iii) must not contain "[i]nformation detailing special offers, discounts, inducements to visit any betting establishment (including on-line), references to betting odds available or any promotional offer intended to encourage the use of [betting] services.[131]

Premium-rate Telecommunication Services

Under the BCI General Advertising Code, commercial communications for premium- [6-45] rate telecommunication services must: state clearly all charges arising for accessing same, such statement to be in terms that do not in any way mislead (whether by exaggeration or omission)[132]; and comply with the code of practice issued by the Regulator of Premium-Rate Telecommunication Services (RegTel).[133] Broadcasters are expected to have measures in place to make sure that any use of premium-rate services during competitions, etc. complies with RegTel's code of practice.[134]

Prohibited Communications

Without prejudice to any prohibitions contained in other legislative or regulatory [6-46] provisions, commercial communications that either (a) come within the recognised character of, or (b) are specifically concerned with, the following are prohibited under the BCI General Advertising Code: (i) products, treatments or services which are only available on medical prescription; (ii) cigarettes and tobacco; (iii) infant formula; (iv) advertisements directed towards a political end or which have any relation to an industrial dispute; (v) certain advertisements directed towards a religious end.[135] In

---

[127] BCI General Advertising Code, 15, para 8.8.1.
[128] BCI General Advertising Code, 15, para 8.8.2.
[129] *ibid.*
[130] BCI Guidance Notes, 35. This rule does not apply to the National Lottery. (BCI Guidance Notes, 35).
[131] BCI General Advertising Code, 15, para 8.8.2.
[132] BCI General Advertising Code, 15, para 8.9.1.
[133] *ibid.*
[134] BCI Guidance Notes, 35.
[135] BCI General Advertising Code, 16, para 9.

(iv) the term "political end", per the BCI Guidance Notes, is intended to embrace, amongst other matters, activities intended to influence legislation or executive action by the Oireachtas or foreign legislatures.[136]

---

[136] BCI Guidance Notes, 36. Where there is a risk that a particular commercial communication may breach the prohibition on advertisements directed towards a political end or which have any relation to an industrial dispute, broadcasters are in effect required to seek guidance. (BCI Guidance Notes, 36). As regards which religious advertisements are prohibited, cf. the exceptions prescribed in BCI General Advertising Code, 16, para 9.

Chapter 7

THE BCI CHILDREN'S ADVERTISING CODE[1]

Overview

Pursuant to s 19(1)(c) of the Broadcasting Act, 2001,[2] the Broadcasting Commission of Ireland has published its Children's Advertising Code which came fully into effect on 1 January 2005.[3] Although the BCI Children's Advertising Code is not directed at financial product or service providers, it nonetheless is of practical significance

[7–01]

---

[1] Broadcasting Commission of Ireland, *Children's Advertising Code* (Dublin: 2005). The BCI Children's Advertising Code is published in the English and Irish languages and the comments on, and quotes from, the Children's Advertising Code are concerned with, and drawn from, the English-language version. As of 21 April 2008, the text of the BCI Children's Advertising Code was available on-line at www.bci.ie/documents/childrens_code_oct_04.pdf.

[2] No 4 of 2001.

[3] s 19(1) of the Broadcasting Act 2001 provides that "The Commission shall, upon being directed by the Minister to do so and in accordance with the provisions of this section, prepare- . . .(b) a code specifying standards to be complied with, and rules and practices to be observed, in

for those providers in that the provisions of the Code will be applied by affected broadcasters in Ireland to any radio or television advertising that such providers may seek to broadcast, whether because the advertisement is broadcast at a time when children may view it or because the product or service that is the subject of the advertisement is for children (exclusively or among others), or both. Consequently, the provisions of the BCI Children's Advertising Code are considered in this work. The Children's Advertising Code is comprised of an introductory section and then various sections focused on specific issues that arise in the context of children's advertising. Clearly any person minded to publish a financial advertisement directed at children should be mindful at all times of the prohibition in s 139 of the Consumer Credit Act on knowingly, with a view to financial gain, sending to a minor any document inviting the minor to (a) borrow credit, (b) obtain goods on credit or hire, (c) obtain services on credit, or (d) apply for information or advice on borrowing credit or otherwise obtaining credit or hiring goods. Breach of s 139 is a summary criminal offence.[4]

Introduction

Definitions

[7–02]   The BCI Children's Advertising Code commences by defining a limited number of terms, including "child", "children's advertising", "children's programmes". A "child" is defined as anyone under 18 years of age (the Code does not indicate whether this means anyone who has not yet commenced or anyone who has not yet completed their eighteenth year).[5] Notwithstanding that it defines a child as anyone under 18 years of age, the Code recognises that children of different ages require varying levels of protection. Thus the Code distinguishes between children under six years of age, children under 15 years of age, and children aged 15 years or over. (Again, in each instance the Code does not indicate whether, for example, in its references to a child of six or 15 it means to refer to a child who has not commenced, or has not completed, their sixth or fifteenth year). Thus the Code prescribes certain provisions in respect of all children's advertising and also makes particular provision for under-six year olds and under-15 year olds. As for the term "children's advertising", this "refers to advertising that promotes products, services or activities that are deemed to be of particular interest to children and/or are broadcast during and between children's programmes."[6] The term "advertising" is not defined but (although this is not stated in the BCI Children's Advertising Code) it seems reasonably safe to assume that the Broadcasting Commission would apply the same definition of advertising as is contained in the BCI General Advertising Code, as considered in Chapter 6 of this book. The term "children's programmes" is defined as

---

respect of advertising, teleshopping material, sponsorship and other forms of commercial promotion employed in any broadcasting service or sound broadcasting service, being advertised and other activities as aforesaid which relate to matters likely to be of direct or indirect interest to children."

[4] Consumer Credit Act, 1995, s 12(1)(j).
[5] BCI Children's Advertising Code, 4.
[6] *ibid.*

embracing "programmes that are commonly referred to as such and/or have an audience profile of which over 50 percent are under 18 years of age. Where provisions of the Code are categorised as pertaining to those under 15 years or those under 6 years of age, these provisions apply to (i) advertising targeting these age groups; (ii) advertising broadcast during programmes where over 50 percent of the audience are of these age groups."[7]

Scope

The BCI Children's Advertising Code applies to broadcasters under the jurisdiction of Ireland or who make use of a frequency, satellite capacity or up-link based in Ireland.[8] In practical terms, the Code applies to RTÉ and TG4 radio and television broadcasts and also to radio and television services licensed under the Radio and Television Act, 1988, which includes TV3, as well as services licensed by the Broadcasting Commission of Ireland under the Broadcasting Act 2001.[9]

[7–03]

Parents/the 'watershed'

The Code acknowledges "the principle of parental responsibility".[10] However, it does not elaborate on same, except to state that after 9pm programmes are not regarded as children's programmes and parents/guardians have primary responsibility from this time for what a child is watching.[11] (This 9pm threshold is often referred to as the 'watershed'). Notwithstanding the foregoing, the Code offers a degree of protection for the first hour after the watershed in that if a programme is broadcast between 9pm and 10pm and its audience figures are comprised of over 50 percent of under-18s, "the provisions [of the Children's Advertising Code] pertaining to under 18s will apply".[12] Obviously all the provisions of the Children's Advertising Code are concerned with under-18 year olds, given that the definition of a "child" for the purposes of the Children's Advertising Code is someone under 18 years of age. However, some provisions of the Children's Advertising Code state themselves to apply to under-15 year olds or under-six year olds and it would seem the reference to under-18 year olds means to refer to those provisions expressly stated to apply to under-18 year olds. The Children's Advertising Code does not state at what time of night or morning the watershed ends.

[7–04]

Audience composition

As mentioned above, the term "children's programmes" is defined by reference to audience composition. This immediately raises the question of how audience composition is to be determined. In this regard the Code states that audience profiling will be the primary means of implementing the Code.[13] However, it may not always be possible to predict audience profile (e.g. in the case of one-off programmes

[7–05]

---

[7] *ibid.*
[8] *ibid.*
[9] *ibid.*
[10] *ibid.*
[11] *ibid.*
[12] *ibid.*
[13] BCI Children's Advertising Code, 6.

or short-run series). In such instances, the Code prescribes certain 'indicative scheduling guidelines' that indicate times during which particular age groups most often watch television. When scheduling children's advertising and determining the appropriateness of an advertisement for children, broadcasters are "requested" by the Broadcasting Commission to have reference to the guidelines. The guidelines are as follows:

> "[1] If broadcasters, using reasonable judgement, consider, that particular children's advertising is inappropriate for children under 6 years of age, having regard in particular to the provisions of this code, then it should not be broadcast during and between children's programmes which target that age group. [2] If broadcasters, using reasonable judgement, consider that particular children's advertising is inappropriate or likely to cause distress to children under 15 years of age, having regard in particular to the provisions of this code, then it should be broadcast after 9 p.m. [3] If broadcasters, using reasonable judgement, consider that children's advertising contains material of a sexual or violent nature not suitable for children under 15, having regard in particular to the provisions of this code then a post 11 p.m. restriction must be considered."[14]

[7–06] In the case of long-running programmes, broadcasters must take the average audience figures over a reasonable time in order to determine whether such programme is a children's programme or not.[15] There can be instances where a programme that is not typically a children's programme nonetheless attracts an audience of which over 50 per cent is comprised of children.[16]

Assessment

[7–07] An advertisement is assessed on its own merit, by reference to its content and the context in which it is broadcast.[17] By 'context' the Broadcasting Commission means to refer in this regard to one or more of the following: the time the advertisement is broadcast; the type of programme which is on when it is broadcast; the likely profile of the audience watching when it is broadcast; and the target audience of the advertised product.[18]

Age codes

[7–08] The BCI Children's Advertising Code uses a variety of shorthand terms to indicate whether a provision of the Code applies to under-18 year olds ("U/18"), under-15 year olds ("U/15") or under-six year olds ("U/6"). These shorthand terms are also used in the following sections, with each new heading below indicating a new section of the Code.

Section 1 - Social values

[7–09] Children's advertising must not, per the Children's Advertising Code, reflect a range of values that are inconsistent with the moral or ethical standards or the diversity of

---

[14] *ibid.*
[15] BCI Children's Advertising Code, 4.
[16] BCI Children's Advertising Code, 6.
[17] *ibid.*
[18] *ibid.*

contemporary Irish society.[19] Moreover, such advertising is required to respect human dignity and cannot discriminate on the basis of age, disability, family status, gender, marital status, race, religion, sexual orientation or membership of the Traveller community.[20] In addition it must not offend religious or political beliefs or encourage behaviour damaging to the environment. It must respect the principle of equality, avoid sexual stereotyping and any demeaning/exploitation of men, women or children.[21] All of the foregoing requirements are 'U/18'.

Section 2 - Inexperience and Credulity

The Children's Advertising Code requires that children's advertising not take advantage of the natural credulity and sense of loyalty of children. It must not (whether by ambiguity, exaggerated claim, implication, or omission): mislead or deceive or be likely to mislead or deceive children; abuse children's trust; or exploit their lack of knowledge.[22] Such advertising must not exploit or, without justifiable reason, play on children's fears.[23] All of the foregoing requirements are 'U/18'. It is open to question whether there is ever a justifiable reason for playing on children's fears.

[7–10]

Facts

In terms of facts presented in advertisements, children's advertising must: (i) clearly indicate what accessories, elements or parts are included as standard with the purchase or service (and identify those which are only available at extra cost) ('U/18')[24]; (ii) ensure that on-screen messages and 'small print' are clear, legible, simple, and remain on-screen long enough for a child to read same ('U/15')[25]; (iii) indicate (to children) the actual size of a product ('U/15')[26]; (iv) clearly indicate whether batteries are required and if supplied with the product ('U/15')[27]; (v) clearly indicate whether product assembly is required (and what age level is required to assemble it ('U/15')[28]; (vi) avoid the use of imaginative scenes, language or special effects that could confuse a child or cause them to believe that the advertised product or service has capabilities/characteristics that it does not possess in reality ('U/15')[29]; (vii) in the case of toys or children's possessions that children aged under 15 years could ordinarily be expected to possess, not make direct comparisons between new and improved versus existing models/versions, even where such comparisons are valid ('U/15')[30]; and (viii) read out any on-screen messages or small print so as to ensure that children aged under six

[7–11]

---

[19] BCI Children's Advertising Code, 8, para 1.1.
[20] *ibid.*
[21] *ibid.*
[22] BCI Children's Advertising Code, 8, para 2.1.
[23] *ibid.*
[24] BCI Children's Advertising Code, 8, para 2.2.1.
[25] BCI Children's Advertising Code, 8, para 2.2.2.
[26] BCI Children's Advertising Code, 8, para 2.2.3.
[27] BCI Children's Advertising Code, 8, para 2.2.4.
[28] BCI Children's Advertising Code, 8, para 2.2.5.
[29] BCI Children's Advertising Code, 8, para 2.2.6.
[30] BCI Children's Advertising Code, 8, para 2.2.7.

years of age understand the message ('U/6').[31] Clearly not all of these requirements are of immediate relevance to an advertisement for a financial product or service, even where directed at children but requirements (ii), (vi) and (viii) (in the last case, in the unlikely event that a financial product or service was being targeted at the very young) would seem of potential relevance.

Price

[7–12]   As regards how the price of a product/service is presented in children's advertising, the following requirements apply: (i) price when given must be in euro and inclusive of VAT and any other charges ('U/18')[32]; (ii) if the price is dependent on purchase of another item, this must be made clear ('U/18')[33]; (iii) if there are a number of products in an advertisement and the price of one or more items is highlighted, it must be clear that the highlighted price applies to the said item(s) only ('U/18')[34]; (iv) references to free gifts or offers must detail any qualifying terms and conditions ('U/18')[35]; (v) advertising must not offer children prizes/rewards for attracting any new purchasers for "the product or service" (presumably the advertised product or service) ('U/18')[36]; (vi) the price must be presented in clear, legible and simple font and, if appropriate, also spoken ('U/15')[37]; (vii) language minimising cost such as 'only' or 'just' must not be used ('U/15')[38]; (viii) the price of any expensive toys (i.e. toys which, with essential accessories, are available at a price specified by the Broadcasting Commission of Ireland — €30 at the time of writing) must be stated in any advertisement for same ('U/15').[39] Clearly not all of these requirements are of immediate relevance to an advertisement for a financial product or service, even where directed at children but requirements (ii), (vi) and (vii) would seem of relevance.

Section 3 - Undue Pressure

[7–13]   The BCI Children's Advertising Code requires that children's advertising: (i) not directly encourage or exhort children to ask adults to buy the children the products or services advertised ('U/18')[40]; (ii) not imply that possession/use of a product or service will make a child (or the child's family) physically/psychologically/socially superior ('U/18')[41]; (iii) conversely, not imply that for not possessing a product/service a child (or the child's family) will be inferior or open to ridicule or contempt ('U/18')[42]; (iv) not imply that a product is affordable to all families ('U/18')[43]; (v) be particularly

---

[31] BCI Children's Advertising Code, 8, para 2.2.8.
[32] BCI Children's Advertising Code, 10, para 2.3.1.
[33] BCI Children's Advertising Code, 10, para 2.3.2. This and other paras of the Code use the colloquial term "advert" when referring to the undefined term "advertisement".
[34] BCI Children's Advertising Code, 10, para 2.3.3.
[35] BCI Children's Advertising Code, 10, para 2.3.4.
[36] *ibid.*
[37] BCI Children's Advertising Code, 10, para 2.3.5.
[38] BCI Children's Advertising Code, 10, para 2.3.6.
[39] BCI Children's Advertising Code, 10, para 2.3.7.
[40] BCI Children's Advertising Code, 10, para 3.1.
[41] BCI Children's Advertising Code, 10, para 3.2.
[42] BCI Children's Advertising Code, 10, para 3.3.
[43] *ibid.*

careful to avoid implying that possession of a product/service will add to/detract from a child's popularity or winning friends ('U/18')[44]; (vi) not make a child feel disloyal or inferior or doubtful about their self-image ('U/18').[45]

Section 4 - Special Protection for Children in Advertising

Children endorsing products

The BCI Children's Advertising Code states that children may only be used to comment on or endorse products in children's advertising where they could reasonably be expected to use and would usually be interested in such products themselves (which possibly excludes children from commenting on or endorsing most financial products or services).[46] In addition, children may appear in "children's advertising for adult products" if their appearance is as a natural element in the environment depicted or is necessary to demonstrate or explain the use of the advertised product service. Both of the foregoing requirements are 'U/18'. At first glance the notion of 'children's advertising for adult products' may appear unlikely to arise in practice. However, it will be recalled that the term "children's advertising" is defined as "advertising that promotes products, services or activities that are deemed to be of particular interest to children and/or *are broadcast during and between children's programmes*." (Emphasis added).[47] Thus while adult products seem unlikely to be of particular interest to children, it seems likely that advertising for adult products (e.g. for certain financial products or services) could be broadcast during and between children's programmes.

[7–14]

Sexualisation of children

The BCI Children's Advertising Code requires that children's advertising not portray a child in a sexually provocative manner or provoke anxiety in children over their bodily appearance ('U/18').[48]

[7–15]

Privacy and provision of information

The BCI Children's Advertising Code requires that, save where an advertisement is part of a campaign which relates to the safety, health or well-being of children, children's advertising not request children "to submit private information or details regarding themselves, their family or their friends".[49] Where advertising contains such a request it must state "where reasonable" that children must seek the approval of an adult before providing such information.[50] It is perhaps surprising that such advertising is not required invariably to so state and not just "where reasonable". Both of the requirements imposed by the Code in this regard are 'U/18'.

[7–16]

---

[44] BCI Children's Advertising Code, 10, para 3.4.
[45] BCI Children's Advertising Code, 10, para 3.5.
[46] BCI Children's Advertising Code, 12, para 4.1.
[47] The quoted text appears in the BCI Children's Advertising Code at 4.
[48] BCI Children's Advertising Code, 12, para 4.2.
[49] BCI Children's Advertising Code, 12, para 4.3.
[50] *ibid.*

Adults pretending to be children

[7–17]   Any use, in children's advertising, of adults pretending to be children, must not be offensive to children's dignity.[51]

Section 5 - General Safety

[7–18]   The BCI Children's Advertising Code requires that children's advertising: (i) not encourage children to enter into unsafe situations/strange places or to speak with strangers ('U/18')[52]; (ii) not show children in morally/physically dangerous situations or behaving dangerously (whether at home or outside), including road and street scenes, except when the only purpose of the advertisement is to promote child safety ('U/18')[53]; (iii) show children using appropriate safety equipment and respecting applicable safety rules when engaged in activities that require same (and with adult supervision where appropriate) ('U/18')[54]; (iv) not using the internet without appropriate adult supervision ('U/18')[55]; (v) not unreasonably portray children close to/using dangerous equipment/substances or administering (or in possession of) medicines without appropriate adult supervision ('U/15').[56]

Behaviour

[7–19]   The BCI Children's Advertising Code requires that, except where an advertisement is to discourage such behaviour, children's advertising must not encourage children to join in (or portray them as engaged in) anti-social behaviour, particularly bullying, teasing or taunting of other children ('U/18').[57] Moreover, children's advertising must not, under the Code, disparage education or condone aggression or greed as admirable qualities ('U/18').[58]

Section 6 - Violence

[7–20]   Under the BCI Children's Advertising Code, children's advertising should not "in principle" include violence or scenes that will cause distress to children ('U/18').[59] Where violent scenes need to be included as part of a public service message or to demonstrate a product, the advertising must be scheduled responsibly by broadcasters in order that the advertising does not cause distress to "this age group".[60] There is no reference to an age group in the preceding text of the Code. However, this last

---

[51] BCI Children's Advertising Code, 12, para 4.4.
[52] BCI Children's Advertising Code, 12, para 5.1.
[53] BCI Children's Advertising Code, 12, para 5.2.
[54] BCI Children's Advertising Code, 12, para 5.3. Examples of the activities referred to include where children are portrayed as passengers in vehicles, as pedestrians, or when portrayed cycling, horse-riding, rollerblading, skateboarding, or engaged in water-sports. (BCI Children's Advertising Code, 12, para 5.3).
[55] BCI Children's Advertising Code, 12, para 5.4.
[56] BCI Children's Advertising Code, 12, para 5.5. Examples of such equipment/substances as are referred to in para 5.5 are "matches, gas appliances, petrol, certain household substances".
[57] BCI Children's Advertising Code, 14, para 5.6.
[58] BCI Children's Advertising Code, 14, para 5.7.
[59] BCI Children's Advertising Code, 14, para 6.1.
[60] BCI Children's Advertising Code, 14, para 6.2.

provision is tagged as 'U/6' and presumably the phrase "this age group" means to refer to under-six year olds. It is perhaps open to question whether a public service message, let alone a product demonstration should ever include violent scenes.

Section 7 - Diet and Nutrition

The BCI Children's Advertising Code contains a number of provisions concerning the manner in which food and drink are portrayed or advertised. Not all of these provisions are relevant to financial advertisements. However, some may be relevant if there was an incidental reference to diet/nutrition in such an advertisement. Thus, per the Code, children's advertising: (i) must be responsible in the manner in which it portrays food and drink ('U/18')[61]; and (ii) must not encourage an unhealthy lifestyle or unhealthy drinking/eating habits (e.g. immoderate consumption; over- or compulsive eating) ('U/18').[62] Apart from these general requirements, the other provisions under this heading seem unlikely generally (if ever) to be of interest to persons placing financial advertisements.

[7–21]

Section 8 - Parental Responsibility

As in the introductory text to the BCI Children's Advertising Code, section 8 of the Code affirms that parents and guardians have primary responsibility for children.[63] Even so, the Code requires that advertisers support parents/guardians in discharging their primary responsibility "by scheduling responsibly and by not undermining the authority, responsibility or judgement of parents or guardians in the content of the advertisement".[64] Two matters of particular concern are touched upon by the Code in this regard. Thus advertisement plot lines that encourage children to deceive/manipulate adults into providing or purchasing an advertised product or service are to be avoided.[65] Moreover, children's advertising must not suggest that an adult or a parent who provides/purchases a product or service for a child is better, more generous or more intelligent than one who does not.[66] Both of the requirements imposed by the Code in this regard are 'U/18'.

[7–22]

Section 9 - Programme Characters

Characters and personalities from children's programmes that are "currently broadcast on indigenous services" must not advertise or endorse products or services in children's advertising.[67] The term "currently" is stated by the Code to 'include' — it is not clear if it is limited to — "regular programming due for return in the next broadcast season".[68] This general prohibition does not apply to children's advertising for events, products or services directly associated with a programme in which a

[7–23]

---

[61] BCI Children's Advertising Code, 12, para 7.1.
[62] *ibid.*
[63] BCI Children's Advertising Code, 16, para 8.1.
[64] *ibid.*
[65] *ibid.*
[66] *ibid.*
[67] BCI Children's Advertising Code, 16, para 9.1.
[68] *ibid.*

particular character or personality normally appears.[69] However, such advertisements must not be broadcast for two hours before the start and after the end of such programme.[70] The requirements imposed by the Code in this regard are stated to be 'U/18'.

Section 10 - Product Prohibitions and Restrictions

[7–24]   It will be recalled that under the BCI General Advertising Code there are a number of prohibited commercial communications.[71] The BCI Children's Advertising Code adds to the list of prohibited commercial communications in the General Advertising Code a further number of establishments, products, services and treatments that must not be advertised in children's advertising, of which the only one of potential relevance to financial service providers is the prohibition on betting or gaming services or products (except the National Lottery).[72] This requirement is stated by the Code to be 'U/18'.

Section 11 - Identification and Separation

[7–25]   Under the BCI Children's Advertising Code, children's advertising must be clearly distinguishable from programme content as regards image, sound and text.[73] In particular, it must not include excerpts from children's programmes that might blur the distinction between advertising and those programmes.[74] Both of these requirements are stated by the Code to be 'U/18'. In addition to being clearly distinguishable from, children's advertising must be clearly separated from, programming content.[75] Broadcasters must provide an acoustic or visual cue to a child denoting the beginning and end of a commercial break and such cue must not be sponsored or contain advertising material.[76] These requirements are stated by the Code to be 'U/18'.

Section 12 - Insertion of Advertising

[7–26]   Christmas-themed children's advertising (i.e. advertising that contains acoustic or visual references to Christmas) must not be broadcast before 1 November in any one year ('U/18').[77] There can be no advertising in a children's programme of less than 30 minutes' scheduled duration ('U/15').[78]

---

[69] *ibid.*
[70] *ibid.*
[71] See the consideration of para 9 of the BCI General Advertising Code in Chapter 6.
[72] BCI Children's Advertising Code, 18, para 10.1.
[73] BCI Children's Advertising Code, 18, para 11.1.
[74] *ibid.*
[75] BCI Children's Advertising Code, 18, para 11.2.
[76] *ibid.*
[77] BCI Children's Advertising Code, 18, para 12.1.
[78] BCI Children's Advertising Code, 18, para 12.2.

Chapter 8

OTHER MEASURES AND LAW OF INTEREST

Introduction

The preceding chapters have considered the principal measures that impact on the **[8–01]** content and substance of financial advertisements in Ireland. This Chapter outlines in summary fashion some of the principal other legal measures or aspects of the law that may or may not be of interest in the context of financial advertising. No one book could seek to be a comprehensive and authoritative source on the various aspects of the law that are considered below and a reader interested in a particular law or aspect of the law mentioned hereunder is encouraged to consult a work more directly concerned with the particular area of interest.

Some Other Measures and Law of Interest[1]

- *Betting Act, 1931[2]*

Section 32(1) of the Betting Act, 1931 provides that, except as is otherwise permitted **[8–02]** by s 32, it is not lawful for any person to write, print, publish or knowingly circulate any advertisement,[3] circular or coupon advocating or inviting or otherwise relating to betting on football games or knowingly to cause or procure, or attempt to cause or

---

[1] As elsewhere in this book, any reference in this Chapter to any enactment or other legislation is to such enactment or other legislation as and where amended from time to time.

[2] No 27 of 1931.

[3] The term "advertisement" is not defined in the 1931 Act.

procure, any such advertisement, circular or coupon to be written, printed, published or circulated.[4]

- *Building Societies Act, 1989*[5]

[8–03]   Under s 17 of the Building Societies Act, 1989, a building society incorporated or deemed to be incorporated under that Act, or a person acting or purporting to act on its behalf, is prohibited from raising funds or advertising for or otherwise soliciting deposits or loans or subscriptions for shares unless authorised or deemed to be authorised by the Central Bank and Financial Services Authority to do so. Under s 42(1) of the 1989 Act, if the Authority considers it expedient to do so it may give, to a building society, a direction in relation to the matter and form of: any advertisement or other means of soliciting deposits or subscriptions for shares in such building society; or any advertisement relating to any service provided or business being undertaken by such building society.[6] In addition, the Authority may direct such building society to withdraw an advertisement or cease advertising.[7]

- *Central Bank Acts*

[8–04]   Under the Central Bank Act, 1971, a person must not advertise for or otherwise solicit deposits or other repayable funds from the public on behalf of such (or any other) person.[8] This general prohibition does not apply to advertising for or otherwise soliciting deposits or other repayable funds from the public by, amongst others, a bank licensed in Ireland or a bank duly 'passporting' its services into Ireland.[9] If an advertisement or other solicitation for deposits or other repayable funds from the public is published and does not include the name and address of the person who arranged with the publisher for the advertisement/solicitation, the Central Bank and Financial Services Authority may, at any time within 12 months thereafter, request the publisher to supply the name and address of such person to it and the publisher must forthwith comply with that request.[10]

---

[4] Betting Act, 1931, s 32(1). Per s 31(2) of the 1931 Act and s 26(2) of the Gaming and Lotteries Act, 1956 (No 2 of 1956), the prohibition in s 32(1) does not apply in respect of registered proprietors of registered bookmaking offices or in respect of a lottery conducted wholly within Ireland in accordance with a permit or licence issued under the 1956 Act, as amended. For a brief summary of the law generally applicable, and the self-regulation potentially applicable, to the operation of lotteries, see the chapter on Ireland by Barrett, G and D Voigt in Micklitz. HW and J Kessler, eds., *Marketing Practices Regulation and Consumer Protection in the EC Member States and the US* (Baden-Baden: 2002) at 186ff.

[5] No 17 of 1989.

[6] The term "advertisement" is defined as including "every form of recommendation of any matter to which this section relates, including in particular the display or publication of any such matters by way of leaflet, notice, circular, pamphlet, brochure, photograph, film, video, sound broadcasting, television, electronic communication or personal canvassing and references to the issue of advertisements shall be construed accordingly". (Building Societies Act, 1989, s 42(3)(a)).

[7] Building Societies Act, 1989, s 42(1).

[8] Central Bank Act, 1971 (No 24 of 1971), s 27(1), as inserted by s 70 of the Central Bank Act, 1997.

[9] Central Bank Act, 1971, s 27(2), as inserted by the Central Bank and Financial Services Authority of Ireland Act 2004, s 3 and Schedule 3, Part 4, Item 8.

[10] Central Bank Act, 1971, s 27(3), as substituted by s 70(e) of the Central Bank Act, 1997 (No 8 of 1997).

Breach of s 27 is a criminal offence.[11] Section 22(1) of the Central Bank Act, 1971, provides that the Central Bank and Financial Services Authority may give a direction in writing to a credit institution as regards information contained in such entity's advertisements.[12] Section 22(2) provides that the Authority may direct a credit institution to refrain from publishing or continuing to publish, or causing to be published or to be continued to be published: during such period as is specified in the direction, an advertisement inviting deposits from the public; an advertisement containing information in respect of any service provided or to be provided to the public or any charge, term or condition upon which a service is so provided (or to be so provided) which, in the opinion of the Authority is false, misleading or calculated to deceive.[13] No direction may issue under s 22 of the 1971 Act unless the Authority is satisfied that the issuance of such direction is desirable in the interest of the orderly and proper regulation of banking.[14]

- *Copyright*

Subject to various exceptions prescribed in the Copyright and Related Rights Act, **[8–05]** 2000[15], the owner of the copyright in a work has the exclusive right to undertake or authorise others to undertake all or any of the following: "(a) to copy the work; (b) to make available to the public the work; (c) to make an adaptation of the work or to undertake either of the acts referred to in...(a) or (b) in relation to an adaptation".[16] Copyright is infringed where a person, without the licence of the copyright owner, undertakes or authorises another to undertake any of the acts restricted by copyright.[17] Infringement can arise in relation to the whole or any substantial part of the work in which copyright subsists.[18] An added incentive for caution in this regard is the fact that innocent infringement of copyright is no defence to infringement proceedings: it merely precludes a court from awarding damages against the infringer.[19] In the context of financial advertisements, copyright infringement tends to arise as a potential concern when, for example, a substantial part of a previously recorded song or broadcast is being used in same

---

[11] Central Bank Act, 1971, s 58, as amended by the Central Bank Act, 1989 (No 16 of 1989), s 9, and the Central Bank and Financial Services Authority of Ireland Act 2003 (No 12 of 2003), s 35 and Schedule 1, Part 6, Item 5.

[12] The term "advertisement" when used in s 22 of the 1971 Act "includes every form of recommendation of any matter to which this section relates including, in particular, the display or publication of any such matter by way of notice, leaflet, circular, pamphlet, brochure, photograph, film, video, sound broadcasting, television, electronic communication or personal canvassing." (1971 Act, s 22(4), as substituted by s 39 of the Central Bank Act, 1989).

[13] Central Bank Act, 1971, s 22(2) and (2A), as substituted by the Central Bank Act, 1989, s 39.

[14] Central Bank Act, 1971, s 22(3).

[15] No 28 of 2000.

[16] Copyright and Related Rights Act, 2000, s 37(1).

[17] Copyright and Related Rights Act, 2000, s 37(2).

[18] Copyright and Related Rights Act, 2000, s 37(3). There can also be secondary infringement of copyright e.g. dealing with infringing copies, providing the means for making infringing copies, permitting the use of premises for infringing performances, and permitting the use of apparatus for infringing performances. (Cf. the Copyright and Related Rights Act, 2000, ss 44 to 48 (inclusive)).

[19] Copyright and Related Rights Act, 2000, s 128(2).

- *Credit Union Act*

[8–06]   Section 10(6) of the Credit Union Act, 1997,[20] requires that the registered name of a credit union be set out in legible characters in, amongst other matters, all advertisements of the credit union. Section 86(1) of that Act provides that if the Central Bank and Financial Services Authority considers it necessary to do so in the case of any "body"[21], it may give such body directions in writing relating to the content or form (or both) "(a) of any advertisement or other means of soliciting deposits or subscriptions for shares in any one or more credit unions or credit unions generally; or (b) of any advertisement relating to any service provided or business undertaken by any one or more credit unions or credit unions generally; and the Authority may also give directions in writing requiring any such body to withdraw or amend an advertisement." A credit union or any other body that fails to comply with any direction(s) made under s 86 is guilty of an offence.[22]

- *Data protection*

[8–07]   Insofar as data protection law is concerned, the principal statutory measures are the Data Protection Acts 1988 and 2003.[23] The key provision of interest from an advertising perspective is s 2D of the 1988 Act, as amended. Section 2D provides that personal data shall not be treated as 'processed fairly' for the purposes of s 2(1)(a) of the 1988 Act[24] unless, amongst other matters, the data controller ensures, so far as practicable that, in respect of data obtained from a date subject, that data subject has, is provided with, or has made readily available to him/her certain minimum prescribed data, namely. "(a) the identity of the data controller, (b) if he or she has nominated a representative for the purposes of this Act, the identity of the representative, (c) the purpose or purposes for which the data are intended to be processed, and (d) any other information which is necessary, having regard to the specific circumstances...to enable processing in respect of the data to be fair to the data subject..."[25] Thus, for example, where an advertisement for a financial service provider invites persons viewing the advertisement to supply certain personal data (e.g. name and address) the advertiser should provide its identity. It would also be appropriate to disclose the intended use of such information and the fact that (if such be the case) such information may be transferred to another person. Notwithstanding the foregoing, the principal impact of the Data Protection Acts and other data protection measures in the advertising/marketing arena is on marketing, not on the substance or content of financial advertisements, and thus outside the scope of this book.

---

[20] No 15 of 1997.

[21] i.e. a credit union, group or association of credit unions or otherwise.

[22] Credit Union Act, 1997, s 86(5).

[23] i.e. the Data Protection Act, 1988 (No 25 of 1988) and the Data Protection (Amendment) Act, 2003 (No 6 of 2003).

[24] Section 2(1) of the 1988 Act, as amended, provides that "A data controller shall, as respects personal data kept by him or her, comply with the following provisions: (a) the data or, as the case may be, the information constituting the data shall have been obtained, and the data shall be processed fairly...".

[25] Data Protection Act 1988, as amended, s 2D(2).

- *Distance marketing*

The European Communities (Distance Marketing of Consumer Financial Services)   **[8–08]**
Regulations 2004,[26] apply to the marketing and supply of financial services to
consumers under organised distance marketing schemes. Of particular interest in the
context of the substance/content of financial advertisements (i.e. the subject-matter of
this book) is the requirement in the Regulations that in advertising a financial service[27]
that is proposed to be supplied under a distance contract (or in communicating with a
consumer[28] in relation to the supply or proposed supply of a financial service), a
supplier must comply with all codes made and all directions given by a competent
authority[29] insofar as those codes or directions impose standards on suppliers with
respect to (a) advertising financial services, (b) communicating with consumers (or
potential consumers) of those services, or (c) protecting minors whose capacity to enter
into contracts is limited.[30] Non-compliance with this requirement is an offence.[31]

- *Equal status legislation*

The Equal Status Act, 2000,[32] is principally concerned with legislating against   **[8–09]**
discrimination on grounds of age, disability, family status, gender, marital status, race,
religion, sexual orientation and/or membership of the Traveller community. Under s
12(1) of that Act a person must not publish an advertisement[33] which indicates an
intention to engage in defined prohibited conduct or which might reasonably be
understood as indicating such an intention. A person who makes a statement which s/

---

[26] SI No 853 of 2004.

[27] By "financial service" the Regulations mean "any service of a kind normally provided in the
ordinary course of carrying on a banking business, an insurance business or a business of
providing credit, personal pensions, an investment service or a payment service". (European
Communities (Distance Marketing of Consumer Financial Services) Regulations 2004,
Regulation 3(1)).

[28] By "consumer", the Regulations mean "in relation to a distance contract, or proposed
distance contract, for the supply of a financial service...a natural person who is acting
otherwise than in the course of a business carried on by the person, and, if the rights and
obligations of a consumer under a contract to which these Regulations apply have passed to
another such person (whether by assignment or operation of law), includes that other person".
(European Communities (Distance Marketing of Consumer Financial Services) Regulations
2004, Regulation 3(1)).

[29] The term "competent authority" when used in relation to Ireland means the Central Bank and
Financial Services Authority of Ireland as regards functions imposed on it by or under the
Central Bank Act, 1942, or (b) the National Consumer Agency as regards suppliers to whom
Part XI of the Consumer Credit Act, 1995 applies. (European Communities (Distance
Marketing of Consumer Financial Services) Regulations 2004, Regulation 3(1), as construed in
accordance with s 37(3) of the Consumer Protection Act 2007).

[30] European Communities (Distance Marketing of Consumer Financial Services) Regulations
2004, Regulation 20(2).

[31] European Communities (Distance Marketing of Consumer Financial Services) Regulations
2004, Regulation 20(5).

[32] No 8 of 2000.

[33] The term "advertisement" is defined in the Act as including "every form of advertisement,
whether to the public or not and whether in a newspaper or other publication, on television or
radio or by display of a notice or by any other means and references to the publishing or
display of advertisements shall be construed accordingly. (Equal Status Act, 2000, s 12(3)).

he knows to be false with a view to securing publication/display in breach of s 12(1) is, upon the publication or display being made, guilty of an offence.[34]

- *Investor compensation*

[8–10]   The Investor Compensation Act, 1998[35] established an investor compensation scheme intended to compensate eligible investors of failed investment firms (including credit institutions). Of interest from an advertising perspective is the provision in s 38(3) of the Act that, save with the prior written consent of a supervisory authority,[36] "an investment firm shall not advertise or cause to be advertised the fact (however expressed) that monies or investment instruments placed with the investment firm are protected by or through an investor compensation fund."

- *MifiD legislation*[37]

[8–11]   The MiFID Regulations, insofar as they are concerned with advertising, are concerned not so much with the substance and detail of advertising as the capacity of the Central Bank and Financial Services Authority to regulate advertising concerned with the subject-matter of those Regulations. Regulation 152(1) of the MiFID Regulations provides that a person must not "(a) cause to be advertised, supply or offer to supply, investment or ancillary services, (b) make any other solicitation in respect of investment or ancillary services, or (c) represent that the person is a provider of such services" where the provision of such services would be in breach of Regulation 7 of the MiFID Regulations.[38] Breach of Regulation 152(1) is a criminal offence.[39] Under, amongst other matters, Regulation 152(2) of the MiFID Regulations, the Central Bank and Financial Services Authority may impose conditions or requirements (or both) on, amongst others, investment firms, in respect

---

[34] Equal Status Act, 2000, s 12(2).

[35] No 37 of 1998.

[36] i.e. the Central Bank and Financial Services Authority (per ss 2(1) and 8(1) of the Investor Compensation Act, 1998, as amended by the Central Bank and Financial Services Authority of Ireland Act 2003, s 35 and Schedule 1, Part 26, Item 1.

[37] i.e. the European Communities (Markets in Financial Instruments) Regulations 2007 (SI No 60 of 2007) (as amended and supplemented by the European Communities (Markets in Financial Instruments) (Amendment) Regulations 2007 (SI No 663 of 2007)) and the Markets in Financial Instruments and Miscellaneous Provisions Act 2007 (No 37 of 2007). The European Communities (Markets in Financial Instruments) Regulations 2007, as amended and supplemented by the European Communities (Markets in Financial Instruments) (Amendment) Regulations 2007, are hereafter referred to as the "MiFID Regulations".

[38] Regulation 7 prohibits an investment firm from claiming or representing to be an investment firm in Ireland unless it is duly authorised or deemed to be authorised and is acting as authorised. The term "investment firm" means "any person, other than a tied agent, which person's regular occupation or business is the provision of one or more investment services to third parties on a professional basis, but does not include a natural person [except in certain specified circumstances]" (MiFID Regulations, Regulation 3(1)). Under Regulation 3(2) of the MiFID Regulations, where an individual provides an investment or ancillary service or, alternatively, carries on the activity of dealing on own account, and the service or activity is carried on solely for the account of and under the full and unconditional responsibility of an investment firm, an insurance undertaking or a credit institution, the activity or service, as the case may be, shall be regarded as that of the investment firm, insurance undertaking or credit institution itself.

[39] Markets in Financial Instruments and Miscellaneous Provisions Act 2007, s 5(2)(b).

of advertising by such firms where the Authority considers this necessary for the protection of investors or the orderly and proper regulation and supervision of investment firms or regulated markets. The Authority may also, under Regulation 152(3) of the MiFID Regulations, require any specified (or all authorised) investment firm(s) to display specified information at their premises or to publish specified information. Under Regulation 152(4) and (5) of the MiFID Regulations the Authority is empowered to give various advertising-related directions to, amongst others, an investment firm, including but not limited to a direction: as to the content and form of any advertisement or other means of soliciting money, financial instruments or business from potential or existing clients[40]; as to the content and form of any advertisement relating to any service provided or business undertaken by such firm[41]; requiring such firm to withdraw an advertisement or to cease advertising[42]; prohibiting the issue by such firm of advertisements of all descriptions or any specified description[43]; requiring such firm to modify advertisements of a specified description in a specified manner[44]; prohibiting the issue by such firm of any advertisements which are, or are substantially, repetitions of a specified advertisement[45]; requiring such firm to withdraw any specified advertisement or any advertisement of a specified description[46]; and/or requiring such firm to include specified information in any advertisement to be published by it or on its behalf or in any statement to the public to be made by it or on its behalf.[47] Regulation 152 does not apply to any class of advertisement specified from time to time by the Authority, for the purpose of exempting from Regulation 152, advertisements that appear to the Authority to have a private character, to deal with investment or ancillary services only incidentally, or to be issued to persons whom the Authority considers sufficiently expert to understand any risks involved.[48] Any such exemption may be subject to any such conditions as the Authority may specify.[49] The principal civil effect of publishing an advertisement in breach of Regulation 152(1) of the MiFID Regulations (or a direction under Regulation 152) is to render any related agreement or obligation unenforceable and to render compensation payable.[50] The compensation payable under Regulation 153(1)/(2) of the MiFID Regulations can be agreed between the parties or application may be made to the High Court to determine what compensation it considers appropriate.[51] The Central Bank and Financial Services Authority is empowered by the MiFID Regulations, at any time within 12 months after the publication of any advertisement or solicitation to which Regulation 153 relates, to request the relevant publisher to supply the name and address of the person

---

[40] MiFID Regulations, Regulation 152(4)(i).
[41] MiFID Regulations, Regulation 152(4)(ii).
[42] MiFID Regulations, Regulation 152(4)(iii).
[43] MiFID Regulations, Regulation 152(5)(a).
[44] MiFID Regulations, Regulation 152(5)(b).
[45] MiFID Regulations, Regulation 152(5)(c).
[46] MiFID Regulations, Regulation 152(5)(d).
[47] MiFID Regulations, Regulation 152(5)(e).
[48] MiFID Regulations, Regulation 156(1).
[49] MiFID Regulations, Regulation 156 (2).
[50] MiFID Regulations, Regulation 153.
[51] MiFID Regulations, Regulation 153(3).

who arranged with the publisher for the advertisement or solicitation, and the publisher must comply with the request without delay.[52] Regulation 154(1) of the MiFID Regulations empowers the Authority to: direct a person to arrange the publication of a correction of a misleading advertisement concerning services of investment firms or regulated markets; direct a person to arrange the publication of a correction of an advertisement which contravenes the provisions of Regulation 154; direct a person to publish the fact that an offence under Regulation 154 has taken place and that a fine or administrative sanction (if any) has been imposed; arrange the publication of an advertisement correcting any misleading aspects of advertisements published by, amongst others, an investment firm. All of the foregoing must be done in whatever manner is specified by the Authority.[53]

- *Misrepresentation*[54]

[8–12] Misrepresentation (making a statement of fact which is untrue or, exceptionally, remaining silent as to a material fact) may ground a successful action in contract or tort. An action for contract will succeed where a pre-contractual misrepresentation is held to be a part of the relevant contract. An action in tort will succeed where the misrepresentation is fraudulent, innocent or negligent. In the context of the law and regulation concerning the content and substance of financial advertisements, it is sufficient to note that, insofar as liability under general contract law is concerned, care should be taken in such advertisements not to utter a statement of fact that is untrue and not to remain silent as to a material fact. There is a long line of case-law that draws a distinction between, statements of opinion, statements of future intention and actionable misrepresentations on the other.[55] This line of authority may be relevant in the context of financial advertising which by its nature can often be concerned with speculative products in respect of which the line between opinion and misrepresentation can be difficult to draw. Even so, it would be imprudent for any financial institution to make extravagant claims about a product or service in an advertisement and then seek to resile from those claims in the detailed terms and conditions applicable to the relevant product or service. While such financial institution might manage to avoid contractual or tortious liability, it could, depending on the circumstances, expose itself to a successful action under the Consumer Protection Act and/or the Misleading and Comparative Marketing Communications Regulations, as well as the possibility of criminal sanction under the Consumer Protection Act and administrative sanction under the Consumer Protection Code.

- *Supply of service*

[8–13] In general, under s 39 of the Sale of Goods and Supply of Services Act, 1980,[56] certain defined terms are implied into a contract for the supply of services where the supplier is acting in the course of, amongst other matters, a business or profession (e.g. that the supplier has the necessary skill to render the service and that s/he will supply the

---

[52] MiFID Regulations, Regulation 153(7).
[53] MiFID Regulations, Regulation 154(1).
[54] On misrepresentation generally, see further Clark, R. *Contract Law in Ireland*, 5th edition (Dublin: 2004), Chapter 11.
[55] *ibid.* at 290ff.
[56] No 16 of 1980.

service with due skill, care and diligence). Under s 40(1) of the 1980 Act, any term of a contract implied by virtue of s 39 may be negatived or varied by an express term of contract or by a course of dealing between parties or by usage (subject to certain constraints in the case of consumers).[57] Section 41 of the 1980 Act makes certain provision in respect of statements likely to be taken as indicating that a right or the exercise of a right conferred by, or a liability arising by virtue of s 39 is restricted or excluded other than under s 40. Section 41(2) provides that it shall be an offence for a person in the course of a business to do a number of matters of the following things in relation to a statement to which s 41(1) refers, including: "[i]...to display on any part of the premises a notice that includes any such statement, or [ii]...to publish or cause to be published an advertisement which contains any such statement."

- *Tort*

The torts of passing off, defamation, deceit and injurious falsehood may arise for consideration in the context of a particular financial advertisement. It is outside the scope of this work to engage in a detailed examination of each of these four torts and the interested reader is referred to one of the many specialist books on torts.[58]   **[8–14]**

The tort of passing off involves a trader representing its goods or services as those of another and so being likely to mislead the public and involve an appreciable risk of detriment to that other. An intention to deceive is not essential. Insofar as financial advertising is concerned, advertisers will naturally want to ensure that the content or substance of their advertisement (and the product that is being advertised) do not satisfy the various elements of the tort of passing off and thus expose them to an action for damages. One of the more prominent passing off cases in Ireland in recent years arose in the financial sector. In *An Post, National Treasury Management Agency and The Minister for Finance* v. *Irish Permanent plc*,[59] the plaintiffs sought an interlocutory injunction restraining the defendant from using the words 'Savings Certificates'. At the time the injunction was sought, the plaintiffs and their predecessors in title had promoted and marketed for 65 years a State-guaranteed, tax-free savings product known as 'Savings Certificates'. In July 1994, the defendant launched a new savings product, also called 'Savings Certificates' and initially marketed as being 'free of tax' and later marketed as 'tax paid'. (It appears from the report of the case that this change in description followed a complaint by the plaintiffs to the Advertising Standards Authority for Ireland). The plaintiffs contended that they had acquired a significant, substantial and exclusive reputation (as well as immensely valuable goodwill) in the name/trademark 'Savings Certificates' and, further, that the words were a generic term use to describe investment funds guaranteed by the State. The defendant contended that the words 'Savings Certificates' were not capable of constituting a trade mark, being a generic and/or descriptive name in which the plaintiffs had no rights or no exclusive rights. The defendant further contended that when selling or supplying its 'Savings Certificates' it had sold them as its own products and under (or by reference to) the name 'Irish Permanent Savings Certificates'. It denied that its use of the words 'Savings   **[8–15]**

---

[57] Sale of Goods and Supply of Services Act, 1980, s 40(1).
[58] See, for example, McMahon, B. and W. Binchy, *Law of Torts*, 3rd edition (Dublin: 2000).
[59] [1995] 1 IR 140.

Certificates' had led to (or was likely to lead to) any public deception or confusion, or that it had passed off its goods or any of them for those of the plaintiff. It also made certain arguments under European Community and competition law that are not considered here. As is increasingly typical in passing off actions, market survey evidence was adduced by the plaintiffs and the defendant to support their respective cases. In the High Court, Kinlen J granted the interlocutory injunction sought, holding that there was a serious case for the defendant to answer.

[8–16] The tort of defamation occurs where there is wrongful publication of a false statement about a person to a third party which tends to: lower that person in the eyes of right-thinking members of society: hold that person up to contempt, hatred or ridicule; or cause such person to be avoided or shunned by right-thinking members of society.[60] The tort of deceit occurs where there is a representation as to a past or existing fact by the defendant, such representation is made knowingly or without belief in its truth or recklessly, careless as to whether it is true or false, it is intended by the defendant that the representation is acted on by the plaintiff, and the plaintiff so acts and suffers damages as a result.[61] The tort of injurious falsehood involves maliciously deceiving others about the plaintiff and thus engendering loss to the plaintiff.[62] The injurious falsehood need not be defamatory and — unlike deceit — involves deceiving others, not the plaintiff. A corporate entity may bring an action for defamation, deceit or injurious falsehood. It is conceivable that a financial advertisement could involve an advertiser in committing one or more of the torts of deceit, defamation or injurious falsehood. However, the legal, regulatory and self-regulatory constraints applicable to the advertising and financial sectors, as considered in the preceding chapters, mean that the chances of such torts being committed solely by means of an advertisement are perhaps relatively low.

• *Trade marks*

[8–17] A trade mark is any sign capable of being represented graphically which is capable of distinguishing goods or services of one undertaking from those of other under-takings.[63] Many financial service providers have trade marks. Trade marks may be registered or unregistered. If registered, they enjoy certain protections under statute. If unregistered, they may be the subject of a passing-off claim. Where a trade mark is registered, the effective period of the registration is 10 years in the first instance, renewable for further 10-year periods at the election of the proprietor and on payment of a prescribed renewal fee.[64] The proprietor of a registered trade mark has exclusive rights in the trade mark.[65] Section 14(6) of the Trade Marks Act represents a significant change on previously existing law, in effect allowing use of the registered trade mark of a business rival in comparative advertising, provided certain criteria are satisfied. Thus, per s 14(6):

---

[60] McMahon, B and W. Binchy, *Law of Torts*, 3rd edition (Dublin: 2000), 882.
[61] *Cf* the judgment of Shanley J in *Forshall and Fine Arts and Collections Limited v Walsh*, High Court (18 June 1997), para 128.
[62] McMahon, B and W Binchy, *Law of Torts*, 3rd edition (Dublin: 2000), 997.
[63] Trade Marks Act, 1996 (No 6 of 1996), s 6(1).
[64] Trade Marks Act, 1996, ss 47 and 48.
[65] Trade Marks Act, 1996, s 13(1).

"Nothing in the preceding provisions of this section shall be construed as preventing the use of a registered trade mark by any person for the purpose of identifying goods or services as those of the proprietor or licensee of the registered trade mark; but any such use, otherwise than in accordance with honest practices in industrial or commercial matters, shall be treated as infringing the registered trade mark if the use without due cause takes unfair advantage of, or is otherwise detrimental to, the distinctive character or reputation of the trade mark."

Financial providers often use their own registered trade marks in any advertisements   **[8–18]**
that they publish. Where a financial provider publishes an advertisement containing another person's registered trade mark that financial provider needs to ensure that it acts in compliance with the requirements of s 14(6) of the Trade Marks Act or, in instances where a particular use is not excepted under the 1996 Act, that it acts under licence or sub-licence from the relevant trade mark proprietor.[66]

- *Trustee Savings Banks*

Section 27(1) of the Trustee Savings Bank Act, 1989,[67] provides that the Central Bank   **[8–19]**
and Financial Services Authority may give a direction to the trustees of a trustee savings bank in relation to the information that is to be included in any advertisement[68] published by or on behalf of them or the bank or in any public statement made by or on behalf of them or the bank. Section 27(2) provides that the Authority may give a direction to the trustees of a trustee savings bank to refrain or cause the bank to refrain (for such period as the Authority may specify) "(a) from publishing or continuing to publish an advertisement inviting deposits from the public payable on demand or on notice or at a fixed or determinable future date, or (b) from inviting or continuing to invite such deposits as aforesaid." Section 27(3) prohibits the Authority from giving a direction under s 27 unless it is satisfied "that it is desirable to do so in the interest of the orderly and proper regulation of banking." Failure or refusal to comply with a direction under s 27 is a criminal offence.[69] Under s 14(2) of the 1989 Act a person other than a trustee savings bank must not, in an advertisement, business card, circular or other document, use either the phrase "trustee savings bank" or "savings bank" or any phrase that is a derivative, translation or variation of such phrases if by so doing such person would hold that person out, or represent such person as being, a trustee savings bank.[70]

---

[66] On the use of signs identical with, or similar to, a trade mark in a comparative advertisement, see further the recent decision of the European Court of Justice in *O2 Holding Limited, O2 (UK) Limited v Hutchison 3G UK Limited* (Case C-533/06, Decision of the European Court of Justice of 12 June 2008).

[67] No 21 of 1989.

[68] The term "advertisement" is not defined in the 1989 Act.

[69] Trustee Savings Bank Act, 1989, s 27(4).

[70] Trustee Savings Bank Act, 1989, s 14(2). By contrast the said phrases must, unless the Central Bank and Financial Services Authority otherwise consents, be included in the name of a trustee savings bank. (Trustee Savings Bank Act, 1989, s 14(1)).

• *Unit Trusts*

[8–20] Section 10(1) of the Unit Trusts Act, 1990,[71] provides that, absent the approval of the Central Bank and Financial Services Authority, no advertisement[72] in relation to (or referring to), in effect, an unauthorised trust scheme or certain like schemes may be published or communicated. If it is shown to the satisfaction of the Authority (in respect of a magazine/newspaper that is printed outside Ireland and which in the opinion of the Authority has only a small circulation in Ireland) that compliance with s 10(1) would necessitate the production for circulation in Ireland of a special edition of the said magazine/newspaper and the cost of such production would impose an unreasonably heavy burden on the newspaper/magazine owner, the Authority may exempt (conditionally or otherwise) any advertisements published in the said magazine/newspaper from the application of s 10 of the 1990 Act.[73] Where an advertisement is published or communicated in breach of s 10(1), the person who publishes or communicates the advertisement and the person who procured such publication/communication commits an offence.[74]

---

[71] No 37 of 1990.

[72] The term "advertisement" is defined in s 10(4) of the 1990 Act as including "every form of recommendation of any matter to which [section 10]…relates, including, in particular the display or publication of any such matter by way of leaflet, circular, pamphlet, brochure, photograph, film, video, sound broadcasting, television, electronic communication or personal canvassing."

[73] Unit Trusts Act, 1990, s 10(2)(a).

[74] Unit Trusts Act, 1990, s 10(3).

114

PART 2
SELF-REGULATION

Chapter 9

THE CODE OF STANDARDS FOR ADVERTISING, PROMOTIONAL AND DIRECT MARKETING IN IRELAND[1]

---

[1] The full text of the Code is contained in the Advertising Standards Authority for Ireland's *Manual of Advertising Self-Regulation with the Code of Standards for Advertising, Promotional and Direct Marketing in Ireland*, 6th edition (Dublin: 2007), available on-line, as of 21 April 2008, at www.asai.ie/asai%20codebook.pdf.

Introduction

[9–01]   The Code of Standards for Advertising, Promotional and Direct Marketing in Ireland is published by the Advertising Standards Authority for Ireland. The Authority has been established by the advertising industry as an independent self-regulatory body that seeks to promote the highest standards of advertising, promotional marketing and direct marketing. The Authority is a company limited by guarantee and without a share capital. It has three categories of member: advertiser members, media members and agency members, It also has an independent chairman appointed by its Board. It is financed entirely by the advertising industry, its principal source of income being an annual subscription from its advertiser members. This subscription is collected and remitted by advertising agencies or media-buying companies.[2]

[9–02]   The Advertising Standards Authority is itself a founder member of the European Advertising Standards Alliance (EASA), a Brussels-based, non-profit organisation that seeks to promote best practice in self-regulation in the field of advertising, develops best practice, supervises the cross-border complaints process (considered further below), provides information, conducts research and works with the European Union law-making bodies to ensure that new legislation affecting advertising makes due acknowledgement of self-regulation.

[9–03]   The Code of Standards published by the Authority is based on principles that were established by the International Chamber of Commerce and which require that all marketing communications "be legal, decent, honest and truthful. . .be prepared with a sense of responsibility to consumers and to society. . .[and] respect the principles of fair competition generally accepted in business".[3] (In the 'rough and tumble' of commercial life it is perhaps open to question whether there are any generally accepted principles of fair competition apart from those imposed by law or regulation or perhaps agreed to by business out of self-interest).

[9–04]   The Code of Standards applies to most commercial 'marketing communications' and also to sales promotions which promote the sale of goods or services.[4] The term

---

[2] At the time of writing the levy is set at 0.2 percent of media spend (or €2 per €1000 spent). (Code of Standards, 84, para 7).

[3] Code of Standards, 75, para 1.

[4] Code of Standards, 75, para 2.

'marketing communication' is a (broadly) defined term for the purposes of the Code and includes but is not limited to "advertising, as well as other techniques such as promotions, sponsorships and direct marketing, and should be interpreted broadly to mean any form of communication produced directly by or on behalf of advertisers intended primarily to promote products, to influence the behaviour of and/or to inform those to whom it is addressed".[5]

The Code of Standards is contained in Chapter 1 of the Advertising Standards Authority's Manual of Self-Regulation and is comprised of a series of general (and then sector-specific) rules which are intended to ensure that marketing communications do not mislead or cause general offence.[6] The Code also makes extensive provision as regards 'promotional marketing practices', defined as follows: "Promotional marketing practices, including sales promotions, are those marketing techniques which involve the provision of direct or indirect additional benefits, usually on a temporary basis, designed to make goods or services more attractive to purchasers."[7] **[9–05]**

Financial product and service providers publish marketing communications and engage in promotional marketing practices. Many financial product and service providers and media outlets are members of the Advertising Standards Authority for Ireland. As a result an entity seeking to advertise financial products and services in Ireland cannot generally avoid encountering the Code, thus making it worthy of consideration in this book. **[9–06]**

Members of the Advertising Standards Authority for Ireland are required to observe, and not knowingly or recklessly to publish an advertisement or undertake a promotion in breach of, the Authority's Code of Standards.[8] A comprehensive complaints procedure exists whereby complaints from any person or body and, in certain circumstances, intra-industry disputes may be investigated and ruled upon (free of charge) by the Advertising Standards Authority. The complaints procedure is considered later below. **[9–07]**

Any marketing communication that contravenes the provisions of the Code of Standards is required to be withdrawn.[9] (Media members of the Advertising Standards Authority will not in any event deliberately publish a marketing communication that has been found to be in breach of the Code of Standards).[10] In addition, in the case of a sales promotion, the promoter may be requested to make changes to the way a promotion is communicated or conducted and recompense of adversely affected consumers may also be requested.[11] A member of the Advertising Standards Authority who does not accept (comply with) a decision of the Authority may be disciplined by the Board of the Authority and subject to penalties such as fines **[9–08]**

---

[5] Code of Standards, 8, para 1.3(b).
[6] Code of Standards, 75, para 3.
[7] Code of Standards, 9, para 1.4(h).
[8] Code of Standards, 69, para 4.
[9] Code of Standards, 79, para 14.
[10] Code of Standards, 81, para 18.
[11] Code of Standards, 79, para 14.

and/or suspension of membership of the Authority.[12] Perhaps most significantly, by way of a 'name and shame' exercise, case reports of the Complaints Committee, including the names of advertisers, promoters and agencies, but not complainants, are made public by the Advertising Standards Authority and often reported in the mainstream media, generating adverse publicity that advertiser members of the Authority are doubtless keen to avoid.[13]

[9–09] Before proceeding to a detailed consideration of the Code of Standards, it is perhaps worth considering why an advertiser member of the Advertising Standards Authority for Ireland would accede to the Code of Standards and submit itself to the Authority's complaints procedure. The Chairman of the Advertising Standards Authority, in his introduction to the current edition of the Code of Standards suggests a number of reasons why an advertiser member might do so, writing:

> "The Code supplements the law, fills gaps where the law does not reach and generally provides a relatively simple and less expensive means of resolving disputes than by civil litigation. In many cases, advertising self-regulation ensures that litigation is not necessary.... Everybody in advertising shares an interest in seeing that advertisements and promotions are welcomed and trusted by those to whom they are addressed. Unless the commercial message is accepted and believed, it cannot be successful. An advertisement or promotion which misleads or offends brings discredit on everyone involved and on the advertising industry as a whole. All advertising interests see the freedom to advertise as part of the basic freedom of expression. They believe that the best way to safeguard this freedom is to ensure that it is exercised in a responsible manner."[14]

[9–10] The text quoted above suggests that there are three key advantages to advertiser members of subscribing to the Code of Standards (and accepting the related complaints procedure). First, it offers a less expensive avenue for the resolution of complaints that could otherwise fall to be resolved in the law courts (even though, as the Code later states,[15] matters of taste and decency might be difficult to judge in law).[16] Second, advertisements are more effective if broadly credible and are more likely to be thought credible where the advertising industry subscribes to a code of standards that favours advertising which is legal, decent, honest and truthful. Third, advertising is an aspect of the basic human freedom of expression and if that expression is not to be circumscribed (whether by legislation or otherwise) it must be seen to be exercised responsibly. Of course, it would be cynical to suggest that the Advertising Standards Authority for Ireland exists or that the Code of Standards is administered solely because of advantages arising for advertiser members. After all, the Code of Standards and the complaints procedure also operate to the benefit of the general public. In particular, the complaints procedure offers ordinary members of the public, who do not have the financial wherewithal to engage in expensive legal

---

[12] Code of Standards, 81, para 19.

[13] Code of Standards, 79, para 13.

[14] Code of Standards, 4 *et seq.*

[15] Code of Standards, 73, para 5.

[16] It is, of course, open to query whether such matters are any easier to resolve in a non-legal forum.

proceedings, a free means whereby complaints about marketing communications may be aired, considered and adjudicated upon.

The Code of Standards commences by distilling 'the essence of good advertising' into three general principles. The first principle is that all marketing communications should be legal, decent, honest and truthful.[17] The second such principle is that all marketing communications should be prepared with a sense of responsibility to the consumer and society.[18] The third principle is that all marketing communications should conform to "the principles of fair competition as generally accepted in business."[19] With regard to this last principle, it is perhaps open to question whether capitalist enterprises bent on maximising profit are instinctively inclined to recognise and accept any principles of fair competition. [9–11]

The Code of Standards next prescribes what it describes as 'the essence of the code', namely that the Code be applied "in the spirit as well as in the letter" and that "[t]he Code rules are indivisible; advertisers should comply, where appropriate, with all rules".[20] Presumably in its reference to "all rules", the Code means to refer to all rules applicable to particular advertisers, as some of the rules contained in the Code are specific to certain types of business. [9–12]

The main part of the Code of Standards is divided into two Chapters. The first Chapter prescribes various standards or rules, not all of which are applicable to the financial services sector. The second Chapter is concerned with the work and workings of the Advertising Standards Authority for Ireland and, in particular, its complaints procedure. Section 1 of the first chapter prescribes the scope and application of the Code of Standards. Section 2 outlines various general principles applicable to 'marketing communications' (defined below). Sections 3, 4 and 5 prescribe various standards or rules applicable respectively to promotional marketing practices, distance selling and children. Section 10 is specifically concerned with marketing communications concerned with financial services and products. [9–13]

Chapter 1, Section 1 - Scope and Application

Section 1.1 of the Code states the primary objective of the Code to be "the regulation of commercial marketing communications in the interest of consumers".[21] [9–14]

Section 1.2 prescribes certain basic rules of interpretation that apply throughout the Code. Thus singular terms are to be construed as importing the plural sense and vice versa; the term "person" is to be construed "as including legal persons and groups, as appropriate"; and (unless the contrary intention appears) words importing the masculine gender are to be construed as also importing the feminine gender and vice versa. [9–15]

---

[17] Code of Standards, 3.
[18] *ibid.*
[19] *ibid.*
[20] *ibid.*
[21] Code of Standards, 8, para 1.1.

[9–16]   Section 1.3 of the Code defines various terms used throughout the Code. In sourcing these defined terms, the Broadcasting Commission looked to a variety of sources, including the Television Without Frontiers Directive[22] and the BCI Children's Advertising Code.

[9–17]   The broad meaning afforded the term "marketing communication" has been considered elsewhere above.

[9–18]   The term "advertising" and the related term "advertisement" are also broadly defined as including but not being limited to "a form of marketing communication carried by the media, usually in return for payment or other valuable consideration".[23]

[9–19]   The term "advertiser" is defined as including "anyone disseminating marketing communications, including promoters and direct marketers; references to advertisers should be interpreted as including intermediaries and agencies unless the context indicates otherwise". Although this definition is broad, it is notable that the term "advertiser" is defined as including and not (unlike the definitions of "marketing communication" and "advertising") as 'including but not being limited to' the categories of individual listed. Thus it seems reasonable to assume that only a person coming within the stated categories of individual recited in the definition of "advertiser" actually constitutes an advertiser. By contrast the use of the term "includes but is not limited to" in the definitions of the terms "marketing communication" and "advertising" indicates that those definitions are not exhaustive.

[9–20]   The terms "promoter" and "intermediary" used in the definition of the term "advertiser" are respectively defined as "any person or body by whom a sales promotion is initiated or commissioned"[24] and "any person or body, other than the promoter, responsible for the implementation of any form of sales promotional activity".[25] The term "agency" is not defined.

[9–21]   Significantly for entities operating in the financial services sector, the term "product" embraces not only 'products' in the conventionally understood sense but "can encompass goods, services, facilities, opportunities, fundraising and gifts".[26] The term "consumer" is defined as "anyone who is likely to see or hear a particular marketing communication".[27] This is a very wide definition of the term "consumer", so wide that any person from the largest company to an ordinary individual would appear to come within the definition.

[9–22]   After these initial definitions (there are others but these are considered, as and where appropriate below), the Code of Standards proceeds to define its breadth of

---

[22] Council Directive 89/552/EEC of 3 October 1989 on the co-ordination of certain provisions laid down by law, regulation or administrative action in Member States concerning the pursuit of television broadcasting activities (OJ No L298, 17 October 1989, 23), as amended.

[23] Code of Standards, 9, para 1.3(c). The term "media" is not defined in the Code of Standards.

[24] Code of Standards, 9, para 1.3(j).

[25] Code of Standards, 9, para 1.3(k).

[26] Code of Standards, 9, para 1.3(e).

[27] Code of Standards, 9, para 1.3(f).

application. Thus the Code of Standards states itself to apply to: (i) marketing communications in newspapers, magazines and other printed publications, including 'free sheets'; (ii) marketing communications in posters and other promotional media in public places, including moving images; (iii) marketing communications in brochures, leaflets, circulars, mailings, facsimile transmissions, e-mails and text transmissions; (iv) marketing communications broadcast on television or radio or screened in cinemas; (v) marketing communications carried on electronic storage materials and all other electronic media and computer systems; (vi) promotional marketing and sales promotions; and (g) advertisement features.[28] Clearly the Code of Standards applies to a wide array of advertisements and advertising practices, though there is also a wide array of communications to which the Code of Standards states itself not to apply, namely: (i) statutory, public, Garda and other official notices; (ii) material published as a matter of record only; (iii) fly-posting; (iv) packages, wrappers, labels, tickets, timetables and menus "unless they advertise another product or a sales promotion or are recognisable in a marketing communication"[29]; (v) point-of-sale displays, except those covered by the promotional marketing rules or when part of a wider advertising campaign; (vi) marketing communications whose principal purpose is to express the advertiser's position on a political, religious, industrial relations, social or aesthetic matter or on an issue of public interest or concern; (vii) classified private advertisements, including those on-line; (viii) press releases and other public relations material; (ix) the content of books and editorial material in media; (x) oral communications, including telephone calls; (xi) works of art; (xii) specialised marketing communications addressed to the medical, veterinary and allied professions; (xiii) the content of premium rate services; (xiv) marketing communications in foreign media[30]; (xv) website content (apart from sales promotions and marketing communications in "paid-for space"[31]); and (xvi) sponsorship.[32]

The last part of Section 1 of Chapter 1 of the Code of Standards prescribes certain **[9–23]** criteria in accordance with which the Code is applied. Thus the Code of Standards states that: (i) the rules of the Code of Standards are indivisible and advertisers should comply, where appropriate, with all of the rules; (ii) the Code is primarily concerned with the content of advertisements, promotions and direct marketing communications and not with terms of business or products themselves[33]; (iii) the Code of Standards

---

[28] Code of Standards, 9 *et seq.*, para 1.4.

[29] Code of Standards, 10, para 1.5 (d).

[30] Such communications may be subject to State or self-regulation in the relevant foreign jurisdiction.

[31] Code of Standards, 11, para 1.5(o).

[32] All the exempted categories are set out in the Code of Standards, 10 *et seq.*, para 1.5. Although the Code of Standards does not apply to sponsorship per se, it does apply to marketing communications that refer to sponsorship. (Code of Standards, 11).

[33] Code of Standards, 12, para 1.6 (d). As the Code of Standards itself notes (at para 1.6 (d), *infra.*) some of the rules do go beyond regulation of content, for example, the rules concerning the administration of sales promotions, the suitability of promotional items and the delivery of advertisements ordered through an advertisement.

does not deal with contractual relationships between advertisers and consumers.[34] In addition to these general criteria, the Code recites at this point certain other criteria that are of a more administrative/procedural nature more directly concerned with the work and workings of the Advertising Standards Authority for Ireland and its operation of the complaints process. Thus the Code states in this regard that: (i) compliance with the Code is assessed in light of a marketing communication's probable effect when taken as a whole and in context[35]; (ii) an invitation from the Advertising Standards Authority to comment on a complaint does not mean that the Authority accepts the complainant's view; (iii) the Advertising Standards Authority does not act as an arbitrator between competing ideologies; (iv) no legal advice can be given or should be presumed in any communications from the Authority (whether from the Board, the Complaints Committee or the Secretariat of the Authority); and (v) the judgment of the Advertising Standards Authority on any matter of interpretation of the Code is final.[36]

Chapter 1, Section 2 - General Rules

[9–24] Section 2 of Chapter 1 establishes a number of general rules under various headings. These are considered below.

Principles

[9–25] The first three principles are a very slightly modified form of the three principles (considered above) that are identified at the outset of the Code of Standards as being 'the essence of good advertising'.[37] Thus it is (re-) stated that marketing communications should: (i) be legal, decent, honest and truthful[38]; (ii) be prepared with a sense of responsibility to consumers and to society[39]; and (iii) respect the principles of fair competition generally accepted in business (again it is perhaps open to question whether capitalist enterprises are instinctively inclined to adhere to such principles).[40] The next principle is also identified at the outset of the Code of Standards[41] as being of 'the essence of the Code', namely that the Code of Standards "is applied in the spirit as well as in the letter".[42] Section 2 of Chapter 2 then proceeds to establish a number of principles that have not previously been encountered in the Code of Standards. Thus the Code of Standards states that: (i) a marketing communication should not bring advertising into disrepute[43]; (ii) primary responsibility for observing

---

[34] So, for example, "[i]t does not presume to judge whether a product represents value for money nor does it seek to regulate terms of business." (Code of Standards, 12).
[35] In this regard, Chapter 1 states (at 11 *et seq.*, para 1.6) that "[p]articular attention is paid to... [i] the characteristics of the likely audience...[ii] the media by means of which the marketing communication is communicated...[iii] the location and context of the marketing communication...[iv] the nature of the advertised product and the nature, content and form of any associated material made available or action recommended to consumers."
[36] Code of Standards, 11 *et seq.*, para 1.6
[37] Cf. Code of Standards, 3.
[38] Code of Standards, 13, para 2.1.
[39] Code of Standards, 13, para 2.2.
[40] Code of Standards, 13, para 2.3.
[41] Code of Standards, 3.
[42] Code of Standards, 13, para 2.4.
[43] Code of Standards, 13, para 2.5.

the Code of Standards rests with advertisers[44]; (iii) a marketing communication (or an advertiser/promoter) may be found to have breached the Code if an advertiser/promoter does not respond, or unreasonably delays a response, to the Advertising Standards Authority[45]; (iv) in its dealings the Advertising Standards Authority will treat in strict secrecy any "truly confidential material" with which it is supplied and that it is requested to so treat "unless the courts or an official agency acting within its statutory powers compel its disclosure".[46] It is worth emphasising that this strict secrecy, in the Code's own terms, is dependent upon a request for same being made.

Substantiation

Under the heading 'Substantiation', the Code of Standards identifies a number of rules intended to ensure that advertisers can prove or support claims made in any market communications. Thus the Code of Standards requires that prior to offering a marketing communication for publication (it is not clear whether this means to an agency or publisher for intended publication or whether it simply means immediately prior to publishing a marketing communication to the world), "advertisers should satisfy themselves that they will be able to provide documentary evidence to substantiate all claims, whether direct or indirect, expressed or implied, that are capable of objective assessment. Relevant evidence should be sent without delay if requested by the Authority and should be adequate to support both detailed claims and the overall impression created by the marketing communication."[47] [9–26]

Substantiation was at issue in a complaint made against Halifax/Royal Bank of Scotland in 2007.[48] A press advertisement had been published for Halifax/Royal Bank of Scotland in which it was indicated that Allied Irish Banks plc was only offering "credit interest and free banking" to new customers (whereas Halifax/Royal Bank of Scotland was offering 10 percent interest on current accounts to all customers). The complainants were all customers of Allied Irish Banks plc who indicated that, despite being existing (not new) customers of Allied Irish Banks plc, they had received an offer of free banking and credit interest. The Complaints Committee decided in favour of the consumer, indicating that they did not consider that the claim in the advertisement had been substantiated. (The advertiser had agreed to withdraw the advertisement by way of response to the complaint so no further direction was made). [9–27]

The Code of Standards requires that: "[t]he full name and geographical business address of advertisers should be provided without delay if requested by the Authority [9–28]

---

[44] Code of Standards, 13, para 2.6. However, the Code goes on to acknowledge that "[o]thers involved in the preparation and publication of marketing communications, such as agencies, media and other service providers, also accept an obligation to abide by the Code". (Code of Standards, 13, para 2.6).

[45] Code of Standards, 13, para 2.7.

[46] Code of Standards, 13, para 2.8.

[47] Code of Standards, 14, para 2.9. It is perhaps worth noting that the Code of Standards later provides that testimonials per se do not constitute substantiation (and must themselves be substantiated, where necessary, with independent evidence of their accuracy). Code of Standards, 20, para 2.38.

[48] Advertising Standards Authority for Ireland, Case No AC/0704/0542.

from an agency or relevant third party"[49]; marketing communications should not present statistics in such a way as to exaggerate the validity of a claim (or give the unjustified impression that there is any validity to a claim)[50]; marketing data should neither misuse, mischaracterise or misleadingly cite any technical data nor use scientific terminology or vocabulary in such a way as to falsely or misleadingly suggest that an advertising claim has scientific validity[51]; if there is a significant division of opinion ("significant" is not defined) about any claim in a marketing communication, the claim should not be portrayed as universally accepted[52]; and marketing communications should not exaggerate the value, the accuracy or the usefulness of unsubstantiated claims made in books, tapes, videos, DVDs, etc.[53]

Legality

[9–29] The Code of Standards provides that the primary responsibility for ensuring that marketing communications are in conformity with the law rests with advertisers (and not, for example, with any external advertising agents or intermediaries that they may engage).[54] Moreover the Code requires that a marketing communication should not contain anything that breaks the law or incites anyone to break it, nor omit anything that the law requires.[55] Having made provision for the legality of advertisements, the Code acknowledges that the issue of legality is a matter for the State and State authorities, providing that "The determination as to whether or not a marketing communication is legal is primarily a matter for the courts or other appropriate regulatory authorities."[56]

Decency and propriety

[9–30] The Code of Standards requires that a marketing communication should contain nothing that is likely to cause grave or widespread offence.[57] The Code acknowledges that a marketing communication which is considered by some to be distasteful may not breach this general prohibition on content likely to cause grave or widespread offence.[58] However, the Code of Standards urges advertisers to consider public sensitivities before using material that is potentially offensive (but not likely to cause grave or widespread offence).[59]

[9–31] The Code of Standards requires that marketing communications should respect the dignity of all persons and avoid causing offence on grounds of gender, marital status, family status, sexual orientation, religion, age, disability, race or membership of the

---

[49] Code of Standards, 14, para 2.9
[50] Code of Standards, 14, para 2.10.
[51] Code of Standards, 14, para 2.11. Examples of "technical data" include research results and quotations from technical and scientific publications (Code of Standards, 14, para 2.11(a)).
[52] Code of Standards, 14, para 2.12.
[53] Code of Standards, 15, para 2.13.
[54] Code of Standards, 15, para 2.14.
[55] *ibid.*
[56] *ibid.*
[57] Code of Standards, 15, para 2.15.
[58] Code of Standards, 16, para 2.19.
[59] Code of Standards, 16, para 2.9.

Traveller community.[60] Though these terms derive from the equal status legislation, there is no indication in the Code of Standards that the Advertising Standards Authority would seek to interpret the terms in accordance with any judicial interpretation of the terms as employed in such legislation.

In addition to requiring that advertising should avoid causing offence on grounds of gender, the Code of Standards further requires that marketing communications respect the principle of gender equality.[61] Thus, per the Code, marketing communications "should avoid sex stereotyping and any exploitation or demeaning of men and women. Where appropriate, marketing communications should use generic terms that include both the masculine and feminine gender; for example the term 'business executive' covers both men and women."[62] **[9–32]**

Diversity within Irish society is also a matter to which marketing communications are required to be responsive, the Code of Standards requiring, in paragraph 2.18, that "marketing communications which portray or refer to people within the groups mentioned in [paragraph] 2.16 should: (a) respect the principle of equality in any depiction of these groups; (b) fully respect their dignity and not subject them to ridicule or offensive humour; (c) avoid stereotyping and negative or hurtful images; (d) not exploit them for unrelated marketing purposes; and (e) not ridicule or exploit religious beliefs, symbols, rites or practices."[63] As it happens, paragraph 2.16 of the Code of Standards does not generally refer to groups as such. Thus "gender", "marital status", "family status", "sexual orientation", "religion", "age", "disability" are not groups, though "race" and "membership of the traveller [*sic*] community" are. However, the intent of paragraph 2.18 seems reasonably clear, namely that advertisements must not, in essence, be disrespectful of a particular gender, marital status, family status, sexual orientation, religion age, disability or race, or of the Traveller community. **[9–33]**

Advertisers are required to take account of public sensitivities in the preparation and publication of marketing communications.[64] They are required to avoid the exploitation of sexuality and the use of coarseness and undesirable innuendo.[65] Moreover, the Code of Standards directs that advertisers should not use offensive or provocative copy or images merely to attract attention.[66] As stated above, the Code of Standards urges advertisers to consider public sensitivities before using material that is potentially offensive, presumably in circumstances where that offensive material would not suffice to cause grave or widespread offence in breach of paragraph 2.15 of the Code of Standards.[67] Continuing in a similar vein, the Code of Standards requires that advertisers should avoid causing offence in marketing communications while acknowledging that the fact that a product (as opposed to an advertisement) is **[9–34]**

---

[60] Code of Standards, 14, para 2.16.
[61] Code of Standards, 15, para 2.17.
[62] *ibid.*
[63] Code of Standards, 16.
[64] Code of Standards, 16, para 2.19.
[65] *ibid.*
[66] *ibid.*
[67] *ibid.*

offensive to some is not in itself sufficient basis for objecting to a marketing communication,[68] i.e. it is the marketing communication that should prompt offence.

[9–35] Decency and propriety are highly subjective matters and the litmus test by which such matters are to be gauged is not easily defined. The Code of Standards states in this regard that "Compliance with the Code is assessed on the basis of the standards of taste, decency and propriety generally accepted in Ireland, taking account of the characteristics of the likely audience, the media by means of which the marketing communication is communicated, the location and context of the marketing communication, the nature of the advertised product and the nature, content and form of any associated material made available or action recommended to consumers."[69] Given the subjective nature of these tests, the composition of the Complaints Committee, of the Advertising Standards Authority (and the need for it to be both diverse and reflective of the various elements within Irish society) assumes a central importance.

Honesty

[9–36] The Code of Standards requires that advertisers should not exploit the credulity, inexperience or lack of knowledge of consumers.[70] Like the Consumer Protection Code, the Code of Standards requires that "The design and presentation of marketing communications should allow them to be easily and clearly understood. Where footnotes or 'small print' sections are used, they should be of sufficient size and prominence and easily legible; where appropriate they should be linked to the relevant part of the main copy."[71]

Truthfulness

[9–37] The Code of Standards requires that a marketing communication not mislead or be likely to mislead by inaccuracy, ambiguity, exaggeration, omission or otherwise.[72] This echoes the (wider) requirement in the Consumer Protection Code that "An advertisement must not influence a consumer's attitude to the advertised product or service or the regulated entity either by inaccuracy, ambiguity, exaggeration or omission."[73] However, except perhaps insofar as the provision regarding spelling is concerned, it is unlikely that the Financial Regulator would be minded to agree with the next succeeding provision of the Code of Standards which provides that "Obvious untruths or deliberate hyperbole that are unlikely to mislead, incidental minor inaccuracies and unorthodox spellings are not necessarily in conflict with the Code provided they do not affect the accuracy or perception of the marketing

---

[68] Code of Standards, 16, para 2.20.

[69] Code of Standards, 16, *et seq.*, para 2.21.

[70] Code of Standards, 17, para 2.22.

[71] Code of Standards, 17, para 2.23. It will be recalled that the Consumer Protection Code requires that "The design and presentation of an advertisement must allow it to be clearly understood. Where small print or footnotes are used, they should be of sufficient size and prominence to be clearly legible. Where appropriate they should be linked to the relevant part of the main copy." (Consumer Protection Code, 35, Chapter 7, para 6).

[72] Code of Standards, 17, para 2.24.

[73] Consumer Protection Code, 35, Chapter 7, para 2.

communication in any material way."[74] Claims such as 'Up to' and 'From' in marketing communications are required by the Code of Standards not to exaggerate the value or range of benefits that are likely to be achieved in practice by consumers.[75]

Matters of opinion

The Code of Standards allows advertisers to state an opinion about the desirability or quality of a product, so long as: (i) it is clear that they are expressing their own opinion and not a matter of fact; and (ii) there is no likelihood of consumers being misled about any matter that is capable of objective assessment.[76] Where assertions/comparisons go beyond subjective opinions, the Code of Standards requires that such assertions/comparisons be capable of substantiation.[77]

[9–38]

Fear and distress

The Code of Standards requires that a marketing communication should not, "without good reason" cause fear or distress.[78] 'Good reason' includes the encouragement of prudent behaviour or the discouragement of imprudent behaviour (specifically "dangerous or ill-advised actions").[79] However, where fear or distress is aroused for good reason, "the fear aroused should not be disproportionate to the risk",[80] presumably the risk that the imprudent behaviour would be pursued. The Code of Standards does not contain an express requirement that any distress (as opposed to fear) aroused for good reason should not be disproportionate to the risk.

[9–39]

Safety

A marketing communication, per the Code of Standards "should not encourage or condone dangerous behaviour or unsafe practices except in the context of promoting safety".[81]

[9–40]

Violence and anti-social behaviour

The Code of Standards requires that a marketing communication should contain nothing that condones or is likely to provoke violence, anti-social behaviour, nuisance, personal injury or damage to property.[82] Offhand, it may seem unlikely that a financial advertisement would be excessively violent. However, in 2007, a television advertisement for Halifax was the subject of complaints that, amongst other matters, it: was excessively violent; inappropriately depicted anti-social behaviour as a means of resolving conflict, communicating or competing; and condoned and glamourised

[9–41]

---

[74] Code of Standards, 17, para 2.25.
[75] Code of Standards, 17, para 2.26.
[76] Code of Standards, 18, para 2.27.
[77] *ibid*. 'Substantiation', for the purposes of the Code of Standards, has been considered elsewhere in the main text above.
[78] Code of Standards, 18, para 2.28.
[79] *ibid*.
[80] *ibid*.
[81] Code of Standards, 18, para 2.29.
[82] Code of Standards, 18, para 2.30.

violence.[83] One complainant also alleged that the advertisement implied that non-Halifax bank officials were thugs. The advertisement complained of affected to show a fight between Halifax bank staff and other bankers. The fight was slap-stick in execution and depicted one 'banker' being thrown through a window and another being hit over the head with a poster. The Complaints Committee accepted that the advertisement had been slap-stick in execution but considered that the scene where someone was thrown from a window and had a poster smashed over his head was inappropriate, even given the nature of the commercial. The Committee did not consider that the advertisement implied all non-Halifax bank officials to be thugs.

Portrayal of persons or property

[9–42]   The Code of Standards requires that, save in certain expressly excepted circumstances, advertisers should have prior written permission from living persons portrayed or referred to in a marketing communication.[84] In addition, the Code of Standards requires that permission (the Code does not expressly mention that this permission be prior or written) is also required before "any person's house or other possessions can be featured in a manner which identifies the owner to the public".[85] There is no reference to the fact that such person must be a living person. Exceptions to the requirement that permission be obtained, "include" (it is not clear whether they are limited to): "(a) the use of crowd scenes or property depicted in general outdoor locations, or where the purpose of the marketing communication is to promote a product such as a book, newspaper article, broadcast programme or film of which the person concerned is a subject; (b) in the case of people with a public profile, references that accurately reflect the contents of books, newspaper articles, broadcast programmes, films or other electronic communications etc."[86] The Code of Standards further provides that: marketing communications should not (a) exploit the public reputation of persons in a manner which is humiliating or offensive[87] or (b) claim or imply an endorsement where none exists[88]; and references to deceased persons should be particularly carefully handled so as to avoid causing offence or distress.[89] The Code of Standards notes that persons who do not wish to be associated with a marketing communication may take legal action against advertisers[90], thus highlighting the need for care in this regard.

Testimonials and endorsements

[9–43]   At the time of writing, testimonials and endorsements appear to have become an increasingly popular form of advertising in the financial services sector, in part perhaps because such forms of advertising generally tend to require fewer regulatory statements and warnings (i.e. less 'small print'). The Code of Standards makes

---

[83] Advertising Standards Authority for Ireland, Case No AC/0701/0081.
[84] Code of Standards, 18, *et seq.*, para 2.32.
[85] *ibid.*
[86] Code of Standards, 19, para 2.33.
[87] Code of Standards, 19, para 2.34.
[88] *ibid.*
[89] Code of Standards, 19, para 2.35.
[90] Code of Standards, 18, para 2.31.

reasonably extensive provision as regards testimonials and endorsements. Thus, per the Code of Standards: (i) advertisers who use testimonials should be able to provide relevant supporting documentation and should hold signed and dated proof for any testimonials used (which information must be provided to the Advertising Standards Authority on request[91]; (ii) testimonials by persons named or depicted in a marketing communication may be used only with the prior permission of those persons (and only where such permission continues to be extant)[92]; (iii) testimonials could be considered misleading if the formulation of a product or its market environment changes significantly and should therefore relate to a product — presumably the advertised product — "as currently offered", presumably as at the date of publication)[93]; testimonials do not constitute substantiation and any opinions expressed in them should be supported, where necessary, with independent evidence of their accuracy (any claims based on a testimonial being required also to be otherwise in conformity with the Code of Standards)[94]; endorsements by fictitious or historical characters should not be presented as though they were genuine testimonials (unless, presumably, such endorsements are genuine and otherwise in conformity with the Code of Standards)[95]; references to research tests, trials, professional endorsements, research facilities and professional journals may only be used with the permission of those concerned and should be relevant and current (with all such tests, trials and endorsements being signed and dated, and any establishment referred to being under appropriate professional supervision).[96]

Prices

The Code of Standards states, with respect to prices that if a price is stated in a marketing communication, it should relate to the product depicted or specified in such communication (care being taken to ensure that prices and illustrated products in fact match).[97] Any prices quoted should be quoted inclusive of Value Added Tax and other taxes, duties or inescapable costs to the consumer.[98] Moreover, where applicable, the amounts of any other charges arising (for example, those arising from the method of payment or purchase) should be stated.[99] The requirements as to inclusion of VAT, taxes, etc. do not apply "in marketing communications addressed primarily to the trade".[100] It is not clear from the text of the Code of Standards whether this latter reference to "the trade" is intended to refer to the advertising trade only or to all trades and whether the term is intended to embrace businesses and/or professions. The Code of Standards further requires as regards prices that: if the price of one product is

[9–44]

---

[91] Code of Standards, 20, para 2.36.
[92] *ibid.*
[93] Code of Standards, 20, para 2.37.
[94] Code of Standards, 20, para 2.38.
[95] Code of Standards, 20, para 2.39.
[96] Code of Standards, 20, para 2.40.
[97] Code of Standards, 21, para 2.41.
[98] Code of Standards, 21, para 2.42.
[99] *ibid.*
[100] *ibid.* Where marketing communications are addressed to "the trade" and quote a VAT-exclusive price, it must, per the Code, be clear that the price is VAT-exclusive. (Code of Standards, 21, para 2.42).

dependent on the purchase of another, the extent of any commitment required of consumers should be made clear[101]; and if the price of accessing a message/service, or communicating with advertisers, is greater than the relevant standard rate applicable, this should be made clear in any (applicable) marketing communications.[102]

Availability of products

[9–45] The Code of Standards requires that advertisers should be in a position to meet any reasonable demand created by their advertising.[103] If there is insufficient quantity of a product, advertisers are required under the Code to take immediate action to ensure that any further marketing communications are amended or withdrawn.[104] The Code of Standards further states that where there is limited availability of some or all products advertised, then apart from indicating that there may be other terms and conditions applicable, advertisers should not exaggerate the availability of any such products and should be able to demonstrate a reasonable supply or proportion of the various products available.[105] There is related provision in the Consumer Protection Code which requires that "An advertisement must not be misleading in relation to... [amongst other matters] the scarcity of the advertised product or service."[106]

[9–46] The Code of Standards requires that products should not be advertised as a way of gauging possible demand unless the marketing communication makes this clear.[107] The Code of Standards further requires that advertisers not engage in 'switching' (the practice whereby sales staff indicate an advertised product is unavailable or else criticise that product and suggest that a more expensive alternative product be bought).[108] Moreover, advertisers are required not to create obstacles to purchasing a product or delivering it promptly.[109]

Comparisons

[9–47] The Code of Standards allows comparative advertising which it justifies as being "in the interests of public information and vigorous competition."[110] It sanctions comparisons whether explicit or implied and whether they relate to an advertiser's own products or those of their competitors.[111] However, the Code requires that advertisers should not unfairly attack or discredit rival businesses or products[112] and establishes a number of constraints on an area of advertising that is perhaps particularly prone to abuse and also perhaps likely to bring advertisers (and advertising) into disrepute if not subject to some form of restraint. Thus the Code

---

[101] Code of Standards, 21, para 2.43.
[102] Code of Standards, 21, para 2.44.
[103] Code of Standards, 21, para 2.45.
[104] *ibid.*
[105] Code of Standards, 21 *et seq.*, para 2.46.
[106] Consumer Protection Code, 35, *et seq.*, Chapter 7, para 11.
[107] Code of Standards, 22, para 2.47.
[108] Code of Standards, 22, para 2.48.
[109] *ibid.*
[110] Code of Standards, 22, para 2.49.
[111] *ibid.*
[112] Code of Standards, 22, para 2.52.

provides that: (i) comparisons should be fair and should be so designed that there is no likelihood of a consumer being misled[113]; (ii) the basis of selection for the comparisons should be clear and the elements of comparison should not be unfairly selected in a way that gives the advertisers an artificial advantage[114]; a claim as to the superiority of a product should only be made where there is clear evidence to support such claim[115]; wording such as 'number one', 'leading', 'largest', i.e. wording which intimates superior or even superlative status being capable of substantiation by reference to market share data or similar proof.[116]

Guarantees

The Code of Standards requires that: where a marketing communication refers to a guarantee, the full terms of such guarantee should be available, for consumers to inspect pre-purchase, with any substantial limitations thereon being clearly indicated in the marketing communication[117]; and use of the term 'guarantee' in a colloquial sense should not cause any confusion about the statutory rights available to a consumer.[118]   **[9–48]**

Exploitation of goodwill

Advertisers are not permitted, under the Code of Standards, to exploit or make unfair use of the goodwill attaching to the name/trademark/brand/slogan/marketing communications campaign of any other person.[119] Any advertiser who did so would be in breach of the Code of Standards but would also be exposing itself to general legal liability for doing so.   **[9–49]**

Imitation

The Code of Standards requires that one marketing communication should not so closely resemble another as to be likely to mislead or cause confusion. Any advertiser in breach of this requirement would be in breach of the Code of Standards and also exposing itself to general legal liability for so doing.   **[9–50]**

Recognisability

By 'recognisability', the Code of Standards means that a marketing communication should be recognisable as such. Thus the Code of Standards requires that a marketing communication be designed and presented in such a way that it is clear that the marketing communication is just that.[120]   **[9–51]**

---

[113] Code of Standards, 22, para 2.50.
[114] *ibid.*
[115] Code of Standards, 22, *et seq.*, para 2.51.
[116] *ibid.*
[117] Code of Standards, 23, para 2.53.
[118] Code of Standards, 23, para 2.54.
[119] Code of Standards, 23, para 2.55.
[120] Code of Standards, 23, para 2.57. Likewise, the Consumer Protection Code requires that "An advertisement must be designed and presented so that any reasonable consumer knows immediately that it is an advertisement." (Consumer Protection Code, 35, Chapter 7, para 5).

[9–52] The Code of Standards further requires that an advertisement feature, announcement or promotion that is published or electronically broadcast in exchange for payment (or other reciprocal arrangement) in circumstances where the content is controlled by the advertiser must comply with the Code of Standards and must be clearly identified and distinguished from editorial matter.[121]

[9–52] The Code of Standards requires that the identity of an advertiser, product or service should be apparent, except in the case of 'teaser advertisements'.[122] The Code of Standards further requires that marketing communications should, where appropriate, include contact information so that a consumer can get in touch with the advertiser without difficulty, though presumably this is only appropriate where an advertiser is expressly inviting a consumer to make such contact.

[9–53] Consistent with the general requirement that marketing communications should be recognisable as such, the Code of Standards requires that marketing communications: should not misrepresent their true purpose and so should not, for example, be presented as market research or consumer surveys if their purpose is marketing (i.e. promoting) a product[123]; and, likewise, marketing communications soliciting orders should not be presented in a form which might be mistaken for an invoice or which otherwise (and falsely) suggests that payment is due.[124]

[9–54] The Code of Standards further requires that marketing communications which seek a response which would constitute an order (for which payment will have to be made) should make this clear.[125] The example given in the Code of Standards of when such a situation would arise is a letter soliciting a response as to whether entry in a particular publication is sought (a positive response being an order for which payment is required).[126]

Chapter 1, Section 3 - Promotional Marketing Practices

[9–55] The Code of Standards states that "promotional marketing practices, including sales promotions are those marketing techniques which involve the provision of direct or indirect additional benefits, usually on a temporary basis, designed to make goods or services more attractive to purchasers".[127] Engagement by advertisers in such practices is comprehensively addressed in Chapter 1, Section 3 of the Code of Standards. The introductory paragraph to Section 3 expressly identifies the following promotional marketing practices, though the list is not exhaustive: premium offers; reduced price and free offers; the distribution of vouchers, coupons and samples;

---

[121] Code of Standards, 23 *et seq.*, para 2.58.

[122] Code of Standards, 24, para 2.59. The term "teaser advertisement" is defined in para 2.59 as meaning "marketing communications with the sole purpose of attracting attention to communication activities to follow". It will be recalled that the Consumer Protection Code similarly requires that "The name of the regulated entity publishing an advertisement must be clearly shown in all advertisements." (Consumer Protection Code, 35, Chapter 7, para 3).

[123] Code of Standards, 24, para 2.61.

[124] Code of Standards, 24, para 2.63.

[125] Code of Standards, 24, para 2.62.

[126] *ibid.*

[127] Code of Standards, 25, para 3.1.

personality promotions; charity-linked promotions; and prize promotions.[128] It is possible that a financial product or service provider would engage in any or all such (or other) promotional marketing practices from time to time and hence it is useful to consider this aspect of the Code of Standards in this book.

The provisions of Section 3 are designed primarily to protect the ordinary public.[129] However, they also apply to "trade promotions" and incentive schemes and to "the promotional elements of sponsorship".[130] The precise meaning of the quoted text is somewhat unclear. Also, it is not clear whether the reference to "trade" means the advertising trade or all trades and also whether or not it embraces business and professions. [9–56]

By way of general provision, the Code of Standards states that "Sales promotions should be conducted equitably, promptly and efficiently and should be seen to deal fairly and honourably with consumers. Promoters should avoid causing unnecessary disappointment."[131] It will be recalled that the definition of "consumer" for the purposes of the Code of Standards is extremely wide.[132] [9–57]

Protection of Consumers

Promoters are required to have proper regard for normal safety precautions.[133] Thus promotional products and samples are required to be distributed in such a way as to avoid even the risk of harm to consumers.[134] Moreover, the Code of Standards requires that special care be taken when engaging in sales promotions addressed to children (or where promotional products) intended for adults may fall into the hands of children.[135] Safety warnings are required to be included in any literature that accompanies promotional items, though the Code of Standards shrinks from requiring that literature containing necessary warnings must accompany promotional items.[136] Sales promotions are required by the Code of Standards to be conducted and designed in a way that respects the rights of consumers to a reasonable degree of privacy and freedom from annoyance.[137] The Code also requires that consumers be told before entry in a sales promotion whether, as participants in the sales promotion, they may be required to become involved in any promoter advertising or publicity (whether such advertising or publicity is itself connected with the promotion or not).[138] On a related note, the Code requires that the interests of prize-winners should not be compromised through the publication of excessively detailed information.[139] [9–58]

---

[128] *ibid.*
[129] Per Code of Standards, 25, para 3.2.
[130] *ibid.*
[131] Code of Standards, 25, para 3.3.
[132] See the consideration of the term "consumer" elsewhere in the main text above.
[133] Code of Standards, 25, para 3.4.
[134] *ibid.*
[135] *ibid.*
[136] *ibid.*
[137] Code of Standards, 25, para 3.5.
[138] Code of Standards, 26, para 3.6.
[139] *ibid.*

Suitability

[9–59] Under the Code of Standards, promoters are required not to offer (let alone provide) promotional products which are of a nature likely to cause offence, or to offer products which (in the context of the promotion) may reasonably be considered to be socially undesirable.

Availability

[9–60] It will be recalled that the Code of Standards requires that advertisers should be in a position to meet any reasonable demand created by their advertising.[140] Likewise, when it comes to promotional marketing practices, promoters are required "to be able to demonstrate that they have made a reasonable estimate of the likely response and that they are capable of meeting that response".[141] This requirement arises with regard to all promotional marketing practices, except prize promotions.[142] In the case of the latter, the number of prizes to be awarded is required to be made clear to participants.[143] Interestingly (and, it might be contended, somewhat unfairly) the Code of Standards provides that phrases such as 'Subject to Availability' do not relieve promoters of the obligation to take all reasonable steps to avoid disappointing participants in a promotion.[144] On a related note, the Code of Standards provides that if promoters cannot meet demand for a promotional offer because of an unexpectedly high response (or some other unexpected factor outside their control), then products of a similar or greater quality and value or a cash payment should normally be substituted.[145]

Quality

[9–61] The Code of Standards requires that promotional products should meet satisfactory standards of safety, durability and performance in use (and, where appropriate, matters such as guarantees and after-sales service should be clearly explained).[146]

Presentation

[9–62] The Code of Standards requires that the presentation of sales promotions and the associated publicity should not mislead consumers.[147] Moreover, the Code requires that all supporting advertising material should conform both to the law and to the general and (applicable) sectoral rules of the Code of Standards, as appropriate.[148] In particular, the Code requires that descriptions of promotional products should not overstate their availability, quality, uses or value.[149] Specifically, the Code states that

---

[140] Code of Standards, 21, para 2.45.
[141] Code of Standards, 26, para 3.8.
[142] *ibid.*
[143] *ibid.*
[144] Code of Standards, 26, para 3.9.
[145] Code of Standards, 26, para 3.10.
[146] Code of Standards, 27, para 3.11.
[147] Code of Standards, 27, para 3.12.
[148] Code of Standards, 27, para 3.13.
[149] *ibid.*

just because promotional products may be "acquired" (presumably by the persons to whom they are distributed) free of charge, does not eliminate the need for a full and complete description of such products by the advertiser.[150]

Terms of the promotion

Paragraph 3.15 of the Code of Standards requires that the terms of a promotion must be presented in such a way as to be clear, complete and also easy for a consumer to understand.[151] It will be recalled that the term "consumer" is very broadly defined in the Code of Standards and it would seem prudent for an advertiser to have a relatively unsophisticated consumer in mind when drafting the terms of a promotion. The following are required to be clearly explained: (i) how to participate in the promotion (including any conditions and costs); (ii) the promoter's full name and business address in a form that can be retained by consumers; (iii) the closing date (which must be prominently displayed); (iv) any 'proof of purchase' requirements; (v) any geographical or personal restrictions; (vi) any necessary permissions that must be obtained (e.g. from parents/guardians); (vii) any limit on the number of applications permitted; (viii) any limit on the number of promotional products or prizes that an individual consumer/household may claim or win; and (ix) any other factor likely to influence a consumer's decisions or understanding about the promotion.[152] Lastly, as regards terms of a promotion, paragraph 3.16 of the Code of Standards requires the clear and prominent statement (so as to be clear to a consumer before any commitment is made) of any "terms or conditions" which either (a) exclude some consumers from the opportunity to participate in a promotion, or (b) impose requirements likely to affect a consumer's decision whether or not to participate in the promotion. Having consistently referred throughout paragraph 3.15 to the 'terms' of a promotion, it is not clear why paragraph 3.16 then refers to "terms or conditions", though the additional text seems to have no practical effect.

[9–63]

Administration

Sales promotions are required, under the Code, to be conducted under proper supervision and with adequate resources.[153] Moreover, promoters (and intermediaries) are required not to give consumers any justifiable grounds for complaint.[154] The Code of Standards requires that promoters allow ample time for each phase of a promotion, namely. notifying "the trade" (again, as mentioned above, the precise ambit of this

[9–64]

---

[150] Code of Standards, 27, para 3.14.

[151] Code of Standards, 27, *et seq.,* para 3.15.

[152] *ibid.* With regard to point (iii) in the main text above, the Code of Standards further provides that where the final date for purchase of a promoted product differs from the closing date for submission of claims/entries, this must be made clear to participants. (Code of Standards, 27, para 3.15(c)). As regards point (iv) in the main text above, any 'proof-of-purchase' requirements must be emphasised by separating them from the other terms or using a different colour. Moreover, any requirement to purchase more than one unit of a product to participate in a promotion must "ideally" (so not necessarily) state this on the front of any label/material carrying details of the relevant promotion. (Code of Standards, 28, para 3.15(d)).

[153] Code of Standards, 28, para 3.17.

[154] *ibid.*

term is not clear as it is not defined in the Code), distributing "the goods"[155], issuing rules where appropriate, collecting wrappers and such like, and judging and announcing the results.[156] Promoters are required to fulfil applications within 30 days, save where: (i) participants in a promotion have been told that it is impractical for a promoter so to do; or (ii) participants are informed promptly of any unforeseen delays and offered either (a) another delivery date or (b) an opportunity to recover any money paid for the offer.[157] Paragraph 3.20 of the Code of Standards provides that "[w]hen damaged or faulty goods are received by a consumer, promoters should ensure either that they are replaced without delay or that a refund is sent immediately".[158] Presumably the Code of Standards means to refer in this regard to damaged/faulty goods provided as part of a promotional marketing practice. Promoters for their part are, per the Code of Standards, entitled to seek the return of such damaged/faulty goods and (where possible) the original packaging at their expense.[159] Where damaged/faulty goods fall to be replaced in accordance with the aforesaid provisions of the Code, the full cost of replacing them must (per the Code) fall on promoters. Where an applicant does not receive goods (again, presumably, goods that are offered as part of a promotional marketing exercise) promoters are required normally (though not invariably) to replace them free of charge.[160]

Free offers

[9–65] An offer need not quite be free before it can be described as a free offer in accordance with the Code of Standards. For the purposes of the Code, an offer may be described as free if consumers do not pay anything more than: (i) the minimum unavoidable cost of responding to the promotion[161]; (ii) the actual cost of delivery/ freight; (iii) the cost (including incidental expenses) of any travel involved if consumers "collect the offer".[162] It is not clear from the text of the Code whether only one of the costs referred to may be met before an offer may be described as free or whether all of the costs may be met and the offer may still be described as free. It appears that the quoted reference to "the offer" is a typographical error as it is not possible to "collect" an offer. It seems more likely that the Code intends to refer at this point to collecting a product that is offered as part of the relevant promotional marketing practice. The Code further requires that in all cases consumer liability for costs should be made clear and there should be no additional charges for packaging or handling.[163]

---

[155] The Code does not define the term "goods" but refers instead to them as one class of "product". The term "product" is defined as encompassing "goods, services, facilities, opportunities, fundraising, prizes and gifts". (Code of Standards, 9, para 1.3(e)).

[156] Code of Standards, 29, para 3.18.

[157] Code of Standards, 29, para 3.19.

[158] Code of Standards, 29, para 3.20.

[159] *ibid.*

[160] *ibid.*

[161] E.g. the current public postage rate, the cost of telephoning (up to and including the national rate) or the minimum unavoidable cost of sending an e-mail or SMS text. (Code of Standards, 29, para 3.21(a)).

[162] Code of Standards, 29 *et seq*, para 3.21.

[163] *ibid.*

"Marketers" (it is not clear whether the term embraces advertisers or producers) are **[9–66]** required not to seek to recover costs (presumably the costs incurred as a result of providing a product consequent upon a free offer) "by reducing the quality or composition of a product by imposing additional charges or inflating incidental expenses or by increasing the price of any other product that must be purchased as a pre-condition of obtaining a free item".[164]

Various further provision is made as regards 'free offers'. Thus the Code of Standards **[9–67]** requires that: (i) a trial must not be described as free if the consumer is expected to pay the cost of returning any goods (save where this is made clear to the consumer when the offer is made)[165]; (ii) where a product features an offer and, to avail of that offer, further purchases of the product need to be made, the need to make such further purchases must be clearly indicated[166]; (iii) where an offer covers two or more items, one free and the other(s) not, it must be made clear to a consumer what is free and what is not[167]; where unsolicited samples/gifts are distributed by way of promotion it must be made clear to the consumer (presumably the recipient consumer) that there is no obligation to pay or return the said samples/gifts.[168]

Promotions with prizes

The Code of Standards notes by way of general comment that promotions with prizes **[9–68]** are subject to legal requirements and exhorts promoters to seek legal advice when effecting such promotions.[169] Notwithstanding the foregoing, the Code makes certain supplementary provision as regards such promotions. Thus paragraph 3.28 of the Code requires that entry conditions should be clearly worded and recite the following details: the closing date[170]; any age, eligibility or geographical restrictions; any

---

[164] Code of Standards, 30, para 3.22.

[165] Code of Standards, 30, para 3.23.

[166] Code of Standards, 30, para 3.24.

[167] Code of Standards, 30, para 3.25.

[168] Code of Standards, 30, para 3.26.

[169] Code of Standards, 30, para 3.27. The Gaming and Lotteries Acts are clearly of relevance as regards the operation of such promotions. A consideration of Ireland's gaming and lotteries legislation is outside the scope of this book. For a brief summary of the law generally applicable, and the self-regulation potentially applicable, to the operation of lotteries, see the chapter on Ireland by Barrett, G and D Voigt in Micklitz. HW and J. Kessler, eds., *Marketing Practices Regulation and Consumer Protection in the EC Member States and the US* (Baden-Baden: 2002) at 186ff.

[170] Para 3.30 of the Code of Standards (at 32) provides further that: "The closing date should be clearly stated in each advertisement, on each entry form and on the outer surface of any relevant pack, wrapper or label. This date should not be changed unless circumstances outside the reasonable control of the promoters make it unavoidable." On a related note, para 3.32 of the Code (at 32) states that "A poor response or a low level of entries is not an acceptable basis for extending the duration of a promotion or withholding prizes unless the promoters have explicitly reserved their right to do so at the outset." The Code of Standards mentions one exception to this but the precise ambit of this exception is not clear from the wording of the Code itself. Thus, per the Code of Standards "[W]here, in a promotion involving a collection or redemption mechanic, a poor response may be an acceptable basis for extending the promotion for a reasonable duration." (Code of Standards, 32, para 3.31).

restrictions on entry or prize numbers; any proof of purchase requirements; any permissions (for example, parental or guardian permissions) required; the judging criteria[171]; a full, accurate description of any prizes; any limitations pertaining to acceptance of the prizes[172]; any duties/obligations arising for winners (for example, as regards post-promotion publicity); whether a cash alternative may be taken in lieu of a prize; how and when winners will be notified and results will be published[173]; who owns the copyright of entries (where appropriate); and if and how entries will be returned. The Code further requires that complex rules should be avoided and that promoters "should not need to" supplement entry conditions with additional rules.[174] Where additional rules cannot be avoided, the Code of Standards requires that: participants must be advised how to obtain them; and they should contain nothing that would have influenced a consumer against making a purchase or participating.[175] In all instances, the Code of Standards requires that participants should be able to retain any entry instructions/rules.[176] The Code of Standards further provides that: (i) where a prize promotion involves a draw, the promoters must ensure that any numbers/tickets/tokens are distributed fairly and randomly (with an independent observer supervising the prize draw to ensure an equal chance of success for individual entries)[177]; (ii) when prize promotions are widely advertised, promoters should ensure that entry forms (and any goods required as proof of purchase) are widely available[178]; (iii) the distinction between a prize and a gift should always be clear to consumers[179]; and (iv) the likelihood of a consumer winning a prize in a particular promotion should not be exaggerated by promoters (presumably, though the Code does not state this, the promoters of the relevant promotion).[180]

---

[171] On a related note, when it comes to judging entries, para 3.34 (at 32) of the Code of Standards provides that "If the selection of winning entries is open to subjective interpretation, an independent judge, or a panel including one member who is independent of the competition's promoters and intermediaries, should be appointed. Those appointed to act as judges should be competent to judge the subject matter of the competition. The identity of the judges should be made available to the Authority on request."

[172] On a related note, the Code of Standards later requires in para 3.33 (at 32) that "[u]nless otherwise stated in advance, prizewinners should receive their prizes no more than six weeks after the promotion has ended."

[173] On a related note, para 3.32 of the Code of Standards (at 32) provides, as regards the publication of results, that "Promoters should either publish or make available on request details of the name and country of residence of major prizewinners. Promoters should bear in mind the risk of theft or harassment that may arise if the details given are sufficient to allow the address of a winner of a prize of substantial value to be pinpointed."

[174] Code of Standards, 31, para 3.29.

[175] *ibid.*

[176] *ibid.*

[177] Code of Standards, 33, para 3.35.

[178] Code of Standards, 33, para 3.36.

[179] Code of Standards, 33, para 3.37. Para 3.37 further provides that "Gifts offered to all or most participants in a promotion should not be described as prizes. If promoters offer a gift to all entrants in addition to giving a prize to those who win, particular care is needed to avoid confusing the two."

[180] Code of Standards, 33, para 3.38.

Advertisement promotions

The Code of Standards requires that: (i) advertisement promotions should be designed and presented so that they can be distinguished easily from editorial material[181]; (ii) announcements/features/promotions published for payment (or other reciprocal arrangements in which content is controlled by a promoter) should comply with the Code of Standards[182]; (iii) publishers announcing reader promotions on the front cover/page of a publication must ensure that consumers know (a) whether they are expected to buy later issues of that publication and (b) whether any financial contribution is required. In addition the front page/cover must mention any major qualifications that may significantly influence customers in any decision as to whether or not to buy the publication.[183]   [9–69]

Charity-linked promotions

It is not uncommon for financial product or service providers to operate charity-linked promotions. Under paragraph 3.42 of the Code of Standards, a promotion which claims that participation in it will benefit a charity or good cause must: (i) name the charity or good cause that will benefit; (ii) be able to demonstrate that the charity/good cause that so benefits agrees to the advertising or promotion; (iii) define the nature and objectives of the charity/good cause (unless such information is already widely available); (iv) specify the extent and nature of the advantage that will accrue to the charity/good cause; (v) identify any self-imposed limitation on the contributions that the promoter will make; (vi) not limit consumer contributions[184]; (vii) not exaggerate any benefit to a charity/good cause that is to be derived from individual purchases of a promoted product; and (viii) make available (on request) a current/final total of contributions made.[185]   [9–70]

Promotions and the trade

As mentioned previously above, it is not clear from the text of the Code of Standards whether references to 'the trade' within the Code are intended to be construed as references to the advertising trade to the exclusion of any other business or profession. Fortunately this absence of clarity does not entirely obfuscate the requirements made under the heading 'Promotions and the Trade'. Thus paragraph 3.43 of the Code of Standards provides that promotion and incentive schemes should be designed and implemented in such manner as to take account of the interests of everyone involved and must not conflict with the duty of employees to their employer or their obligation to give honest advice to consumers. Paragraph 3.44 states that promoters should secure the prior agreement of employers (or the manager responsible) if they offer incentives to, or if they intend to request assistance from, the employees of any other company. In such instances promoters must observe any procedures established by   [9–71]

---

[181] Code of Standards, 33, para 3.39.

[182] Code of Standards, 33, para 3.40.

[183] Code of Standards, 34, para 3.41.

[184] Para 3.42(e) of the Code of Standards requires that any extra money collected (presumably from consumers) must be given to the named charity/good cause on the same basis as contributions below "that level". It is not clear from the text of the Code of Standards to which level the quoted text means to refer.

[185] Code of Standards, 34, para 3.42.

companies for their employees (including rules for participating in promotions).[186] Where a trade incentive scheme has been advertised (as opposed to individually targeted), employees must be advised to obtain employer permission before participating.[187] Paragraph 3.45 of the Code requires that it be made clear to persons benefiting from an incentive scheme that they may be liable to taxation.

Data protection and other legal requirements

[9–72]   In the context of promotional marketing practices, the Code of Standards notes the particular relevance of the Data Protection Acts 1988 and 2003[188] (and their requirements as regards the processing, retention, use and disclosure of personal data) and the gaming and lotteries legislation (and the specific need for a prize promotion to include a game of skill).[189]

Chapter 1, Section 4 - Distance Selling (Mail Order and Direct Response)

[9–73]   The Code of Standards prescribes various rules for transactions for goods or services in which the buyer and seller, after being brought into communication through a marketing communication, conduct their business with each other without a face-to-face meeting. Thus if there is, at any stage, a face-to-face meeting between buyer and seller, these requirements do not apply. Although many of these standards established in the distance-selling context are focused on marketing and not on advertising per se, they are considered in their entirety here for the sake of completeness. Thus the Code of Standards requires: (i) that mail order and direct response marketing communications state the name and full address of the advertiser in the marketing communication (in a print marketing communication, this must be stated separate from any response coupon); or (ii) that alternative arrangements be made for enquirers to be informed by the media of the name and full address of the advertiser.[190] Non-compliance with the foregoing renders the relevant mail order or direct response marketing communication "not acceptable".[191] It is permissible for a separate address for orders to be given in a mail order or direct response marketing communications, which address need not be full and may be a Freepost or box number.[192] Paragraph 4.2 of the Code of Standards further requires that distance selling marketing communications: (i) include the main characteristics of the products; (ii) include the price (including any VAT, taxes, other inescapable costs for the consumer and the applicable payment arrangements); (iii) identify how the advertiser's details may be accessed if the offer is sent by Short Message Service (SMS) or Wireless Application Protocol (WAP) and all the advertiser's details cannot be included in the relevant distance selling marketing communication. The Code of Standards requires that orders placed should generally be fulfilled within 30 days

---

[186] Code of Standards, 35, para 3.44.

[187] *ibid.*

[188] i.e. the Data Protection Act, 1988 (No 25 of 1988) and the Data Protection (Amendment) Act 2003 (No 6 of 2003).

[189] Code of Standards, 35, paras. 3.46 and 3.47.

[190] Code of Standards, 36, para 4.1.

[191] *ibid.*

[192] *ibid.*

(presumably from the date of placement of the order).[193] However, this general time limit does not apply in three instances. First, where security is provided for the purchaser's money through an independent scheme.[194] Second, in respect of goods such as plants and made-to-measure products (in respect of which the estimated time of delivery must, per the Code of Standards, be made clear).[195] Third, where a series of goods is to be despatched in sequence.[196] (In such instances only the first delivery need be made within 30 days. However, the period within which deliveries will be made must be stated). Any goods supplied in the distance selling context are required to conform to any relevant and accepted standard and also to the description given in the relevant marketing communication.[197] Under paragraph 4.5 of the Code, advertisers are required to refund all money promptly (and not later than 30 days after notice of cancellation of an agreement being given) where: (i) consumers have not received their goods/services[198]; (ii) goods are returned because they are damaged or faulty or not as described[199]; (iii) consumers cancel the contract of sale within seven clear working days after delivery[200]; (iv) an unconditional money-back guarantee is given and the goods are returned within a reasonable period; (v) returned goods have not been received but the relevant consumer can produce proof of posting.[201]

The full refund obligation does not arise in respect of "(a) perishable, personalised or **[9–74]** made-to-measure goods provided all contractual and statutory obligations to the consumer are met; [or] (b) goods that can be copied unless they fall under [category (i), (ii) or (iii) above]...with the exception of audio or video recordings or computer software if unsealed by the consumer."[202] When, in the distance selling context, an advertiser offers to supply goods on approval, the consumer will, per the Code of Standards and subject to (b) above, suffer the cost of returning any unwanted goods (unless the advertiser has undertaken to refund such costs).[203] Continuing with its provision in respect of distance selling, the Code of Standards requires that: (i) advertisers should be in a position to meet any reasonable demand created by their advertising[204];

---

[193] Code of Standards, 37, para 4.3.

[194] Code of Standards, 37, para 4.3(a).

[195] Code of Standards, 37, para 4.3(b).

[196] Code of Standards, 37, para 4.3(c).

[197] Code of Standards, 37, para 4.4.

[198] In such instances, advertisers may, if requested, provide a replacement. (Code of Standards, 37, para 4.5(a)).

[199] In such instances, advertisers must suffer the cost of their return provided notice of cancellation has been given by the relevant consumer within a reasonable period of time. (Code of Standards, 37, para 4.5(b)).

[200] The Code of Standards further states in this regard (albeit that this is not, in truth, an advertising standard) that "consumers should assume that they can try out goods unless the marketing communication says otherwise; such goods nevertheless should be returned undamaged." (Code of Standards, 37, para 4.5(c)).

[201] Code of Standards, 37 *et seq.*

[202] Code of Standards, 38, para 4.6.

[203] Code of Standards, 38, para 4.7.

[204] Code of Standards, 48, para 4.8. The Code goes on to provide that "If a product proves to be available in insufficient quantity, advertisers should take immediate action to ensure that any further marketing communications are amended or withdrawn". (*Infra.*).

(ii) if advertisers intend to call on respondents personally this must be made clear in either the marketing communication or a follow-up letter (and advertisers must provide a reply-paid postcard or telephone contact to allow a consumer an adequate opportunity to refuse such home visit)[205]; (iii) advertisers, when using media primarily targeted at children should not promote products unsuitable for children;[206] and (iv) goods and (where applicable) samples must be packaged in such a way as to be suitable for delivery to the customer, particular care being required where packaging products may fall into the hands of children (a possibility that perhaps invariably prevails).[207]

---

[205] Code of Standards, 38, para 4.9. Obviously the 'cold-calling' requirements of the Consumer Protection Code are of relevance in this context. The Consumer Protection Code states in this regard (at 15, Chapter 2, paras, 32-38 (inclusive)) that:

"32 When contacting a consumer who is an existing customer: A regulated entity may make an unsolicited contact to a consumer, who is an individual, by way of a personal visit or telephone call, only if: a) the regulated entity has, within the previous twelve months, provided that consumer with a product or service similar to the purpose of the unsolicited contact; b) the consumer holds a product, which requires the regulated entity to maintain contact with the consumer in relation to that product; c) the purpose of the contact is limited to offering protection policies only; or d) the consumer has given his/her consent in writing to being contacted in this way by the regulated entity.

33 When contacting a consumer other than an existing customer: A regulated entity may make an unsolicited contact to a consumer, who is an individual, by way of a personal visit or telephone call, only if: a) the consumer has signed a statement, within the previous 6 months, giving the regulated entity permission to make personal visits or telephone calls to him/her; b) the consumer has a listing in the business listing section of the current telephone directory, classified telephone directory or in trade/ professional directories circulating in the State; c)the consumer is a director of a company, or a partner of a firm with an entry in one of the directories listed in b) above; d) the consumer is the subject of a referral, received from an entity authorised to provide financial services in Ireland, another entity within the same group, a solicitor, a certified person or an existing customer; e) the purpose of the contact is limited to offering protection policies. In relation to d) above, such a referral must be followed up by an indication to the consumer by the regulated entity that the referral has been made and asking for consent to proceed.

34 A regulated entity must ensure that, where it makes an unsolicited contact on foot of a referral, it retains a record of the referral.

35 Unsolicited contact, made in accordance with this Code, may only be made between 9.00 a.m. and 9.00 p.m. Monday to Saturday (excluding bank holidays and public holidays), unless otherwise requested by the consumer.

36 When making an unsolicited contact in accordance with this Code, the representative of a regulated entity must immediately and in the following order: a) identify himself by name, the name of the regulated entity on whose behalf he/she is calling and the commercial purpose of the contact; b) inform the consumer that the call is being recorded, if this is the case; c) disclose to the consumer, the source of the business lead or referral supporting the contact; and d) establish if the consumer wishes the call to proceed; if not, the caller must end the contact immediately.

37 A regulated entity must abide by a request from a consumer not to make an unsolicited contact to him/her again.

38 A regulated entity must not reach a binding agreement with a consumer on the basis of an unsolicited contact alone, except in the circumstances permitted under the European Communities (Distance Marketing of Consumer Financial Services) Regulations 2004."

[206] Code of Standards, 38, para 4.10.
[207] Code of Standards, 39, para 4.11.

Chapter 1, Section 5 - Children

Financial product and service providers generally offer a limited array of products (such as savings accounts) to children. Section 5 of Chapter 1 of the Code of Standards makes provision in respect of advertising to children.[208] Section 5 commences by 'acknowledging' (it is perhaps more a case of 'highlighting') that parents and guardians, i.e. not advertisers and not the Advertising Standards Authority, have primary responsibility for children.[209] Even so, the Code of Standards accepts that children lack the experience, knowledge and maturity of judgment that adults enjoy.[210] The Code therefore concludes that "Marketing communications addressed directly or indirectly to children or marketing communications likely to be seen or heard by a significant proportion of them should have regard to the special characteristics of children and the ways in which they perceive and react to marketing communications."[211] The Code of Standards recognises that the way in which children perceive and react to marketing communications is in part conditioned by age, experience and the context in which the message is delivered.[212] Thus it recognises that marketing communications for young teenagers may not be suitable for younger children.[213] According to the Code of Standards, "The Authority will take these factors into account when assessing marketing communications."[214] These general provisions aside, the Code proceeds to prescribe a variety of detailed requirements that seek to protect children in the advertising context. Curiously, although Section 5 of the Code of Standards mentions at the outset "[m]arketing communications addressed directly or indirectly to children or marketing communications likely to be seen or heard by a significant proportion of them", the first seven of the detailed requirements prescribed by the Code under the heading 'Children' appear to pertain to all advertisements (a conclusion buttressed by the fact that subsequent requirements are expressly stated to apply to marketing communications "addressed to children"). It is notable that an advertisement not targeted at children and not intended to be seen by children may nonetheless be subject to requirements that are aimed at the protection of children. Thus the Code provides by way of general requirement that marketing communications "contain nothing that is likely to result in physical, mental or moral harm to children or that is likely to frighten or disturb them, except to promote safety or in the public interest."[215] One would not generally expect advertisements for financial services to contain material that might frighten children. Yet in 2007, Bank of Ireland was the subject of complaints from a number of parents who maintained that a particular character in a Bank of Ireland advertisement had been frightening to

---

[208] It will be recalled that for the purposes of the Code of Standards, a child is a person aged less than 18 years. (Code of Standards, 41, para 5.1).

[209] Code of Standards, 41, para 5.2.

[210] Code of Standards, 41, para 5.3.

[211] *ibid.*

[212] Code of Standards, 41, para 5.4.

[213] *ibid.*

[214] *ibid.*

[215] Code of Standards, 41, para 5.5. It is perhaps open to question whether any safety promotion exercise or public interest ever justifies exposing children to marketing communications likely to frighten or disturb them.

children and ought to have been shown after the 9pm. 'watershed'.[216] The advertisement complained of contained a number of fictional monsters, including 'Dave Bogeyman' who lived under a child's bed and was hoping to find a new place to live. Several parents complained to the Advertising Standards Authority for Ireland that their children had been afraid to go to bed after seeing the advertisement and a number queried why the advertisement had not been shown after the 9pm 'watershed'. By way of response, the advertisers indicated, amongst other matters, that: they always sought to avoid contravening the advertising codes applicable to them; they had exercised care during the production process of the relevant advertising campaign; the 'bogeyman' was part of children's folklore; they had presented the 'bogeyman' as having the typical concerns of ordinary consumers, e.g. money and mortgage concerns; and 'Dave Bogeyman' had been modelled on the tarsier monkey, "a very cute, tiny, wide-eyed furry creature" and was innocuous and charming by comparison to what children regularly encountered on television, computer games and in the cinema. The Complaints Committee did not uphold the complaints made. It accepted that the advertisement had upset a small number of children but noted that the advertisers had deliberately avoided programming exclusively aimed at children. The Committee did not consider that the advertisement had breached the Code of Standards but suggested that it should also be excluded from programmes which, though not aimed directly at young children, were known to attract reasonable numbers of them.

[9–76]   Paragraph 5.5 of the Code requires that "[i]n principle" (a phrase which seems almost to caveat the binding nature of what follows) and subject to the qualifications previously expressed in Section 5 (such as, for example, the fact that parents and guardians have primary responsibility for their children), the following rules apply (again, it appears, to all advertisements), namely: (i) children must not be portrayed in a manner that offends against accepted standards of taste and decency[217]; (ii) children must not be encouraged to enter into unsafe situations or strange places to talk to strangers[218]; (iii) children must not be shown in morally or physically dangerous situations or behaving dangerously in the home or outside[219]; (iv) children must not be encouraged to engage in (or be portrayed engaging in) anti-social behaviour[220]; (v) younger children "in particular" (the quoted text suggests that there is perhaps a concern about all children in this regard, though especial concern for younger children) must not be shown either using or in close proximity to dangerous

---

[216] Advertising Standards Authority for Ireland, Case No AC0708/1003.

[217] Determining what are "accepted standards" is, of course, a subjective and difficult exercise.

[218] E.g. for the purpose of making collections or accumulating coupons, labels or wrappers (Code of Standards, 42, para 5.5(b)).

[219] In particular, the Code provides, "Children should not be shown unattended in street scenes unless they are old enough to take responsibility for their own safety." (Code of Standards, 42, para 5.5(c)).

[220] Moreover, per the Code, "where they appear as pedestrians or cyclists they should be seen to observe the Rules of the Road. Special attention should be paid, where relevant, to the use of child car seats and the wearing of car seat-belts and safety helmets." (Code of Standards, 42, para 5.5(d)).

equipment or substances absent adult supervision[221]; (vi) on a related note, when portraying a domestic scene an open fire is required always to be shown with a clearly visible fireguard in circumstances where a young child is included in the scene[222]; (vii) for fear that they may imitate what they see, children must not, in marketing communications, be encouraged to copy any potentially unsafe practice.[223] Further to these requirements which appear to be applicable to all marketing communications, including advertisements, the Code provides that marketing communications specifically addressed to children must not: (i) exploit the credulity, loyalty, vulnerability or lack of experience of children[224]; (ii) exaggerate what is attainable by an ordinary child using the product[225]; (iii) make it difficult to judge the actual size, characteristics and performance of any product advertised[226]; (iv) ask a child to disclose personal information about themselves or their families without first obtaining permission from their parents or guardians[227]; or (v) minimise the price of products through the use of such words as 'only' or 'just'.[228] The Code further provides that when packaging products that may fall into the hands of younger children "[a]dvertisers should take particular care".[229] It is not clear from the text of the Code in this regard whether this particular injunction extends to taking care from a safety perspective or a content perspective or both. The Code then makes certain provision in respect of marketing communications for food and beverages to children, which provision falls outside the ambit of this text.[230] In addition to the extensive provision made by the Code in respect of promotional marketing practices (as considered elsewhere in the above text), paragraph 5.11 of the Code of Standards establishes the following requirements in respect of promotions addressed to or likely to attract children, namely that such promotions "(a) should not offer promotional products that are unsuitable for distribution to children; (b) should be carried out responsibly, taking into account the location in which the promotion is conducted; (c) should make it clear that parental permission is required if prizes and incentives might cause conflict between children and their parents; examples include animals, bicycles, outings, concerts and holidays; (d) should allow a sufficient timeframe for participation in a

---

[221] Code of Standards, 42, para 5.5(e).

[222] Code of Standards, 42, para 5.5(f).

[223] Code of Standards, 42, para 5.5(g).

[224] Code of Standards, 43, para 5.6. The Code gives examples of what it means in this regard: "For example: (a) They should not be made to feel inferior or unpopular for not buying an advertised product. (b) They should not be made to feel that they are lacking in courage, duty or loyalty if they do not buy or do not encourage others to buy a particular product. (c) Marketing communications should not undermine the authority, responsibility or judgment of parents, guardians or other appropriate authority figures. Marketing communications should not include any appeal to children to persuade their parents or other adults to buy advertised products for them. (d) A product that is part of a series should be clearly indicated as such and marketing communications should include the method of acquiring the series." (Code of Standards, 43, para 5.6).

[225] Code of Standards, 43, para 5.7(b).

[226] *ibid*.

[227] Code of Standards, 43, para 5.7(c).

[228] Code of Standards, 43, para 5.7(d).

[229] Code of Standards, 44, para 5.8.

[230] The relevant provisions are at Code of Standards, 44, paras. 5.9 and 5.10.

manner that will reflect moderate consumption of a product; (e) should clearly explain the number and type of any additional proofs of purchase needed to participate; (f) should contain a prominent closing date; (g) should not exaggerate the value of the prizes or the chances of winning them; (h) should not exploit children's susceptibility to charitable appeals."[231]

Chapter 1, Section 10 - Financial Services and Products

[9–77] Section 10 of Chapter 1 of the Code of Standards is expressly concerned with financial products and is the last section of Chapter 1 of the Code of Standards considered in this book. The other sections which have not been considered address a variety of areas that fall outside the ambit of this book.[232] Given that financial services and products are now so comprehensively addressed in the Consumer Protection Code it is perhaps open to question whether the Code of Standards would not be improved in this regard by the deletion from the Code of Standards of the requirements particular to the Code of Standards and the wholesale incorporation into the Code of Standards (whether by reference or otherwise) of the relevant provisions of the Consumer Protection Code. This would not result in any lessening of protection to consumers. However, it would result in there being one less set of requirements to which financial service providers who are also members of the Advertising Standards Authority for Ireland would need to have regard in the advertising context.

[9–78] Paragraph 10.1 of the Code of Standards requires that marketing communications for financial services and products be carefully prepared "with the conscious aim of ensuring that members of the public fully grasp the nature of any commitment into which they may enter as a result of responding to a marketing communication".[233] In particular advertisers are required in this regard not to take advantage of "people's" (presumably 'consumer') gullibility or inexperience.[234]

[9–79] Marketing communications which invite a response by mail are required to contain the advertiser's full address separate from any response coupon.[235] The Code also requires that marketing communications "indicate the nature of the contract being offered and provide information on any limitations on eligibility, any charges, expenses or penalties attached and the terms on which withdrawal may be arranged."[236] Recognising that this requirement involves the provision of a lot of detail in a marketing communication, the Code of Standards provides that "where a marketing communication is short or is general in its content, free explanatory

---

[231] Code of Standards, 33 *et seq.*

[232] Thus Section 6 is concerned with 'Food and Non-Alcoholic Beverages', Section 7 with 'Alcoholic Drinks', Section 8 with 'Health and Beauty', Section 9 with 'Slimming', Section 11 with 'Employment and Business Opportunities', Section 12 with environmental matters, and Section 13 with 'Occasional Trading'.

[233] Code of Standards, 62, para 10.1.

[234] *ibid.*

[235] Code of Standards, 62, para 10.2.

[236] Code of Standards, 62, para 10.3.

material giving full details of the offer should be made available before a binding contract is entered into".[237]

Consistent with the requirement in the Consumer Protection Code that "Any forecast contained in an advertisement must not be misleading at the time it is made and any assumptions on which it is based must be reasonable and stated clearly"[238], the Code of Standards requires that when a marketing communication contains a forecast or projection it must make clear the basis on which such forecast or projection is made.[239] Thus it should explain, for example, "whether reinvestment of income is assumed...whether account has been taken of any applicable taxes...[and] whether any penalties or deductions will arise on premature realisation or otherwise".[240]

[9–80]

As in the Consumer Protection Code, the Code of Standards requires that marketing communications make clear "that the value of investments is variable and, unless guaranteed, can go down as well as up".[241] The Code of Standards also provides that where the value of an investment is guaranteed, details should be included in the relevant marketing communication.[242] It will be recalled that the Consumer Protection Code[243] makes quite comprehensive provision as to when an advertisement may describe a product or an investment as guaranteed or partially guaranteed.

[9–81]

Like the Consumer Protection Code, the Code of Standards requires that marketing communications specify that "past performance or experience" does not necessarily give a guide for the future.[244] Unlike the Consumer Protection Code, the Code of Standards does not expressly limit this requirement to marketing communications which contain information on past performance. Presumably the "experience" referred to is past investment/market experience. If so, the word "experience" seems to add little or nothing to the word "performance". The Code of Standards further requires that any examples of past performance or experience should not be unrepresentative.[245]

[9–82]

Finally, the Code of Standards refers, in the context of financial products and services, to the fact that there are statutory requirements which may impact on advertisements for such products and services. There are also, of course, other non-statutory legal and regulatory requirements, such as the requirements imposed on regulated entities by the Consumer Protection Code. To the extent that the Code of Standards partially duplicates such requirements it is of course open to question whether it ought not to be amended so as to avoid such partial duplication. Such an amendment should not

[9–83]

---

[237] *ibid.*

[238] Consumer Protection Code, 35, Chapter 7, para 10.

[239] Code of Standards, 62, para 10.4.

[240] *ibid.*

[241] Code of Standards, 63, para 10.5. Cf. in this regard the Consumer Protection Code, 39, Chapter 7, para 34.

[242] Code of Standards, 63, para 10.5.

[243] At 38, Chapter 7, para 32.

[244] Code of Standards, 63, para 10.6. The Consumer Protection Code makes similar provision in Chapter 7, para 11(g) (at 36) and this and more general provision in the 'Savings & Investments' section of Chapter 7 (at 37 *et seq*, though see, in particular para 28, at 38).

[245] Code of Standards, 63, para 10.6.

adversely impinge on consumers but would benefit advertisers in removing some unnecessary duplication in the law, regulation and codes now applicable to the advertisement of financial services.

Chapter 2

[9–84] Chapter 2 of the Code of Standards is largely concerned with explaining the work and workings (in particular the complaints process operated by) the Advertising Standards Authority for Ireland. From a legal perspective, Chapter 2 is perhaps of most interest in its description of the complaints process (and the related appeals process) operated by the Advertising Standards Authority for Ireland.

Complaints procedure

[9–85] Any person or body who considers that a marketing communication has breached the Code of Standards may institute a complaint before the Advertising Standards Authority for Ireland.[246] Alternatively, the Authority may itself investigate matters that it identifies as part of its own compliance monitoring programme.[247]

[9–86] To facilitate the making and resolution of complaints the Authority states it to be "essential" that a complainant: (i) write to the Authority (or use its on-line complaints form) with full name and postal address; (ii) briefly outline the grounds of complaint; (iii) include either (a) a copy of the offending marketing communication, if possible, or (b) particulars of the marketing communication, including dates and media involved; (iii) identify the product, the promoter and copies of any labels, leaflets or entry forms involved (in a sales promotion or direct mail activity).[248] It will be recalled that the term "promoter" is a defined term (both as regards the Code and "the procedures for its implementation"[249]. (This latter phrase presumably embraces the rules of operation of the complaints process operated in tandem with the Code). It could be contended that the Advertising Standards Authority for Ireland might usefully have restated the meanings of any defined terms employed in the rules concerning its application as it is possible that an ordinary consumer reading these rules (which sit to the rear of a lengthy document) might not immediately recognise a term as being a defined term.

[9–87] Complaints are investigated free of charge.[250] This is a considerable incentive to ensuring that the complaints process can be (and it is) used by ordinary members of the public who consider an advertisement to be somehow offensive. To the extent permissible by law, the identity of a consumer complainant is kept confidential by the Authority.[251] No such assurance of confidentiality extends to commercial or other interests seeking to make a complaint (and complainants may be asked to indicate that they have no such interest).[252]

---

[246] Code of Standards, 76, para 1.

[247] *ibid.*

[248] *ibid.*

[249] Code of Standards, 8, para 1.3. The term "promoter" is defined as "any person or body by whom a sales promotion is initiated or commissioned". (Code of Standards, 9, para 1.3(j)).

[250] Code of Standards, 76, para 2.

[251] *ibid.*

[252] *ibid.*

Complaints by competitors

The Advertising Standards Authority does not purport to be an arbitration service for commercially interested parties.[253] It considers that such disputes are best resolved by direct discussions between the relevant parties or through their trade associations.[254] However, an intra-industry dispute may be investigated by the Advertising Standards Authority where consumer interests are involved, In these cases: (i) complainants may be asked to substantiate their complaints (perhaps to ensure that the Authority and its complaints process are not used as a weapon to enmesh a competitor in time-consuming but ultimately groundless proceedings); (ii) the identity of the complainants is invariably revealed to the advertiser or promoter and both parties are thereafter named in the concluding report of the Advertising Standards Authority; (iii) the Authority may elect to issue a statement and not a formal decision, where appropriate.[255] There may be instances in which the Advertising Standards Authority is not able to reach a conclusion because, for example, its conclusion would involve it making adverse comment about a third party who/which is not the subject of complaint (though in such instances it would be possible for a complainant to institute separate court proceedings, if so minded).[256]

[9–88]

Resolution process

Once a complaint is made it is evaluated by the Secretariat of the Advertising Standards Authority to determine whether: (i) it comes within the remit of the Advertising Standards Authority; and (ii) there is a prima facie case for investigation.[257] Where a complaint fails on either ground, it is not pursued and the reason for not proceeding further is explained to the relevant complainant.[258] Even if a complaint satisfies both grounds, it will not generally be pursued further if: (i) it is already the subject of legal action (whether by way of litigation or with a view to litigation) or alternative dispute resolution process; (ii) the complaint would more properly be the subject of investigation by another body (in which case the Advertising Standards Authority for Ireland will seek either to provide relevant information, or direct the complainant to such other body).[259]

[9–89]

Where the Secretariat of the Advertising Standards Authority finds that there is a prima facie case for investigation, such investigation is started. The investigation can be accelerated or varied where circumstances merit it.[260] Typically, however, it will proceed as follows. The relevant advertiser/promoter (or advertising/promotional

[9–90]

---

[253] Code of Standards, 76, para 3.

[254] *ibid.*

[255] Code of Standards, 77, para 4.

[256] Code of Standards, 76 *et seq.*, para 3.

[257] Code of Standards, 77, para 5.

[258] Code of Standards, 77, para 6.

[259] Code of Standards, 77, para 7.

[260] Code of Standards, 78, para 15. In addition, "[i]f a case is considered by the Secretariat, in its absolute discretion, to be particularly grave, the Secretariat may request interim action by the advertiser/promoter or agency, including the immediate amendment or withdrawal of a marketing communication or promotion pending completion of the investigation and adjudication by the Complaints Committee." (Code of Standards, 79 *et seq.*, para 15).

marketing agency) is contacted by the Advertising Standards Authority, advised of the complaint and invited to comment (in the context of the Code), such response (and substantiation where necessary), normally being required within a strictly enforced 10-day turnaround period (or such other period as the Secretariat may decide upon).[261] Once the response is received, the Secretariat may prepare a summary of the case (which report, if made, will also include: any facts that the Secretariat has garnered; a recommendation to the Complaints Committee as to (a) what that Committee's decision might be and (b) whether the complaint should be upheld; and (possibly) a recommendation to the Committee as to other courses of action that may be adopted).[262] A significant incentive to promoters/advertisers to be responsive to any investigation commenced by the Secretariat is the fact that a marketing communication and/or advertiser or promoter may be found to be in breach of the Code simply by virtue of a failure to respond (or an unreasonable delay in responding to) the Authority.[263] The next step in the process is that the complainant and the relevant advertiser/agency/promoter (as appropriate) are provided with a copy of the Secretariat's recommendation and invited to comment, before referral to the Complaints Committee, within a period specified by the Secretariat.[264] Thereafter, the case, the recommendation and any further comments are placed before the Complaints Committee.[265] It is the Complaints Committee which decides whether or not the Code has been contravened.[266] Once the Complaints Committee reaches a conclusion, the case details, including the name of the relevant advertiser/agency/ promoter but not the name of the complainant (if a consumer complainant) are set out in a case report which, subject always to the discretion of the Complaints Committee, is generally posted on the website of the Advertising Standards Authority and also released to the media for publication.[267] Where a marketing communication is deemed by the Complaints Committee to have contravened the rules of the Code, such marketing communication "is required to be amended or withdrawn. In the case of a sales promotion, the promoter may be requested to make the necessary changes to the way the promotion is communicated or conducted and, where appropriate, may also be asked to recompense any consumers who have been adversely affected".[268]

The Complaints Committee[269]

[9–91]   The Complaints Committee is a committee appointed by the Board of the Advertising Standards Authority for Ireland. At the time of writing, the Committee is comprised of 13 members under the chairmanship of an independent Chairman. Some of the Committee members have an advertising and/or regulatory background and bring that

---

[261] Code of Standards, 78, para 8.

[262] Code of Standards, 78, para 9.

[263] Code of Standards, 78, para 10.

[264] Code of Standards, 79, para 11.

[265] Code of Standards, 79, para 12.

[266] *ibid.*

[267] Code of Standards, 79, para 13.

[268] Code of Standards, 79, para 14.

[269] See generally the Code of Standards, 82 *et seq*,, paras. 4 and 5.

expertise to the Committee. However, the majority of members are not employed in the advertising industry. Instead they have an interest and expertise in such matters as consumer protection, child and adolescent welfare and community issues, thus ensuring that the Complaints Committee brings a more rounded and objective approach to resolving complaints than if it was, for example, simply a committee of advertising executives adjudicating on the content of advertisements. The Chief Executive of the Advertising Standards Authority acts as secretary to the Complaints Committee and administers the complaints investigation service and the 'copy advice' service. Following the making of a report by the Complaints Committee (or on receipt of notification of an allegation made against or "circumstance involving" a member of the Authority), a specially convened disciplinary meeting of the Board is convened. This meeting hears the relevant parties and then makes a ruling (which ruling can involve the imposition of a fine or the suspension or expulsion of a member from any or all of the privileges that membership of the Authority confers, or, ultimately, expulsion from membership).

Review process[270]

Exceptionally the Complaints Committee can be asked to review its own adjudication.[271] A request for review must be made within 21 days from the date of issue of the initial adjudication on the form provided by the Authority for that purpose.[272] The initial decision remains extant while the matter is reviewed.[273] The following administrative/procedural arrangements apply to any review. A three-person standing Review Panel (comprised of a chairman and two ordinary members) is appointed by the Board of the Authority. The members of the Review Panel are appointed for five years and can be re-appointed once only. The Chairman is independent of both the Authority and the advertising industry. One of the ordinary members has a background in the advertising industry and the other a consumer (or non-advertising industry) background. A review can be sought on any of three grounds, namely: "[1] new, fresh or additional relevant evidence has become available, which could have a significant bearing on the Decision concerned (in such cases, an explanation as to why such evidence was not previously available and/or provided, will be required)...[2] the Decision concerned was clearly and manifestly in error, having regard to the provisions of the Code, wholly irrational, or clearly made against the weight of the evidence before the Complaints Committee at the time of making the Decision...and/or [3] there was a substantial flaw in the process by which the Decision was reached."[274] An applicant must make out a "sufficiently arguable case" on any of these three grounds for a review to proceed.[275] A review will not proceed if the "point

[9–92]

---

[270] See generally the Code of Standards, Appendix I, 88 *et seq.*

[271] Code of Standards, 80, para 17.

[272] *ibid.*

[273] *ibid.*

[274] Code of Standards, 88 *et seq.* The term "Decision" means a decision of the Complaints Committee. (Per the introductory text to Appendix I of the Code of Standards, at 88).

[275] Code of Standards, 89.

at issue" (this ought perhaps more rightly read the 'matter in issue') is the subject of actual or contemplated legal action between anyone directly involved in disputing that point.[276] There are also certain administrative formalities to commencing a request for a review: (i) an application must be submitted on a designated application form (this application can only be made by any of the parties to the original complaint); (ii) application must be made within 21 days of the date that appears on the letter from the Advertising Standards Authority notifying a prospective applicant of the Complaint Committee's initial decision (though this 21-day limit may be waived by the Review Panel if it considers it fair and reasonable to do so). Unlike the complaints process, there is a charge for the review process. For consumer applicants for review, there is, at the time of writing, a nominal application fee of €30. For advertiser applicants for review the application fee is, at the time of writing, €5,000. It will be recalled that the definition of "consumer" for the purposes of the Code of Standards is very wide (being "anyone who is likely to see or hear a particular marketing communication"[277]) and it is perhaps open to question whether all categories of person who/that come within the definition of "consumer" ought rightly to be charged a nominal fee only. The fees are reimbursed to the applicant if the initial decision of the Complaints Committee "is ultimately substantially altered in favour of the applicant, or reversed by the Complaints Committee."[278]

[9–93] The review process commences with a decision by the Review Panel (based on the application form received and any submissions forwarded by the Secretariat of the Advertising Standards Authority) as to whether the application should be accepted. If the Review Panel decides to accept the application, the Secretariat then forwards a copy of the application form to the other parties to the original complaint and seek submissions from those parties. Submissions, when received, are forwarded by the Secretariat to the Review Panel. It then considers all the submissions received and may seek or obtain such further information and submissions as it thinks are appropriate, fair and reasonable in all the circumstances. Its considerations complete, the Review Panel may reach one of two decisions, the burden being on the applicant to make out a sufficiently arguable case, namely that the application does not meet any of the three grounds for review outlined above[279] or, alternatively, that one or more of the three

[276] *ibid.*

[277] Code of Standards, 9, Para 1.3(f).

[278] Code of Standards, 89.

[279] In this regard the Review Panel may find that "[i] new, fresh or additional evidence is not relevant, or sufficiently relevant, and/or that the said evidence could not have a significant bearing on the Decision concerned, and/or that the explanation for the previous non-availability and/or non-provision of the said evidence is unsatisfactory and/or…[ii] no arguable case has been made that the Decision concerned was clearly and manifestly in error, having regard to the provisions of the Code, wholly irrational, or clearly made against the weight of the evidence before the Complaints Committee at the time of the making of the Decision, and/or…[iii] no arguable case has been made that there was a substantial flaw in the process by which the Decision concerned was reached, and that, accordingly, no further action will be taken on foot of the Application." (Code of Standards, 90, *et seq.*).

grounds has been met, in which instance the case is referred back to the Complaints Committee for reconsideration.[280] In either instance, the Review Panel will set out the reasoning for its decision and the decision will be communicated by the Secretariat of the Advertising Standards Authority to all parties involved. The Review Panel in arriving at its decision is not bound by any interpretation in the Complaints Committee decision under review as to any provision of the Code. There is no appeal from a decision of the Review Panel and, as mentioned above, the decision of the Complaints Committee that is under review remains extant pending the outcome of the review process. Where a case is referred back to the Complaints Committee, the Committee, having regard to the decision of the Review Panel may either affirm or vary the Committee's original decision or, alternatively, annul it and make such further decision as it considers proper. The decision of the Complaints Committee in this regard is final. Following the further decision of the Complaints Committee, the Secretariat advises all relevant parties of that further decision. An original decision of the Complaints Committee that has been revised is also published on the website of the Advertising Standards Authority.

Enforcement and sanctions

The Advertising Standards Authority considers its publication of case reports (which is something of a 'name and shame' exercise) to be an important element of the self-regulatory system that it promotes.[281] By way of sanction, as mentioned previously above, a marketing communication that breaches the Code of Standards must either be withdrawn or amended and the mainstream media will not deliberately publish a marketing communication which does not conform with the requirements with the Code.[282] Given the cost of preparing advertising, no advertiser would therefore lightly disregard the provisions of the Code. A member of the Advertising Standards Authority for Ireland who does not "accept" (conform with) a decision of the Authority may be disciplined by the Board of the Authority and may also be subject to penalties, including fines and/or suspension of membership.[283] Where the marketing communications of a particular advertiser "persistently and/or gravely" contravene the Code of Standards, the Advertising Standards Authority may require such advertiser to subject some or all of its proposed advertising to compulsory 'copy advice' (in effect vetting before publication) by the Authority until such time as the

[9–94]

---

[280] In this regard the Review Panel may find that "[i] the new, fresh or additional evidence appears to be relevant, or sufficiently relevant and/or that the said evidence could have a significant bearing on the Decision concerned, and that the explanation for the previous non-availability and/or non-provision of the said evidence is satisfactory and/or...[ii] that an arguable case has been made that the Decision concerned was clearly and manifestly in error, having regard to the provisions of the Code, wholly irrational, or clearly made against the weight of the evidence before the Complaints Committee at the time of the making of the Decision; and/or...[iii] that an arguable case has been made that there was a substantial flaw in the process by which the Decision concerned was reached, and that the case should be referred back to the Complaints Committee to be reconsidered accordingly." (Code of Standards, 91).

[281] Code of Standards, 81, para 18.

[282] *ibid.*

[283] Code of Standards, 81, para 19.

Authority is satisfied that future market communications from such advertiser are likely to comply with the Code.[284] In particular, where an advertiser appears to have purposely flouted the Code with the deliberate intention of generating complaints, notoriety, and 'PR', the Advertising Standards Authority can request the relevant advertiser and "the media", in effect the mainstream media outlets that are members of the Advertising Standards Authority, and not just the particular broadcaster(s) or publisher(s) who published the offending marketing communication(s), to submit for a stated period any further proposed marketing communications by that advertiser with a view to vetting same pre-publication to ensure compliance with the Code of Standards.[285]

Cross-border complaints

[9–95]   Complaints about marketing communications that appear in foreign media do not come within the remit of the Code of Standards and so do not fall to be considered by the Advertising Standards Authority.[286] In accordance with what the Code of Standards describes as the "Cross-Border Complaints System"[287], complaints with an intra-European, cross-border dimension are referred via the European Advertising Standards Alliance to the appropriate national self-regulatory authority for consideration under its Code.[288] "This", the Code states, "ensures that a consumer can have redress against misleading or offensive advertising originating anywhere in Europe."[289]

---

[284] Code of Standards, 81, para 20. The term 'Copy Advice' is capitalised in para 20 but is not a defined term.

[285] Code of Standards, 81, para 21.

[286] Code of Standards, 80, para 16.

[287] *ibid.*

[288] *ibid.*

[289] Code of Standards, 80, para 16.

PART 3
TEXTS AND MATERIALS

Appendix A

CONSOLIDATED EXTRACTS FROM THE CONSUMER CREDIT ACT, 1995

PART I
PRELIMINARY AND GENERAL

... 2. Interpretation ...

"advertisement" includes every form of advertising, whether in a publication, by television or radio, by display of notices, signs, labels, showcards or goods, by distribution of samples, circulars, catalogues, price lists or other material, by exhibition of pictures, models or films, or in any other way, and references to the publishing of advertisements shall be construed accordingly;

"agreement" means an agreement to which this Act applies;

"APR" means the annual percentage rate of charge, being the total cost of credit to the consumer, expressed as an annual percentage of the amount of credit granted and calculated in accordance with s 9;

"Bank" means the Central Bank and Financial Services Authority of Ireland;[1]

"borrower" means a consumer acting as a borrower;

"business" includes trade and profession ...[2]

"cash" includes money in any form ...

"consumer" means-

(a) a natural person acting outside the person's business, or
(b) any person, or person of a class, declared to be a consumer in an order made under subsection (9)[3];

"consumer-hire agreement" means an agreement of more than three months duration for the bailment of goods to a hirer under which the property in the goods remains with the owner ...

---

[1] Inserted by the Central Bank and Financial Services Authority of Ireland Act 2003 (No 12 of 2003), s 35(1) and Schedule 1, Part 21, Item 1(b).

[2] Inserted by the Central Bank and Financial Services Authority of Ireland Act 2004 (No 21 of 2004), s 33 and Schedule 3, Part 12, Item 1(a).

[3] Inserted by the Central Bank and Financial Services Authority of Ireland Act 2004 (No 21 of 2004), s 33 and Schedule 3, Part 12, Item 1(b).

"credit" includes a deferred payment, cash loan or other similar financial accommodation[4];

"credit agreement" means an agreement whereby a creditor grants or promises to grant to a consumer a credit in the form of a deferred payment, a cash loan or other similar financial accommodation ...

"credit institution" means-

(a) the holder of a licence granted under s 9 of the Central Bank Act, 1971,
(b) a body licensed to carry on banking under regulations made under the European Communities Act, 1972,
(c) a building society incorporated or deemed to be incorporated under s 10 of the Building Societies Act, 1989,
(d) a society licensed to carry on the business of a trustee savings bank under s 10 of the Trustee Savings Bank Act, 1989,
(e) such person or class of persons as may be prescribed by the Bank for the purposes of this Act ...[5] [and numerous named institutions];

"credit intermediary" means a person, other than a credit institution or a mortgage lender, who in the course of his business arranges or offers to arrange for a consumer the provision of credit or the letting of goods in return for a commission, payment or consideration of any kind from the provider of the credit or the owner, as the case may be ...

"creditor" means a person who grants credit under a credit agreement in the course of his trade, business or profession, and includes a group of such persons ...

"the Director" means the Director of Consumer Affairs[6];

"financial accommodation" includes credit and the letting of goods ...

"hirer" means a consumer who takes, intends to take or has taken goods from an owner under a hire-purchase agreement or a consumer-hire agreement in return for periodical payments;

---

[4] The words "or other similar financial accommodation" were substituted by Regulation 2(a) of the European Communities (Consumer Credit Act, 1995) (Amendment) Regulations, 1996 (SI No 277 of 1996) for the words "or any other form of financial accommodation" which appeared in the text of the Consumer Credit Act, 1995, as enacted.
[5] Inserted by the Central Bank and Financial Services Authority of Ireland Act 2003 (No 12 of 2003), s 35(1) and Schedule 1, Part 21, Item 1(d).
[6] Notwithstanding that the above text represents the current text of the Consumer Credit Act, 1995, as amended, s 37(3) of the Consumer Protection Act 2007 provides that "References to the Director and the office of the Director contained in any Act...or instrument (including a licence or certificate granted, nomination made or consent or authorisation given thereunder) relating to any functions transferred by subsection (2) shall, on and after the establishment day, be read as references to the [National Consumer Agency]". Regulation 2 of the Consumer Protection Act 2007 (Establishment Day) Order 2007 (SI No 179 of 2007) established 1 May 2007 as the establishment day for the purposes of the Consumer Protection Act.

"hire-purchase agreement" means an agreement for the bailment of goods under which the hirer may buy the goods or under which the property in the goods will, if the terms of the agreement are complied with, pass to the hirer in return for periodical payments; and where by virtue of two or more agreements, none of which by itself constitutes a hire-purchase agreement, there is a bailment of goods and either the hirer may buy the goods, or the property therein will, if the terms of the agreements are complied with, pass to the hirer, the agreements shall be treated for the purpose of this Act as a single agreement made at the time when the last agreement was made;

"house" includes any building or part of a building used or suitable for use as a dwelling and any outoffice, yard, garden or other land appurtenant thereto or usually enjoyed therewith;

"housing loan" means-

(a) an agreement for the provision of credit to a person on the security of a mortgage of a freehold or leasehold estate or interest in land-
    (i) for the purpose of enabling the person to have a house constructed on the land as the principal residence of that person or the person's dependants, or
    (ii) for the purpose of enabling the person to improve a house that is already used as the principal residence of that person or that person's dependants, or
    (iii) for the purpose of enabling the person to buy a house that is already constructed on the land for use as the principal residence of that person or that person's dependants, or
(b) an agreement for refinancing credit provided to a person for a purpose specified in paragraph (a)(i),(ii), or (iii), or
(c) an agreement for the provision of credit to a person on the security of a mortgage of a freehold or leasehold estate or interest in land on which a house is constructed where the house is to be used, or to continue to be used, as the principal residence of the person or the person's dependants, or
(d) an agreement for the provision of credit to a person on the security of a mortgage of a freehold or leasehold estate or interest in land on which a house is, or is to be, constructed where the person to whom the credit is provided is a consumer ...[7]

"mortgage" includes charge;

"mortgage intermediary" means a person (other than a mortgage lender or credit institution) who, in return for commission or some other form of consideration —

(a) arranges, or offers to arrange, for a mortgage lender to provide a consumer with a housing loan, or
(b) introduces a consumer to an intermediary who arranges, or offers to arrange, for a mortgage lender to provide the consumer with such a loan[8];

---

[7] Inserted by the Central Bank and Financial Services Authority of Ireland Act 2004 (No 21 of 2004), s 33 and Schedule 3, Part 12, Item 1(ba).
[8] Inserted by the Central Bank and Financial Services Authority of Ireland Act 2004 (No 21 of 2004), s 33 and Schedule 3, Part 12, Item 1(c).

"mortgage lender" means a person who carries on a business that consists of or includes making housing loans ...[9]

"owner" means the person who lets or has let goods to a hirer under a hire-purchase agreement or a consumer-hire agreement ...

"prescribed" means prescribed by Regulations made under this Act[10] and "prescribe" shall be construed accordingly ...

"total cost of credit" means the total cost of credit to the consumer, being all the costs, comprising interest, collection and all other charges, which the consumer has to pay for the credit exclusive of any sum payable as a penalty or as compensation or damages for breach of the agreement;

... PART II
ADVERTISING AND OFFERING OF FINANCIAL ACCOMMODATION

20. Application of Part II

(1) Subject to subsection (2), this Part applies to any advertisement, published or displayed for the purpose of a business carried on by the advertiser indicating willingness to —

(a) provide or to arrange the provision of credit,
(b) enter into a hire-purchase agreement or consumer-hire agreement for the letting of goods by the advertiser, or
(c) arrange the letting of goods under a hire-purchase or consumer-hire agreement by another person, to a consumer.

(2) This Part does not apply to any advertisement published or displayed by a society referred to in s 3(2)(a).[11]

21. Credit Advertisements

(1) An advertisement in which a person offers to provide or arrange the provision of credit shall, if mentioning a rate of interest or making any claim in relation to the cost of credit[12], contain a clear and prominent statement of the APR, using a representative example if no other means is practicable, provided it is indicated

---

[9] Inserted by the Central Bank and Financial Services Authority of Ireland Act 2004 (No 21 of 2004), s 33 and Schedule 3, Part 12, Item 1(d).

[10] The words "made under this Act" were substituted by the Central Bank and Financial Services Authority of Ireland Act 2003, s 35 and Schedule 1, Part 21, Item 1(i) for the words "made by the Minister" which appeared in the text of the Consumer Credit Act, 1995, as enacted.

[11] i.e. "... a society which is registered as a credit union under the Industrial and Provident Societies Acts, 1893 to 1978, by virtue of the Credit Union Act, 1966 ... [and] any registered society within the meaning of the Friendly Societies Acts, 1896 to 1977".

[12] The words "or making any claim in relation to the cost of credit" were inserted by Regulation 2(a) of the Consumer Credit Act, 1995 (Section 28) Regulations, 1996 (SI No 245 of 1996).

that this is only a representative example, and no other rate of interest shall be included in the advertisement.[13]

(2) The statement of the APR included in any advertisement to which subsection (1) applies shall be afforded in the advertisement no less prominence than a statement relating to —
  (a) any period over which payment is to be made,
  (b) the amount of any advance payment or the fact that no advance payment is required, and
  (c) the amount, number or frequency of any other payments or charges (other than the cash price of the goods or services) or of any repayments.

(3) An advertisement (other than one relating to a housing loan) shall, where the credit offered is subject to conditions involving the payment of any charges other than the repayment of capital and interest on the sum borrowed, specify those conditions.

(4) An advertisement shall, if any security is required or is required in specific circumstances in relation to the credit offered, state that such security is required.

(5) Notwithstanding s 7 of the Consumer Information Act, 1978[14], it shall not be an offence for a person to provide credit at a lower rate than the rate advertised.

(6) Where an advertisement refers to the availability of credit and the credit is subject to any restrictions, those restrictions shall be clearly indicated.

22. Advertising of Financial Accommodation Related to Goods or Services

Where an advertisement refers to the availability of a financial accommodation in relation to the acquisition of goods or the provision of a service, it shall include, where applicable,[15] a statement of-

(a) the nature of the financial accommodation,
(b) the cash price of the goods or service,
(c) the APR and the total cost of credit or the hire-purchase price,[16]
(d) the number and amount of instalments,
(e) the duration of the intervals between instalment payments,
(f) the number of any instalments which have to be paid before delivery of the goods, and
(g) details of any deposit payable.

---

[13] The words "provided it is indicated that this is only a representative example," were inserted by Regulation 2(a) of the Consumer Credit Act, 1995 (Section 28) Regulations, 1996 (SI No 245 of 1996).
[14] The Consumer Information Act, 1978, was repealed in its entirety by s 4(1) and Schedule 2 of the Consumer Protection Act 2007.
[15] The words "where applicable" were inserted by Regulation 3(a) of the Consumer Credit Act, 1995 (S 28) Regulations, 1996 (SI No 245 of 1996).
[16] The words "(c) the APR and the total cost of credit or the hire-purchase price," were inserted by Regulation 3(a) of the Consumer Credit Act, 1995 (Section 28) Regulations, 1996 (SI No 245 of 1996) in place of the words "(c) where applicable, the total cost of credit or the hire-purchase price" which appeared in s 22(c) of the Consumer Credit Act, 1995, as enacted.

23. Advertising of Consumer-Hire Agreements.

(1) An advertisement in which a person offers to arrange the letting of goods under a consumer-hire agreement or indicates the availability of such a letting shall include a statement to the effect that the agreement is for letting, hiring or leasing only and the goods remain the property of the owner,

    (i) which shall be afforded no less prominence than the sum of any amount payable by the hirer, and

    (ii) in the case of a visual advertisement, shall be enclosed by a boxed boundary line.

(2) Where any figures relating to the amount payable by a hirer under a consumer-hire agreement are indicated in any advertisement to which subsection (1) applies, those figures shall be clearly displayed and shall be fully inclusive of all amounts payable, including taxes.

(3) Where any figures relating to the amount payable by a hirer under a consumer-hire agreement are indicated in any advertisement to which subsection (1) applies, and those figures indicate the amount payable for part of the agreement only, that fact shall also be clearly indicated in the advertisement.

24. Comparative Advertising

Where an advertisement purports to compare the level of repayments or cost under one or more forms of financial accommodation, the advertisement shall contain the relevant terms of each of the forms of financial accommodation referred to in the advertisement.

25. Advertising of Credit as Being without Charge

An advertisement shall not describe credit as being without interest, or any other charge, if the availability of the credit is dependent on the consumer concluding with the creditor or any other person a maintenance contract (for any goods involved) or an insurance contract or on any other condition, compliance with which would, or would be likely in the future to, involve the consumer in any cost additional to that payable if the goods were bought for cash.

26. Advertising of Financial Accommodation to Comply with this Part

(1) A person shall not display or publish or cause to be displayed or published an advertisement to which this Part applies which does not comply with this Part.

(2) In any proceedings for contravening subsection (1), it shall be a defence for the accused, being a person other than the provider of credit, to show that he is a person whose business it is to publish or arrange for the publication of advertisements and that he received the advertisement in question for publication in the ordinary course of business and did not know and had no reason to suspect that its publication would constitute a contravention of subsection (1).

(3) For the purposes of this section an advertisement published by displaying it shall be treated as published on every day on which it is displayed.

27. Obligation on Provider of Financial Accommodation to Ensure Advertisements Comply with Part

(1) Where the provider of a financial accommodation, in respect of any financial accommodation provided by him through a credit intermediary, has devised any part of an advertisement or supplied, or has been requested to supply, information in relation to it, but is not the advertiser, the provider shall ensure the advertisement displayed or published complies with this Part.

(2) In any proceedings for contravening this section it shall be a defence for the accused, being the provider of a financial accommodation in relation to an advertisement which does not comply with this Part, to show that it was displayed or published without his consent or connivance or that he made reasonable efforts to ensure that it complied with this Part or to prevent its publication.

28. Regulations Relating to Advertising Availability and Cost of Credit[17]

(1) The Bank may make regulations amending ss 21, 22, 23, 24 or 25 with respect to the form or content of advertisements relating to the availability or the cost or the provision of credit to consumers.

(2) The Bank may exercise the power conferred by subsection (1) only after consulting with, or at the request of the Director and only after obtaining the consent of the Minister for Finance,

(3) The Bank shall consult the Minister for the Environment and Local Government before making regulations under this section relating to housing loans.

... PART IX
HOUSING LOANS MADE BY MORTGAGE LENDERS

115. Application of Definitions, Part IX

(1) This Part shall apply to a housing loan made by a mortgage lender.
(2) In this Part —

..."endowment loan" means a housing loan which is to be repaid out of the proceeds of an insurance policy on its maturity, other than a policy providing mortgage protection insurance only;

"information document", means any document, leaflet, notice, circular, pamphlet, brochure, film, video or facsimile issued to the general public or to certain persons (whether solicited or not) for the purpose of giving information in relation to housing loans;

"insurance intermediary" means an insurance agent or insurance broker within the meaning of the Insurance Act, 1989;

"insurer" has the meaning assigned to it by the Insurance Act, 1989;

---

[17] A new s 28 was inserted into the Consumer Credit Act, 1995, by the Central Bank and Financial Services Authority of Ireland Act, 2003, s 35 and Schedule 1, Part 21, Item 11.

"mortgage agent" means any or all of the following:

(a) a mortgage lender,

(b) a mortgage intermediary,

(c) an insurer, or

(d) an insurance intermediary;

... 128. Warning on Loss of Home

(1) A mortgage agent shall ensure that —

(a) an information document,

(b) an application form for a housing loan, or

(c) any document approving a housing loan,

   shall include the following notice:

> **WARNING: YOUR HOME IS AT RISK IF YOU DO NOT KEEP UP PAYMENTS ON A MORTGAGE OR ANY OTHER LOAN SECURED ON IT.**

(2) A mortgage agent shall ensure that, where the interest rate for a housing loan is variable —

(a) an information document

(b) an application, or

(c) any document approving that loan, shall, following the notice required under subsection (1), include the following:

> **THE PAYMENT RATES ON THIS HOUSING LOAN MAY BE ADJUSTED BY THE LENDER FROM TIME TO TIME.**

... 132. Disclosure of Other Fees

Where a fee is payable by an applicant for a housing loan in respect of any of the following matters —

(a) the making, accepting or administering of an application for a loan,

(b) the valuation of the security for the loan,

(c) legal services in connection with the loan,

(d) services provided by a mortgage agent in relation to the loan, or

(e) non-acceptance of an offer or approval of a loan,

the mortgage agent shall ensure that a statement of reasonable prominence that such a fee is payable and specifying the amount of the fee or how such amount is determined and the circumstances in which it may be refunded, if such is the case shall be included in or attached to:

(i) any information document issued by or on behalf of the mortgage agent which refers or relates to such a loan,

(ii) any application form issued for the purposes of applying for such a loan or, where application for the loan is made otherwise than by way of an application form, issued to the applicant within 10 days of the receipt of the application, and

(iii) any document sent to the applicant approving the loan, in relation to the matters specified in paragraphs (b), (c), (d) and (e).

133. Endowment Loans

(1) A mortgage agent shall ensure that an information document which refers or relates to an endowment loan, an application form issued to a person for the purpose of applying for such a loan, and any document approving such a loan shall contain in a prominent position the following notice:

> **WARNING: THERE IS NO GUARANTEE THAT THE PROCEEDS OF THE INSURANCE POLICY WILL BE SUFFICIENT TO REPAY THE LOAN IN FULL WHEN IT BECOMES DUE FOR REPAYMENT.**

... (3) [Subsection (1)] ... shall not apply where the insurer underwriting the insurance policy in respect of an endowment loan guarantees that the proceeds of the policy at the initial premium will be sufficient to repay the loan in full when it becomes due for repayment or where the mortgage lender undertakes to accept the proceeds in full and final settlement of the loan debt.

... (5) Where the possibility exists that early surrender of the insurance policy in respect of an endowment loan may result in a return to the consumer which would be less than he has paid in premia and other charges, any document referred to in subsection (1) shall contain a statement of this possibility ...

134. Disclosure of Interest Rate and Penalties to be Applied to Arrears on Housing Loans

(1) Where it is the policy of a mortgage lender to charge interest in respect of arrears on housing loans or on housing loans of a particular type the mortgage lender shall ensure that, any information document relating to, application form for, or document approving, such a loan and any communication in relation to arrears of payments due on such a loan shall state the amount of the increase in interest and other charges which a borrower may become liable to pay in respect of such arrears.

... 135. Advertising of Housing Loans

(1) The Bank may, if it[18] considers it expedient to do so, give a direction to a mortgage agent in relation to the matter and form of any advertisement or information document displayed or published by or on behalf of such agent in relation to a housing loan and may direct that such advertisement or information document be withdrawn.

(2) Without prejudice to the generality of subsection (1), a direction under this section may do all or any one or more of the following:

---

[18] The words "The Bank may, if it" were substituted by the Central Bank and Financial Services Authority of Ireland Act 2003, s 35 and Schedule 1, Part 21, Item 37 for the words "The Director may, if he" which appeared in the text of the Consumer Credit Act, 1995, as enacted, and a sub-para (4) which appeared in section 135, as enacted, was deleted.

(a) prohibit the issue by a mortgage agent of advertisements or information documents of any specified description,

(b) require a mortgage agent to modify advertisements or information documents of a specified description in a specified manner;

(c) prohibit the issue by a mortgage agent of any advertisements or information documents which are, or are substantially, repetitions of a specified advertisement or information document,

(d) require a mortgage agent to withdraw any specified advertisement or information document or any advertisement or information document of a specified description, or

(e) require a mortgage agent to include specified information in any advertisement or information document to be published by it or on its behalf or in any statement to the public made by it or on its behalf.

(3) Any mortgage agent so directed under subsection (1) shall comply with the direction.

...PART X
MISCELLANEOUS

...139. Circulars to Minors

A person shall not knowingly, with a view to financial gain, send to a minor any document inviting the minor to —

(a) borrow credit,
(b) obtain goods on credit or hire,
(c) obtain services on credit, or
(d) apply for information or advice on borrowing credit or otherwise obtaining credit or hiring goods.

Appendix B

DIRECTIONS MADE UNDER SECTION 135(1) OF THE CONSUMER CREDIT ACT, 1995

Direction made by the Director of Consumer Affairs under section 135(1) of the Consumer Credit Act, 1995, effective from 24 March 1997

Office of the Director of Consumer Affairs/Direction under Section 135(1) of the Consumer Credit Act 1995

With effect from Monday 24 March, 1997 the following information must be provided by mortgage lenders until further notice in relation to printed advertisements for residential mortgage credit in newspapers, magazines or other direct printed advertisements and on the internet:-

(a) The maximum percentage of the value of the property which will normally be advanced to the borrower(s) and an indication of whether other criteria apply;
(b) The maximum proportion of loan to income of the borrower(s) which will normally be provided and an indication of whether other criteria apply;
(c) The cost per month of a typical €100,000 20-year variable rate mortgage and the additional cost per month of a 1% rise in the rate of interest of such a mortgage;
(d) A health warning stating "the cost of your monthly repayments may increase – if you do not keep up your repayments you may lose your home".

With effect from Monday 24 March, 1997 a statement must be made in all Radio, Television, and Billboard advertisements for residential mortgage credit that "Lending terms and conditions will apply".

I would point out that it is an offence to include any misleading information in advertisements and I will be checking the veracity of statements in advertisements and for compliance with the terms of this direction.

William Fagan
Director of Consumer Affairs

Direction made by the Financial Regulator under section 135(1) of the Consumer Credit Act, 1995, effective from 1 January 2007

[On headed notepaper of the Financial Regulator]

Direction under Section 135(1) of the Consumer Credit Act 1995

Pursuant to section 135(1) of the Consumer Credit Act 1995, the Consumer Director of the Irish Financial Services Regulatory Authority hereby directs that:

(i) the following information must be displayed in all advertisements and information documents that promote debt consolidation housing loans displayed by or on behalf of a mortgage agent:

(a) where sample figures are displayed for the consolidation of two or more debts, the difference between the total cost of credit of the consolidated mortgage and the total cost of credit of the individual debts that are the subject of consolidation, must be indicated.

(b) any examples of existing debts must be based upon generally prevailing interest rates at the time of the advertisement or information document being published.

(c) where the actual repayment frequency of the advertised housing loan is monthly, any repayment amounts displayed must also be monthly. Weekly equivalents may be displayed but must not be more prominent than the monthly amounts.

(d) where sample repayments of the proposed housing loan are displayed, the repayment term on which they are based must be displayed and must be afforded equal prominence to the sample repayments. The repayment term can be no longer than 20 years.

(e) the following warning which must be prominent, i.e. it must be in a box, in bold type and of a font size that is larger than the normal font size used throughout the advertisement or information document:

> **Warning: This new loan may take longer to pay off than your previous loans. This means you pay more than if you paid over a shorter term.**

(ii) interest only housing loans must not be advertised as being suitable for debt consolidation purposes.

This Direction is made without prejudice to, and shall not provide any derogation from, any provision of the Consumer Credit Act 1995 or other law applicable to such an advertisement. This Direction is effective from 1 January 2007 until further notice.

PART 4
COMPLIANCE CHECKLISTS

Appendix C

CONSUMER PROTECTION CODE CHECKLIST

The checklist set out in this Appendix, as compiled by the author of this book, seeks to reduce the entirety of the Consumer Protection Code to a series of questions. The questions have been drafted so that a 'Yes' answer suggests compliance with the Consumer Protection Code and a 'No' answer suggests non-compliance. Certain terms used in the checklist are terms that bear a defined meaning when used in the Consumer Protection Code and when used in the checklist. Where a term used in the checklist is a defined term, it appears in **Bold** format, with the definition appearing in the appendix to the checklist. Of course, before proceeding to the detail of the checklist it is prudent to consider whether the Consumer Protection Code applies at all.

When the Code applies

The Consumer Protection Code is issued by and in the name of the Financial Regulator and applies to the **regulated activities** of all **regulated entities** operating in Ireland, including: (i) the services of all regulated entities operating in Ireland for which they require to be authorised by, or registered with, the Financial Regulator; and (ii) persons with an equivalent authorisation or registration in another EU or EEA **Member State** when providing services in Ireland on a branch or cross-border basis; and (iii) services of a financial or investment nature that are subject to the regulation of the Financial Regulator, for which a separate authorisation is not required.

Chapter 1 of the Consumer Protection Code applies when providing defined services to **customers** resident in Ireland. The other Chapters apply only when providing defined services to **consumers** in Ireland. Chapters 1 (General Principles), 2 (Common Rules) and 7 (Advertising) apply to all regulated entities. Chapter 3 (Banking Products and Services) applies to regulated entities when providing banking products and services. Chapter 4 (Loans) applies to credit providers, mortgage intermediaries and home reversion firms. Chapter 5 (Insurance Products and Services) applies to insurance undertakings and insurance intermediaries. Chapter 6 (Investment Products) applies to regulated entities providing investment services, or providing services in relation to deposits with a term equal to or more than a year (except **MiFID Services**).

When the Code does not apply

The Consumer Protection Code does not apply to regulated entities when:
(i) providing services to persons outside Ireland; (ii) providing **MiFID Services**;
(iii) providing the services of a 'moneylender' (within the meaning of the Consumer
Credit Act, 1995); (iv) carrying on the business of reinsurance/reinsurance mediation;
(v) carrying on the 'bureau de change' or 'money transmission' business (within the
meaning of Part V of the Central Bank Act 1997); (v) in the case of credit unions only,
where such credit union is providing services for which it does not require to be
authorised by or registered with the Financial Regulator: (vi) carrying on the business
of entering into hire purchase agreements; or (vii) carrying on the business of entering
into consumer hire agreements.

Query	*Source*	*Yes*	*No*	*N/A*
Chapter 1, General Principles				
(Applies when providing services to **customers** resident in Ireland)				
(1) Is the regulated entity acting honestly, fairly, and professionally in the best interests of its **customers** and the integrity of the market?	Ch.1, par.1.			
(2) Is the regulated entity acting with due skill, care and diligence in the best interests of its **customers**?	Ch.1, par. 2			
(3) Has the regulated entity avoided recklessly, negligently or deliberately misleading a **customer** as to the real or perceived advantages or disadvantages of any product or service?	Ch.1, par. 3			
(4) Does the regulated entity have and has it employed effectively the resources and procedures, systems and control checks necessary for compliance with the Consumer Protection Code?	Ch.1, par. 4			
(5) Has the regulated entity sought from its **customers** information relevant to the product or service requested?	Ch.1, par.5			
(6) Has the regulated entity made full disclosure of all relevant material information, including all **charges**, in a way that seeks to inform the **customer**?	Ch.1, par.6			
(7) Has the regulated entity sought to avoid conflicts of interest?	Ch.1, par.7			
(8) Does the regulated entity correct errors and handle complaints speedily, efficiently and fairly?	Ch.1, par.8			
(9) Has the regulated entity avoided exerting undue influence or pressure on any **customer**?	Ch.1, par.9			

(Continued)

Query	Source	Yes	No	N/A
(10) Has the regulated entity ensured that any **outsourced activity** complies with the requirements of the Consumer Protection Code?	Ch.1, par.10.			
(11) Without prejudice to the pursuit of its legitimate commercial aims, has the regulated entity avoided preventing access to basic financial services (through its policies, procedures or working practices)?	Ch.1, par.11			
(12) Is the regulated entity in compliance with the letter and spirit of the Consumer Protection Code?	Ch.1, par.12			
Chapter 2, Common Rules for all Regulated Entities (Applies when providing services to **consumers** resident in Ireland)				
General (13) Has the regulated entity ensured that the name of any product or service which it provides is not misleading in terms of the benefits that the product or service can deliver?	Ch.2, par.1			
(14) Does the regulated entity ensure that all instructions from or on behalf of a **consumer** are processed properly and promptly and that the date of both the receipt and transmission of instructions is recorded?	Ch.2, par.2			
(15) Does the regulated entity ensure that, where it accepts an instruction from a **consumer** that is subject to any condition imposed by the **consumer**, it maintains a **record** of the condition to which the instruction is subject?	Ch.2, par.3			
(16) Has the regulated entity avoided making the sale of a product or service contingent on the **consumer** purchasing another product or service from the regulated entity?	Ch.2, par.4			
(17) Has the regulated entity avoided charging a **consumer** a fee for any optional extra(s) offered in conjunction with a product or service, unless that consumer has positively indicated that such consumer wishes to purchase the optional extra(s)?	Ch.2, par.5			
(18) Has the regulated entity ensured that all warnings required by the Consumer Protection Code are prominent, i.e. are they in a box, in bold type and of a font size that is larger than the normal font size used throughout the document or **advertisement**?	Ch.2, par.6			

(Continued)

Query	Source	Yes	No	N/A
Access (19) Does the regulated entity take into consideration the provisions of the relevant anti-money laundering guidance notes issued with the approval of the Money Laundering Steering Committee, and in particular any guidance in such note on how to establish identity, in order to ensure that a **person** is not denied access to financial services solely on the grounds that that **person** does not possess certain specified identification documentation?	Ch. 2, par.7			
Terms of Business (20) Has the regulated entity drawn up its **terms of business,** does it provide each **consumer** with a copy prior to providing the first service to such **consumer**, and do the **terms of business** set out the basis on which the regulated entity provides its services, including (a) the legal name, trading name (if any), address and contact details of the regulated entity, (b) the identity of the **group** to which the regulated entity belongs, if any, (c) confirmation that the regulated entity is authorised and the name of the competent authority that has authorised it, (d) the regulatory status of the regulated entity, (e) a description of the services that the regulated entity provides, (f) if the regulated entity is tied for any of the services outlined in (e), the name of the regulated entity to which it is tied and details of the service for which it is tied, (g) a general statement of the **charges** imposed directly by the regulated entity, (h) a summary of the regulated entity's policy in relation to conflicts of interest, (i) an outline of the actions and remedies which the regulated entity may take in the event of default by a **consumer**, (j) a summary of the **complaints** procedure operated by the regulated entity, (k) if the regulated entity is a member of a compensation scheme, the name of the scheme and the nature and level of protection available from the scheme?	Ch.2, par.8			
(21) If the regulated entity is a **deposit agent**, does it ensure that each **consumer** is given a copy of the relevant **credit institution's terms of business** prior to providing the first service to that **consumer** and do such **terms of business** set out the nature of the relationship between the **credit institution** and the **deposit agent** and the basis on which the **deposit agent's** services are provided?	Ch.2, par.9			

(Continued)

Query	Source	Yes	No	N/A
(22) Does the regulated entity provide its **terms of business** to a consumer as a stand-alone document?	Ch.2, par.10			
(23) If a regulated entity is making a material change to its **terms of business**, will it provide each affected **consumer** with details of the change as soon as possible?	Ch.2, par.11			

Provision of information to the consumer

Query	Source	Yes	No	N/A
(24) Is the regulated entity satisfied that all information it is providing to **consumers** is clear and comprehensible and that key items are brought to the attention of the **consumer** and that the method of presentation does not disguise, diminish or obscure important information?	Ch.2, par.12			
(25) Does the regulated entity supply information to the **consumer** on a timely basis and, in doing so, does the regulated entity have regard to: the urgency of the situation; and the time necessary for the **consumer** to absorb and react to the information provided?	Ch.2, par.13			
(26) If the regulated entity intends to amend or alter the range of services it provides, will it give notice to affected **consumers** at least one month in advance of the amendment being introduced?	Ch.2, par.14			
(27) If the regulated entity intends to cease operating, will it: provide at least two month's notice to affected **consumers** to enable them to make alternative arrangements; and ensure that all outstanding business is properly completed?	Ch.2, par.15			
(28) Does the regulated entity ensure that, where applicable, documents conferring ownership rights are given to a **consumer** in a timely manner or are held for safekeeping under an agreement with the **consumer**, in accordance with the terms of the regulated entity's authorisation?	Ch.2, par.16			
(29) If, when placing a telephone call with a **consumer**, the regulated entity intends to record the call, will it advise the **consumer** at the outset of the conversation, that it is being recorded?	Ch.2, par.17			
(30) Does the regulated entity provide a **consumer** with a receipt for each negotiable or non-negotiable instrument presented by the **consumer** as payment for a financial product or service provided by that regulated entity?	Ch.2, par.18			

(Continued)

Query	*Source*	*Yes*	*No*	*N/A*
(31) Does the regulated entity acknowledge in writing the receipt of a completed direct debit mandate or payroll deduction mandate, received from a **consumer** as a payment instruction for a financial product or service provided by that regulated entity?	Ch.2, par.19			
(32) If the regulated entity is communicating with a **consumer** using electronic media, does it have in place appropriate arrangements to ensure the secure transmission of information to, and receipt of information, from the **consumer**?	Ch.2, par.20			
(33) Does the regulated entity provide each **consumer** with the terms and conditions attaching to a product or service before the **consumer** enters into a contract for that product or service, or before the cooling-off period (if any) expires?	Ch.2, par.21			
(34) Does the regulated entity ensure that all printed information it provides to **consumers** is of a print size that is clearly legible?	Ch.2, par.22			

Preservation of a consumer's rights

(35) Does the regulated entity, in any communication or agreement with a **consumer** (and other than where permitted by applicable legislation) avoid excluding or restricting or seeking to exclude or restrict: (i) any legal liability or duty of care to a **consumer** which it has under applicable law or under the Consumer Protection Code; (ii) any other duty to act with skill, care and diligence which is owed to a **consumer** in connection with the provision to that **consumer** of financial services; or (iii) any liability owed to a **consumer** for failure to exercise the degree of skill, care and diligence that may reasonably be expected of it in the provision of a financial service?	Ch.2, par.23			

Knowing the consumer

(36) Before providing a product or service to a **consumer**, does the regulated entity gather and record sufficient information from the **consumer** to enable it to provide a recommendation or a product or service appropriate to that **consumer**; is the level of information gathered appropriate to the nature and complexity of the product or service being sought by the **consumer** and to a level that allows the regulated entity to provide a professional service? (A 'No'	Ch.2, par.24			

(Continued)

Query	Source	Yes	No	N/A
answer to this question is not indicative of non-compliance where: (i) the **consumer** has specified both the product and the product provider and has not received any advice; (ii) the **consumer** is purchasing or selling foreign currency; (iii) the regulated entity has established that the **consumer** is seeking a **basic banking product or service**)?				
(37) Does the regulated entity gather and record details of any material changes to a **consumer's** circumstances before providing that **consumer** with a subsequent product or service?	Ch.2, par.25			
(38) In the case of a **standard PRSA**, where an employer has chosen a provider and the regulated entity makes a presentation to **employees**, does the minimum relevant information required by the regulated entity establish that the **consumer** is an **employee** of the firm, has no other form of pension provision and intends to select the **default investment strategy** of the provider?	Ch.2, par.26			
(39) Does the regulated entity ensure that, where a **consumer** refuses to provide information sought in compliance with the Code, the refusal is noted on the **consumer's** records?	Ch.2, par.27			
(40) Does the regulated entity endeavour to have the **consumer** certify the accuracy of the information that it has provided to the regulated entity and where the **consumer** declines to do so, does the regulated entity note this on the **consumer's records**?	Ch.2, par.28			
(41) Does the regulated entity maintain a list of its **customers** who are **consumers** and subject to the Code?	Ch.2, par.29			
Suitability (42) Does the regulated entity ensure that, having regard to the facts disclosed by the **consumer** and other relevant facts about the **consumer** of which the regulated entity is aware, that: (i) any product or service offered to a **consumer** is suitable to that **consumer**; (ii) where it offers a selection of product options to the **consumer**, the product options contained in the selection represent the most suitable from the range available to the regulated entity; or (iii) where it recommends a product to a **consumer**, the recommended product is the most suitable product	Ch.2, par.30			

(Continued)

Query	Source	Yes	No	N/A
for that **consumer**? (A 'No' answer to this question is not indicative of non-compliance where: (i) the **consumer** has specified both the product and the provider and has not received any advice; (ii) the **consumer** is purchasing or selling foreign currency; and (iii) in the context of a **basic banking product or service**, the regulated entity has alerted the **consumer** to any restrictions on the account and/or the availability of a lower cost alternative).				
(43) Assuming that the **consumer** (i) has not specified both the product and the provider and has not received any advice, (ii) is not purchasing or selling foreign currency and (iii) is not seeking a **basic banking product or service**, is it the case that, before providing a product or service to a **consumer**, the regulated entity prepares a written statement setting out: (i) the reasons why a product or service offered to a **consumer** is considered to be suitable to that **consumer**; (ii) the reasons why each of a selection of product options offered to a **consumer** are considered to be suitable to that **consumer**, and (iii) the reasons why a recommended product is considered to be the most suitable product for a **consumer**, and does the regulated entity give a copy of this written statement to the **consumer** and retain a copy?	Ch.2, par.31			
Unsolicited contact (44) If a regulated entity is contacting, by way of personal visit or telephone call, a **consumer** who is an individual and an existing **customer**: (i) has the regulated entity within the previous 12 months provided that **consumer** with a product or service similar to the purpose of the unsolicited contact; (ii) does the **consumer** hold a product which requires the regulated entity to maintain contact with the **consumer** in relation to that product; (iii) is the purpose of the contact limited to offering **protection policies** only; or (iv) has the **consumer** given consent in writing to being contacted in this way by the regulated entity?	Ch.2, par.32			

(Continued)

Appendix C

Query	Source	Yes	No	N/A
(45) If a regulated entity is making unsolicited contact, by way of personal visit or telephone call, to a **consumer** (other than an existing **customer**) who is an individual: (i) has the **consumer** signed a statement within the previous six months giving the regulated entity permission to make personal visits or calls to that **consumer**; (ii) does the **consumer** have a listing in the business listing section of the current telephone directory, classified telephone directory or trade/professional directories circulating in Ireland; (iii) is the **consumer** a director of a company or a partner in a firm with an entry in one of the directories listed in (ii); (iii) is the **consumer** the subject of a referral received from an entity authorised to provide financial services in Ireland, another entity within the same **group**, a solicitor, a **certified person**, or an existing **customer**; or (iv) is the purpose of the contact limited to offering **protection policies**? (In relation to (iv), was the referral followed up by an indication to the **consumer** by the regulated entity that the referral had been made and asking for consent to proceed?).	Ch.2, par.33			
(46) Does the regulated entity ensure that, where it makes an unsolicited contact on foot of a referral, it retains a record of the referral?	Ch.2, par.34			
(47) Is unsolicited contact by the regulated entity, assuming such contact otherwise to be in accordance with the Code, made between 9am to 9pm, Monday to Saturday, excluding bank and public holidays (save where otherwise requested by the **consumer** so contacted)?	Ch.2, par.35			
(48) With regard to the unsolicited contact, assuming it to be otherwise in accordance with the Code, does the representative of the regulated entity, immediately and in the following order: (i) identify himself or herself by name, the name of the regulated entity on whose behalf s/he is calling and the commercial purpose of the contact; (ii) inform the **consumer** that the call is being recorded, if so; (iii) disclose to the **consumer**, the source of the business lead or referral supporting the contact; and (iv) establish if the **consumer** wishes the call to proceed (and, if the consumer does not wish the call to proceed, does the caller end the contact immediately)?	Ch.2, par.36			

(*Continued*)

181

Query	Source	Yes	No	N/A
(49) Does the regulated entity abide by a request from any **consumer** not to make an unsolicited contact with such **consumer** again?	Ch.2, par.37.			
(50) Does the regulated entity avoid reaching a binding agreement with a **consumer** on the basis of an unsolicited contact alone, except in the circumstances permitted under the European Communities (Distance Marketing of Consumer Financial Services Regulations) 2004?	Ch.2, par.38			
Disclosure Requirements				
(51) Does the regulated entity include a regulatory disclosure statement (a) on its business stationery; (b) in all **advertisements**; and (c) on all electronic communications with **consumers**, including on the home page of its website, if any?	Ch.2, par. 39			
(52) Does the regulated entity avoid using the regulatory disclosure statement on any business stationery, **advertisement**, or electronic communication in connection with a product or service for which the firm is not regulated by the Financial Regulator?	Ch.2, par. 40			
(53) Does the regulatory disclosure statement take the following form: "[Full name of regulated entity (and trading name, if applicable)] is regulated by the Financial Regulator?"	Ch.2, par. 41			
(54) If the regulated entity is operating in Ireland under EU freedom of services or of establishment provisions has it disclosed the name of the competent authority from which it received its authorisation, or with which it is registered, and the name of the state where that competent authority resides, (a) on its business stationery; (b) in all **advertisements** for services for which the regulated entity is subject to the Consumer Protection Code; and (c) on all electronic communications with *consumers* (including on the home page of its website, if any)?	Ch.2, par.42			
(55) Is the regulatory disclosure statement presented in such a way that it does not appear to be an endorsement by the Financial Regulator of the regulated entity or of its products or services?	Ch.2, par.43			

(Continued)

Query	Source	Yes	No	N/A
Charges (56) Does the regulated entity, where applicable: (i) provide a **consumer** with details of all **charges**, including third party **charges** which the regulated entity will pass on to the **consumer**, prior to providing a service to the **consumer** and where such **charges** cannot be ascertained in advance, does the regulated entity advise the **consumer** that such **charges** will be levied as part of the transaction; (ii) advise affected **consumers** of increases in **charges**, or the introduction of any new **charges**, at least 30 days before the change takes effect; (iii) detail in each statement provided to a **consumer**, all **charges** applied during the period covered by that statement; and (iv) where **charges** are accumulated and applied periodically to accounts, advise **consumers** at least 10 **business days** before deduction of **charges** and give each **consumer** a breakdown of such **charges**, except where **charges** total an amount of _12.70 or less?	Ch.2, par.44			
Errors (57) Does the regulated entity: (i) speedily, efficiently and fairly, correct an error in any charge or price levied on, or quoted to a **consumer** in respect of any product or service the subject of the Consumer Protection Code; (ii) where the regulated entity considers that there may have been a material charging or pricing error, without delay, inform the Financial Regulator of its proposals for correcting any such error as may have occurred in accordance with paragraph (i) (and where such information is provided verbally to the Financial Regulator in the first instance, is it provided in writing on the next business day); and (iii) notify all affected **consumers**, both current and former, in a timely manner and in such form as may be agreed with the Financial Regulator, of any material charging or pricing error that impacts negatively on the cost of the service or the value of the product provided?	Ch.2, par.45			
Handling Complaints (58) Does the regulated entity have in place a written procedure for the proper handling of **complaints** (save in instances where the **complaint** has been resolved to the complainant's satisfaction within five **business**	Ch.2, par.46			

(Continued)

183

Query	Source	Yes	No	N/A
days of the complaint being received; (ii) the regulated entity will provide the complainant with the name of one or more individuals appointed by the regulated entity to be the complainant's point of contact in relation to the **complaint** until the **complaint** is resolved or cannot be processed any further; (iii) the regulated entity will provide the complainant with a regular written update on the progress of the investigation of the **complaint** at intervals of not greater than 20 **business days**; (iv) the regulated entity will attempt to investigate and resolve a **complaint** within 40 **business days** of having received the **complaint**, where the 40 **business days** have elapsed and the **complaint** is not resolved, the regulated entity will inform the complainant of the anticipated timeframe within which the regulated entity hopes to resolve the **complaint** and of the **consumer's** right to refer the matter to the Financial Services Ombudsman or the Pensions Ombudsman, where relevant, and will provide the **consumer** with the contact details of such Ombudsman; and (v) the regulated entity will advise the complainant in writing, within 5 **business days** of the completion of the investigation of the **complaint**, of the outcome of the investigation, and, where applicable, explain the terms of any offer or settlement made and the regulated entity will also inform the complainant of the right to refer to matter to the Financial Services Ombudsman or the Pensions Ombudsman, where relevant, and will provide the **consumer** with the contact details of such Ombudsman?	Ch.2, par.46			
(59) Where the regulated entity receives a verbal complaint, does it offer the **consumer** the opportunity to have the **complaint** treated as a written **complaint**?	Ch.2, par.47			
(60) Does the regulated entity maintain an up-to-date **record** of all **complaints** subject to the complaints procedure and does this **record** contain the details of each **complaint**, a **record** of the regulated entity's response(s), any other relevant correspondence or **records** and the action taken to resolve each **complaint**	Ch.2, par.48			

(Continued)

184

Query	Source	Yes	No	N/A
Consumer Records (61) Does the regulated entity maintain up-to-date **consumer records** containing at least the following: (i) a copy of all documents required for **consumer** identification and profile; (ii) the **consumer's** contact details; (iii) all information and documents prepared in compliance with the Code; (iv) details of products and services provided to the **consumer**; (v) all correspondence with the **consumer** and details of any other information provided to the **consumer** in relation to the product or service; (vi) all documents or applications completed or signed by the **consumer**; (vii) copies of all original documents submitted by the **consumer** in support of an application for the provision of a service or product; and (viii) all other relevant information concerning the **consumer**; and are details of individual transactions retained for six years after the date of the transaction, with all other **records** required under (i) to (viii) above being retained for six years from the date a relationship ends; and are all such **consumer records** aforesaid complete and readily accessible (albeit not kept in a single location)?	Ch.2, par.49			
Fees, commissions and other rewards (62) Does the regulated entity pay a fee, commission, or other reward or remuneration only to a **person** that is: a regulated entity; a **certified person**; an individual for whom a regulated entity has taken full and unconditional responsibility; an entity specifically exempt by law from requiring authorisation; an authorised 'credit intermediary' (within the meaning of the Consumer Credit Act, 1995); or a financial services provider operating in Ireland in accordance with freedom of services or establishment provisions of European Union law?	Ch.2, par.50			
Conflicts of Interest (63) Where conflicts of interest arise and cannot be reasonably avoided, does the regulated entity undertake business with or on behalf of a **consumer** with whom it has directly or indirectly a conflicting interest, only where that **consumer** has acknowledged in writing that the said consumer is aware of the conflict of interest and that the said consumer still wants to proceed?	Ch.2, par.51			

(Continued)

185

Query	Source	Yes	No	N/A
(64) Does the regulated entity take reasonable steps to ensure that neither it nor any of its **officers** or **employees** offers, gives, solicits or accepts any **inducement** likely to conflict with any duties of the recipient or of the recipient's employer?	Ch.2, par.52			
(65) Does the regulated entity avoid entering into a **soft commission agreement** unless such agreement is in writing; does any business transacted under the **soft commission agreement** avoid conflicting with the best interests of the regulated entity's **consumers**; where a regulated entity considers that a **consumer** may be affected by a **soft commission agreement**, is the **consumer** made aware of the **soft commission agreement** and of how the **soft commission agreement** may affect such **consumer**; and is a copy of the **soft commission agreement** made available to the **consumer** on request?	Ch.2, par.53.			
(66) Are goods or services received by the regulated entity under a **soft commission agreement** used to assist in the provision of services to **consumers**?	Ch.2, par.54			
(67) Does the regulated entity provide to any affected **consumer** details of any changes in its policy on **soft commission agreements** promptly after implementation of any such changes?	Ch.2, par.55			
Chinese Walls (68) Does the regulated entity ensure that there are effective **Chinese walls** in place between the different business areas of the regulated entity and between the regulated entity and its **connected parties** in relation to information which could potentially give rise to a conflict of interest or be open to abuse, and are all procedures relating to the maintenance of **Chinese walls** and the consequences and breaches of **Chinese walls** in writing and notified to all relevant **officers** and **employees** of the regulated entity?	Ch.2, par.56			
Compliance with this Code (69) Does the regulated entity have adequate systems and controls in place to ensure compliance with the Consumer Protection Code?	Ch.2, par.57			

(Continued)

Query	Source	Yes	No	N/A
(70) Where the Financial Regulator has required a regulated entity to provide information in respect of the regulated entity's compliance with the Consumer Protection Code, has the regulated entity provided information which is full, fair and accurate in all respects and not misleading and has it done so in such reasonable period of time or format as may have been specified by the Financial Regulator?	Ch.2, par.58			
(71) Where the Financial Regulator has required information in respect of the regulated entity's compliance with the Consumer Protection Code and the Financial Regulator is of the opinion that a meeting with personnel of the regulated entity is necessary in order to procure such information in a satisfactory manner, has the regulated entity used its best endeavours to arrange for appropriate personnel to participate in such a meeting in order to provide the required information to the Financial Regulator?	Ch.2, par.59			
(72) Has the regulated entity, if so required by the Financial Regulator, provided to the Financial Regulator **records** evidencing compliance with the Consumer Protection Code for a period prior to such requirement as the Financial Regulator may specify (up to a maximum period of six years)?	Ch.2, par.60			

Banking Products and Services

Statements

Query	Source	Yes	No	N/A
(73) Does the regulated entity, if a **credit institution**, at least annually issue statements of transactions on all accounts with a balance in excess of _20 unless otherwise agreed with the **consumer** in writing and: (i) does the statement include details of the interest rates applied to the account during the period covered by the statement; (ii) is the statement issued to the **consumer's** last known postal address or made available to the **consumer** electronically if the **consumer** so requests; and (iii) where tax is deducted from interest paid, does the statement provide information on the tax deducted or inform **consumers** how they may obtain a certificate detailing the tax paid?	Ch.3, par.1			

(Continued)

Query	Source	Yes	No	N/A
Branch restructuring/Withdrawal of services (74) If the regulated entity, being a **credit institution** plans to close or move a branch, will it inform affected customers in writing at least three months in advance, and will it advise the Financial Regulator immediately of same, and will the wider local community also be informed, in advance, through notification in the local press?	Ch.3, par.2			
Changes in Interest Rates (75) Does the regulated entity, if a **credit institution**, ensure that when it announces a change in interest rates that the notification states clearly the date from which the changes will apply?	Ch.3, par.3			
(76) When the regulated entity, if a **credit institution**, changes the interest rate on accounts, does it update the information on information services, including any telephone help-lines and web-sites as soon as the change comes into effect?	Ch.3, par.4			
Accounts (77) Does the regulated entity, if a **credit institution**, advise customers who are subject to penalties, including interest surcharges, of the methods by which these penalties may be mitigated?	Ch.3, par.5			
(78) Does the regulated entity, if a **credit institution**, make available to existing deposit holding **consumers** details of the different interest rates that are applied to its other deposit accounts?	Ch.3, par.6			
(79) Does the regulated entity, if a **credit institution**, ensure that at least 10 days before the maturity of a fixed term deposit which has a minimum term of one year, it alerts the **consumer** about its impending maturity?	Ch.3, par.7			
(80) Does the regulated entity, if a **credit institution**, ensure that any funds lodged by a **consumer** to such **consumer's** account directly or via a **deposit agent** are credited to that account on that day?	Ch.3, par.8			
Joint Accounts (81) Does the regulated entity, if a **credit institution**, warn a **consumer**, before such **consumer** opens a joint account which permits full access and use of the funds in the account by either named party, of the consequences of opening and operating a joint account?	Ch.3, par.9			

(Continued)

Query	Source	Yes	No	N/A
(82) Does the regulated entity, if a **credit institution**, ascertain from the accountholders of a joint account any limitations that they wish to impose on the operations of the account?	Ch.3, par.10			
Deposit Agents				
(83) Does the regulated entity, if a **deposit agent**, avoid retaining in its possession an account passbook of a **consumer**?	Ch.3, par.11			
(84) Does the regulated entity, if a **deposit agent**, avoid operating from the same premises as a **deposit broker**?	Ch.3, par.12			
(85) When a deposit agency is terminated by either party, does the regulated entity, if a **deposit agent**: (i) notify its **consumers** of the termination; (ii) advise its **consumers** of the options available; and (iii) properly complete any outstanding business?	Ch.3, par.13			
Loans and Equity Release				
Unsolicited credit facilities				
(86) Does the regulated entity avoid offering pre-approved credit facilities?	Ch.4, par.1			
(87) Does the regulated entity only increase a **consumer's** credit card limit following a request from the **consumer**?	Ch.4, par.2			
Arrears and Guarantees				
(88) Where a loan is being advanced subject to a guarantee, does the guarantee outline the obligations of the guarantor and contain the following warning in a box, in bold type and of a font size that is larger than the normal font size used throughout the guarantee: Warning: As a guarantor of this loan, you will have to pay off the loan, the interest and all associated charges if the borrower does not. Before you sign this guarantee you should get independent legal advice?	Ch.4, par.3			
(89) If the terms of a loan agreement change, does the regulated entity notify the guarantor in writing?	Ch.4, par.4			
(90) Does the regulated entity have in place procedures for the handling of arrears cases?	Ch.4, par.5			
Payment protection insurance				
(91) If the regulated entity offers payment protection insurance in conjunction with a loan, is the initial repayment estimate of the loan advised to the **consumer** exclusive of the payment protection premium?	Ch.4, par.6			

(Continued)

189

Query	Source	Yes	No	N/A
(92) Where a combined application form is used, is all the information relating to payment protection insurance contained in a separate section and does this section also contain a requirement for the **consumer** to sign in order to apply for payment protection insurance?	Ch.4, par.7			
(93) Is a text box indicating that the payment protection insurance optional included in the application form immediately above where the **consumer** is required to sign?	Ch.4, par.8			
Non-mortgage personal lending (94) Prior to a loan being approved, does the regulated entity explain to a **consumer** the effect, if any, of missing any of the scheduled repayments and is this information highlighted in any relevant documentation and does the following notice also appear in a box, in bold type and of a font size that is larger than the normal font size used throughout the documentation: Warning: If you do not meet the repayments on your loan, your account will go into arrears. This may affect your credit rating?	Ch.4, par.9			
Mortgages (95) If a mortgage is offered to a **consumer** for the purpose of consolidating other loans or credit facilities, does the regulated entity provide a **consumer** with a written indicative comparison of the total cost of continuing with the existing facilities and the total cost of the consolidated facility on offer?	Ch.4, par.10			
(96) If a mortgage account is in arrears, does the regulated entity inform the **consumer** in writing of the status of the account as soon as possible after it becomes aware of the arrears and does this information include: (i) the date the mortgage fell into arrears; (ii) the number and total of payments missed; (iii) the amount of the arrears interest charged to date; (iv) the interest rate applicable to the arrears and details of other fees and **charges** used to calculate the arrears interest amount?	Ch.4, par.11			
(97) Does the regulated entity maintain a publicly accessible register of all **mortgage intermediaries** to which it has issued a current appointment?	Ch.4, par.12			

(Continued)

Query	Source	Yes	No	N/A
(98) Upon the termination of the appointment of any **mortgage intermediary**, does the regulated entity provide to the Financial Regulator a confirmation in writing that such **mortgage intermediary** has been removed from the register referred to above, together with details of the consequent amendment made to such register?	Ch.4, par.13			
(99) Before a mortgage can be drawn down, does the regulated entity, if a **mortgage intermediary**, submit to a mortgage lender a signed declaration that such **mortgage intermediary** has had sight of all original supporting documentation including bank statements, P60/certificate of earnings and other supporting documentation evidencing the **consumer's** identity and ability to repay?	Ch.4, par.14.			
(100) Does the regulated entity ensure that it has sight of an original valuation report before drawdown of funds?	Ch.4, par.15			

Lifetime Mortgages

Query	Source	Yes	No	N/A
(101) Does the regulated entity advise a **consumer** of the consequences of **equity release products** including details of the total costs involved, including all interest, **charges** and the effect on an existing mortgage, if any?	Ch.4, par.16			
(102) Does the regulated entity ensure that **consumers** are made aware of the importance of seeking independent legal advice?	Ch.4, par.17			
(103) Does the regulated entity include the following warning on any information document, application form or any other document given to a **consumer** in connection with an **equity release product** and does the warning appear in a box, in bold type and of a font size that is larger than the normal font size used throughout such document or form: "Warning: Purchasing this product may negatively impact on your ability to fund future needs?"	Ch.4, par.18			

Insurance Products and Services

Quotations, proposals and policy documentation

Query	Source	Yes	No	N/A
(104) Does the regulated entity, when providing a quote to a **consumer**, inform the **consumer** of the amount of the quotation and the length of time for which the quotation will be valid, assuming that all details provided by the **consumer** are correct and do not change?	Ch.5, par.1			

(Continued)

Query	Source	Yes	No	N/A
(105) Does the regulated entity express clearly in the quotation documents any warranties or endorsements and are these sections of the document detailed in print that is not smaller than the other information provided in the documents?	Ch.5, par.2			
(106) Does the regulated entity clearly identify any discounts or loadings applying to the policy at the quotation stage?	Ch.5, par.3			
(107) Does the regulated entity state the full legal name of the relevant underwriter on all quotations, policy documentation and renewal notices issued to any **consumer**?	Ch.5, par.4			
(108) Does the regulated entity explain to the **consumer** the consequences of failure to make full disclosure on the proposal form of such **consumer's** medical details or history?	Ch.5, par.5			
(109) Does the regulated entity, before completing a proposal form for a permanent insurance policy, explain to the **consumer** the meaning of disability, the benefit available under the policy and the reductions applied to the benefit where there are disability payments from other sources?	Ch.5, par.6			
(110) If the regulated entity provides serious illness policies, does it, before completing a proposal form, explain clearly to the **consumer** the restrictions, conditions and exclusions that attach to the policies?	Ch.5, par.7			
(111) Does the regulated entity issue policy documents to **consumers** within 10 **business days** of all relevant information being provided by the **consumer and** cover being underwritten?	Ch.5, par.8			
Disclosure				
(112) If the regulated entity offers financial services under a number of business names and product images or through any direct outlets, does it disclose, in all correspondence with **consumers**, the identity of the **group** to which it belongs?	Ch.5, par.9			
(113) If the regulated entity is an **insurance undertaking** that refuses to quote for motor insurance, does it, on request from the **consumer**: state its reasons in writing; and advise the **consumer** immediately of the **consumer's** right to refer the matter to the Declined Cases Committee of the Irish Insurance Federation and the method of doing so?	Ch.5, par.10			

(Continued)

Query	Source	Yes	No	N/A
(114) When a **consumer** advises a regulated entity of the intention to travel to another **Member State**, does the regulated entity provide the **consumer** with details of the regulated entity's appointed claims representative in that **Member State**?	Ch.5, par.11			
(115) In the event of an **insurance intermediary** retiring and the book of business being passed to another **insurance intermediary**, will all **consumers** be informed in writing of the option to decline to have their details transferred?	Ch.5, par.12			
(116) Where a secondary market exists for a life policy, and when the holder of such policy seeks information on its early surrender, does the regulated entity divulge to the holder, at the same time as it discloses the surrender value of the policy, that this secondary market exists and that the policy may be sold on it?	Ch.5, par.13			
Claims Processing (The questions under this heading do not apply to health insurers where a method of direct settlement is used.)				
(117) Does the regulated entity take reasonable steps to verify the validity of a claim before making a decision on its outcome?				
(118) Does the regulated entity have in place a written procedure for the effective and proper handling of claims and, at a minimum, does the procedure provide that: (i) a potential **claimant** is provided with information on how to make a claim, including, where applicable, full details of the **Personal Injuries Assessment Board** process and the manner in which the potential **claimant** can deal with the **Personal Injuries Assessment Board** and what the potential **claimant's** responsibilities are in relation to a claim; (ii) where a claim form is required to be completed, it is issued within five **business days** of receiving notice of a claim; (iii) the regulated entity must offer to assist in the process of making the claim; (iv) details of all conversations with the **claimant** in relation to the claim are noted; (v) the regulated entity must, while the claim is ongoing, provide the **claimant** with updates of any developments affecting the outcome of the claim within 10 **business days** of the development and that when additional documentation or clarification is required from the **claimant**, the **claimant** must be advised of this at an early stage of writing and, if necessary, issued with a reminder?	Ch.5, par.15			

(Continued)

Query	Source	Yes	No	N/A
(119) If the regulated entity is an **insurance inter-mediary** that assists a **consumer** completing a claim, does it, on receipt of completed claims documentation, transmit such documentation to the regulated entity without delay?	Ch.5, par.16			
(120) If there is a requirement to engage the services of a loss adjuster and/or expert appraiser, does the regulated entity inform the **claimant** of the contact details of the loss adjuster and/or expert appraiser it has appointed to assist in the processing of the claim and that such loss adjuster and/or expert appraiser acts in the interests of the regulated entity?	Ch.5, par.17			
(121) Does the regulated entity inform the **claimant** that the claimant may appoint a loss assessor to act in the claimant's interests and that any such appointment shall be at the **claimant's** expense?	Ch.5, par.18			
(122) Is the regulated entity available to confer with a **claimant** in relation to a claim and to discuss assessment of liability and damages during normal office hours or outside those hours if agreed with the **claimant**?	Ch.5, par.19			
(123) Does the regulated entity, within 10 **business days** of the making of a decision in respect of a claim, advise the **claimant** in writing of the outcome of the investigation explaining the terms of any offer of settlement and, if the claim is denied, provide to the **claimant**, in writing, the reasons for the denial?	Ch.5, par.20			
(124) Where the policyholder will not be the beneficiary of the settlement amount, will the policyholder be advised in writing by the regulated entity of the final outcome of the claim, including any details of the settlement amount paid and, where applicable, will the policyholder be informed that settlement of the claim will affect future insurance contracts of that type?	Ch.5, par.21			
(125) Does the regulated entity provide a **claimant** with written details of any internal appeals mechanisms available to the **claimant**?	Ch.5, par.22			
(126) Does the regulated entity pay all claims to a **claimant** within 10 **business days** once the following conditions are satisfied: (i) the insured event has been proven; (ii) all specified documentation has been received by the regulated entity from the **claimant**; (iii) the entitlement of the **claimant** to receive payment	Ch.5, par.23			

(Continued)

194

Query	Source	Yes	No	N/A
under the policy has been established; (iv) the appropriate amount has been agreed subject to finalisation of legal costs, where applicable?				
Premium Handling (127) Does the regulated entity, if an **insurance intermediary**, lodge money it receives in respect of a premium or a premium rebate to a segregated bank account, each such account being designated 'Client Premium Account'?	Ch.5, par.24			
(128) Does the regulated entity, if an **insurance intermediary**, operate separate **client premium accounts** in respect of life and non-life business?	Ch.5, par.25			
(129) Do all payment instructions used to make payments from a **client premium account** clearly state that the payment emanated from a **client premium account**?	Ch.5, par.26			
(130) Is it the case that a **client premium account** is never overdrawn?	Ch.5, par.27			
(131) Does the regulated entity ensure that the following are the only debits and credits passed through a **client premium account**: (A) (Credits (money in)) (i) money received from **consumers** in respect of the renewal of a policy which has been invited by an **insurance undertaking**, or a proposal for insurance accepted by an **insurance undertaking**; (ii) money received from a regulated entity representing premium rebated for onward transmission to the **consumer**; (iii) transfers from another **client premium account** operated by the **insurance intermediary** for the same form of insurance; (iv) transfers from the **insurance intermediary's** office account to allow a 'buffer' amount to be maintained in the **client premium account** (any such transfers being clearly identifiable); (v) proceeds received from a regulated entity in respect of the settlement of a claim for onward transmission to the **claimant**; (vi) bank interest, if appropriate; (vii) where mixed remittances are received, the total amount is first lodged to the appropriate **client premium account**; (B) (Debits (money out)) (i) money paid to a regulated entity on foot of renewal of a policy, which has been accepted by an **insurance undertaking**, or a proposal, accepted by an **insurance undertaking**; (ii) money paid to a **consumer** representing rebates of premiums received	Ch.5, par.28			

(*Continued*)

Query	Source	Yes	No	N/A
from **insurance undertakings**; (iii) commissions and fees paid to the **insurance intermediary** for which there is documentary proof that the funds are properly due to the **insurance intermediary**; (iv) transfers to another **client premium account** operated by the **insurance intermediary** for the same form of insurance; (v) payments of claims settlement amounts to a **consumer**; (vi) bank interest, if appropriate; and (vii) the portion of mixed remittances that does not relate to a premium payment (such remittances should be transferred to, or to the order of, the **consumer** without delay)?				
(132) Does the regulated entity, if an **insurance intermediary**, carry out and retain, on a monthly basis, a detailed reconciliation of amounts due to regulated entities with the balance on each **client premium account** it operates?	Ch.5, par.29			
Premium Rebates				
(133) Does the regulated entity transfer any premium rebate to a **consumer** within five **business days** of the rebate becoming due?	Ch.5, par.30			
(134) Does the regulated entity, if an **insurance intermediary**, handle premium rebates due to **consumers** only where an express agreement exists whereby the **insurance intermediary** acts as an agent of the regulated entity in passing rebates to **consumers** so that in handling the rebated premium the **insurance intermediary** does not become a debtor of the **consumer**?	Ch.5, par.31			
(135) Does the regulated entity, if an **insurance intermediary**, transfer a premium rebate to a **consumer** within five **business days** after receiving payment of such rebate amount from a regulated entity or being notified by a regulated entity that such premium rebate is due to the **consumer**, as applicable?	Ch.5, par.32			
(136) Does the regulated entity, if an **insurance intermediary**, transfer any rebate amount to a **consumer** in full, with any **charges** that such **consumer** may owe the intermediary not being recovered from the rebate amount due to such **consumer** without the prior written agreement of such **consumer**?	Ch.5, par.33			

(Continued)

196

Query	Source	Yes	No	N/A
Investment Products (137) Does the regulated entity issue a statement of **investment product transactions** for each **investment product** held with it at least on an annual basis, either on an actual basis in respect of the previous 12-month period or on a forecast basis in respect of the next 12-month period, unless otherwise agreed in writing, with the **consumer**, such statements including, at a minimum: (i) the opening balance or value; (ii) all additions or withdrawals in the relevant 12-month period; (iii) the total sum invested in the relevant 12-month period; (iv) a closing balance or statement of the value of the investment; and (v) all **charges** and deductions affecting the **investment product** including any **charges** associated with the management, selling, set up and ongoing administration of the **investment product**?	Ch.6, par.1			
(138) Does the regulated entity provide **consumers** with pre-sale product information specific to that **consumer** that contains an estimation of the **investment product's** value after tax, at the end of year 1, 2, 3, 4, 5, 10, 15 and 20 (where applicable) assuming realistic growth rates.	Ch.6, par.2			
(139) Does the regulated entity ensure that all illustrations contained in **investment product** documentation are shown pre- and post-any tax deduction due on surrender or encashment of the **investment product**?	Ch.6, par.3			
(140) Does the regulated entity include the following statement with all illustrations (in a box, in bold type and of a font size that is larger than the normal font size used throughout the relevant document): "Warning: These figures are estimates only. They are not a reliable guide to the future performance of your investment?"	Ch.6, par.4			
(141) Does the regulated entity record and retain in a readily accessible form, the date of both receipt and transmission of any of the following: (i) an instruction to the regulated entity from a **consumer** to effect an **investment product transaction** as agent; (ii) any other instruction to the regulated entity from a **consumer** to effect an **investment product transaction** in similar circumstances as those arising on an instruction to effect an **investment product transaction** as an agent; (iii) a decision by the regulated entity in the exercise of its discretion for the **consumer** with respect to an **investment product**?	Ch.6, par.5			

(Continued)

Query	Source	Yes	No	N/A
(142) Does the regulated entity avoid advising a **consumer** to carry out an **investment product transaction** or a series of **investment product transactions**, with a frequency or in amounts to the extent that those **investment product transactions**, when taken together, are deemed to be excessive and/or detrimental to the **consumer's** best interests, and does the regulated entity make a contemporaneous **record** that it has advised the **consumer** that in its opinion the **investment product transaction(s)** are excessive, if the **consumer** wishes to proceed with the **investment product transaction**?	Ch.6, par.6			
(143) Where a prospectus, other than a prospectus falling within the scope of the Prospectus Directive (2003/71/EC) represents or contains the terms of a contract between the regulated entity and one or more of its **consumers**, is this fact clearly stated in the prospectus?	Ch.6, par.7			
Tracker Bonds (144) Does the regulated entity provide the following information in a prominent position in a **tracker bond** product brochure, if any, and on a **tracker bond** application form with the exception of (iv) below, (in a box, in bold type and of a font size that is larger than the normal font size used throughout the brochure or form, as appropriate): (i) for investments in products that do not promise the 100 percent return of a **consumer's** capital on maturity, the following statement, 'Warning: The value of your investment may go down as well as up. You may get back less than you put in.'; (ii) where the promised return is known but is less than the initial 100 percent invested, the following statement, 'Warning: If you invest in this product you could lose xx% of the money you put in.'; (iii) if the promised 'return of capital' is only applicable on a specific date, this date and the following statement, 'Warning: If you cash in your investment before (specify the particular date) you may lose some or all of the money you put in'; and (iv) the name of the ultimate provider of any guarantee?	Ch.6, par.8			

(Continued)

Query	Source	Yes	No	N/A
(145) Does the regulated entity provide a **consumer**, before the consumer sign an application form for a tracker bond, with a 'Key Features Document' of a type referred to in the Appendix to Chapter 6 of the Consumer Protection Code? (Where information required by the Key Features Document is already provided to the **consumer** under a legal requirement to do so, the regulated entity is not required to include that information in the Key Features Document).	Ch.6, par.9			
(146) Does the regulated entity provide a **consumer** who has invested in a **tracker bond** with a document within two **business days** of the start of a fund, setting out: (i) the name and address of the **consumer**; (ii) the date of investment; (iii) the amount of the investment; (iv) the date/s on which the promised minimum payment is payable; (v) disclosure of the make-up of the investment, if the make-up differs from that shown in the Key Features Document referred to above; and (vi) the date the investment will mature?	Ch.6, par.10			
(147) Where the regulated entity shows an illustration of the projected\return on investment of a **tracker bond**, is the value of the total return expressed and shown as prominently as the equivalent **compound annual rate**?	Ch.6, par.11.			
(148) Does the regulated entity avoid providing an illustration of an investment of a **tracker bond** to a **consumer** where the illustration shows the return that investment could have provided over any prior investment period?	Ch.6, par.12			
(149) Where the regulated entity offers a **consumer** the facility to borrow funds to invest in a **tracker bond**, does the regulated entity give the **consumer** an illustration showing: (i) the year-by-year and total interest payments the **consumer** is likely to have to pay in respect of the funds borrowed to invest in the **tracker bond** until the date the product matures (for this purpose the fixed interest rate offered by the lender for the period to the date of the promised payment under the **tracker bond** should only be used; where the lender does not offer a fixed interest rate over this period, an equivalent open market fixed interest rate should be used for this purpose); (ii) prominently, the **compound annual rate** equivalent of the promised payment under the relevant **tracker bond**; (iii) the difference between the promised should only be used; where the lender does not offer a	Ch.6, par.13			

(Continued)

Query	Source	Yes	No	N/A
fixed interest rate over this period, an equivalent open market fixed interest rate should be used for this purpose); (ii) prominently, the **compound annual rate** equivalent of the promised payment under the relevant **tracker bond**; (iii) the difference between the promised payment under the **tracker bond** and the total projected outgoings of the **consumer** (i.e. interest payments related to the funds borrowed to invest, any capital repayments related to such borrowings and any capital investment by the **consumer** other than the borrowed funds) over the period to the date of the promised payment under the **tracker bond**?				
Advertising (Note: the required warnings prescribed in Chapter 7 do not apply if an **advertisement** does not refer to the benefits of a product but only invites a **consumer** to discuss the product or service in more detail with a regulated entity). (Consumer Protection Code, Chapter 7, par. 16).				
General Requirements (150) Does the regulated entity ensure that all its **advertisements** are fair and not misleading?	Ch, 7, par.1			
(151) If the regulated entity is publishing an **advertisement**, does the **advertisement** avoid influencing a **consumer's** attitude to the **advertised product or service** or the regulated entity either by inaccuracy, ambiguity, exaggeration or omission?	Ch, 7, par.2			
(152) If the regulated entity is publishing an **advertisement**, is the name of the regulated entity publishing an **advertisement** clearly shown in all **advertisements**?	Ch.7, par.3			
(153) If the regulated entity is publishing an **advertisement**, is the nature or type of the **advertised product or service** clear and not disguised in any way?	Ch, 7, par.4			
(154) If the regulated entity is publishing an **advertisement**, is the **advertisement** designed and presented so that any reasonable **consumer** knows immediately that it is an **advertisement**?	Ch, 7, par.5			
(155) If the regulated entity is publishing an **advertisement**, does the design and presentation of an **advertisement** allow it to be clearly understood and where small print or footnotes are used are they of sufficient size and prominence to be clearly legible (and, where appropriate, are they linked to the relevant part of the main copy)?	Ch, 7, par.6			

(Continued)

Query	Source	Yes	No	N/A
(156) If the regulated entity is publishing an **advertisement**, are warnings and product specific information clear and not obscured or disguised in any way by the content, design or format of the **advertisement**?	Ch, 7, par.7			
(157) If the regulated entity is publishing an **advertisement** and the **advertisement** uses promotional or introductory rates and the **advertisement** is not for a loan for which the promotional rate is for a period of less than one year, does the **advertisement** clearly state the expiry date of the promotional/introductory rate and provide an indication of the rate that will apply thereafter?	Ch, 7, par.8			
(158) If the regulated entity is publishing an **advertisement**, is any statement contained in the **advertisement** true and not misleading at the time it is made, and are any assumptions on which it is based reasonable and stated clearly?	Ch, 7, par.9			
(159) If the regulated entity is publishing an **advertisement**, is any forecast contained in the **advertisement** not misleading at the time it is made and are any assumptions on which it is based reasonable and stated clearly?	Ch, 7, par.10			
(160) If the regulated entity is publishing an **advertisement**, does the **advertisement** avoid being misleading in relation to: (i) the regulated entity's independence or the independence of the information it provides; (ii) the regulated entity's ability to provide the **advertised product or service**; (iii) the scale of the regulated entity's activities; (iv) the extent of the resources of the regulated entity; (v) the nature of the regulated entity's or any other **person's** involvement in the **advertised product or service**; (vi) the scarcity of the **advertised product or service**; (vii) past performance or possible future performance of the **advertised product or service**?	Ch, 7, par.11			
(161) If the regulated entity is publishing an **advertisement** and the **advertisement** promotes more than one product, does the **advertisement** set out clearly the different features of each product in such a way that the **consumer** could distinguish between the products?	Ch, 7, par.12			
(162) If the regulated entity is publishing an **advertisement**, are any recommendations or commendations quoted, complete, fair, accurate and not misleading at the time of issue, and relevant to the **advertised product or service**?	Ch, 7, par.13			

(*Continued*)

Query	Source	Yes	No	N/A
(163) If the regulated entity is publishing an **advertisement** and a recommendation or commendation is used, is it used with the consent of the author and, if the author is an **employee** of the regulated entity or a **connected party** of the regulated entity or has received any payment from the regulated entity or a **connected party** of the regulated entity for the recommendation or commendation, does the **advertisement** state this fact?	Ch, 7, par.14			
(164) If the regulated entity is publishing an **advertisement** and comparisons or contrasts are used, are these based either on facts verified by the regulated entity or on reasonable assumptions stated within the **advertisement**, are they presented in a fair and balanced way, do they avoid omitting anything material to the comparison or contrast, and are material differences between products set out clearly?	Ch, 7, par.15			

Lending

Query	Source	Yes	No	N/A
(165) If the regulated entity is publishing an **advertisement** and the **advertisement** includes an annual percentage rate, does the **advertisement** clearly state whether the underlying interest rate is fixed or variable?	Ch.7, par.17			
(166) If the regulated entity is publishing an **advertisement** and the **advertisement** is for a term loan and displays the annual percentage rate and return, does it display the total cost of credit?	Ch.7, par.18			
(167) If the regulated entity is publishing an **advertisement** and the **advertisement** is for a fixed-rate loan, does it, where applicable, state (in a box, in bold type and of a font size that is larger than the normal font size used throughout the **advertisement**): 'Warning: You may have to pay charges if you pay off a fixed-rate loan early.'	Ch.7, par.19			
(168) If the regulated entity is publishing an **advertisement** and the **advertisement** is for the consolidation of two or more debts, and sample figures are offered in the **advertisement**, does the **advertisement** indicate the difference between the total cost of credit of the consolidated mortgage and the total cost of credit of the individual debts that are the subject of consideration?	Ch.7, par.20			
(169) If the regulated entity is publishing an **advertisement** and the **advertisement** is for a debt consolidation mortgage, does it carry the following warning (in a box, in bold type and of a font size that is larger than the normal font size used throughout	Ch.7, par.21			

(Continued)

Query	Source	Yes	No	N/A
the **advertisement**): 'Warning: This new loan may take longer to pay off than your previous loans. This means you may pay more than if you paid over a shorter term.'				
(170) If the regulated entity is publishing an **advertisement** and the **advertisement** is for a variable-rate residential mortgage, does it carry the following warning (in a box, in bold type and of a font size that is larger than the normal font size used throughout the **advertisement**): 'Warning: The cost of your monthly repayments may increase — If you do not keep up your repayments you may lose your home.'	Ch.7, par.22			
(171) If the regulated entity is publishing an **advertisement** and the **advertisement** offers goods on hire purchase, does it carry the following warning (in a box, in bold type and of a font size that is larger than the normal font size used throughout the **advertisement**): 'Warning: You will not own these goods until the final payment is made.'	Ch.7, par.23			
(172) If the regulated entity is publishing an **advertisement** and a free banking period is advertised, is the period for which the free banking applies clearly stated?	Ch.7, par.24			
(173) If the regulated entity is publishing an **advertisement** and (a) the **advertisement** is for an interest-only mortgage, does it carry the following warning: 'Warning: The entire amount that you have borrowed will still be outstanding at the end of the interest-only period.'; (b) the **advertisement** is for an **equity release product,** does if contain the following warning: 'Warning: Purchasing this product may negatively impact on your ability to fund future needs; and is any such warning in a box, in bold type and of a font size that is larger than the normal font size used throughout the **advertisement**?	Ch.7, par.25			
Savings and Investments				
(174) If the regulated entity is publishing an **advertisement** and the interest rate for a savings or deposit account is displayed therein, does it clearly state the following: (i) whether the rate quoted is variable or fixed, and, if fixed, for what period; (ii) the relevant interest rate for each term quoted together with the equivalent annual rate for each rate quoted, with each rate being given equal prominence; (iii) the minimum term and/or minimum amount required to qualify for a specified rate of interest, if applicable; and (iv) whether any tax is payable on the interest earned?	Ch.7, par.26			

(Continued)

Query	Source	Yes	No	N/A
(175) If the regulated entity is publishing an **advertisement,** containing information about the part performance of the **advertised product or service** or of the regulated entity, is/does (as appropriate) such information: (i) based on a product similar to that being advertised; (ii) <u>not</u> selected so as to exaggerate the success or disguise the lack of success of the **advertised product or service**; (iii) state its source; (iv) based on actual performance; (v) state clearly the period chosen (which period must be related to the term of the product being advertised; where that term is open-ended the longest term available should be included); (vi) include the most recent period; (vii) indicate, where they arise, details of transaction costs, interest and taxation that have been taken into account; and (viii) state, where applicable, the basis upon which performance is quoted?	Ch.7, par.27			
(176) If the regulated entity is publishing an **advertisement** and the advertisement contains information on past performance, does it contain the following warning (in a box, in bold type and of a font size that is larger than the normal font size used throughout the **advertisement**): 'Warning: Past performance is not a reliable guide to future performance.'	Ch.7, par.28			
(177) If the regulated entity is publishing an **advertisement** and the regulated entity has a position or holding in a product the subject of an **advertisement**, does it include a statement to this effect in the **advertisement**?	Ch.7, par.29			
(178) If the regulated entity is publishing an **advertisement**, containing information about the simulated performance of the **advertised product or service** or of the regulated entity is/does (as appropriate) such information: (i) based on a simulated performance that is relevant to the performance of the **advertised product or service** or of the regulated entity; (ii) <u>not</u> been selected so as to exaggerate the success or disguise the lack of success of the **advertised product or service** or of the regulated entity; (iii) state the source; and (iv) indicate whether, and to what extent transaction costs, interest and taxation have been taken into account?	Ch.7, par.30			

(Continued)

204

Query	Source	Yes	No	N/A
(179) If the regulated entity is publishing an **advertisement** and the **advertisement** contains information on simulated performance, does it carry the following warning (in a box, in bold type and of a font size that is larger than the normal font size used throughout the **advertisement**): 'Warning: These figures are estimates only. They are not a reliable guide to the future performance of this investment.'	Ch.7, par.31			
(180) If the regulated entity is publishing an **advertisement** and the **advertisement** describes a product or investment as guaranteed or partially guaranteed: (i) is there a legally enforceable agreement with a third party who undertakes to meet, to whatever extent is stated in the **advertisement**, the **consumer's** claim under the guarantee; (ii) has the regulated entity made, and can it demonstrate that it has made, an assessment of the value of the guarantee; (iii) does the **advertisement** give details about both the guarantor and guarantee sufficient for a **consumer** to make a fair assessment about the value of the guarantee; and (iv) where it is the case, does the **advertisement** state that the guarantee is from a **connected party** of the regulated entity?	Ch.7, par.32			
(181) If the regulated entity is publishing an **advertisement** and the **advertisement** contains a reference to the impact of taxation, does it: (i) state the assumed rate of taxation; (ii) state, where applicable, that the tax reliefs are those currently applying, and state the value of the tax reliefs referred to in the **advertisement** apply directly to the **consumer**, to the provider of the **advertised product or service** or its provider, as appropriate; (iii) state, where applicable, that the matters referred to are only relevant to a particular class or classes of **consumer** with particular tax liabilities, identifying the class or classes of **consumer** and the type of liabilities concerned; (iv) state who has the responsibility for obtaining the tax benefits advertised; (v) avoid describing the **advertised product or service** as being free from any liability to income tax unless equal prominence is given to a statement, where applicable, that the income is payable from a product from which income tax has already been paid; and (vi) avoid describing the **advertised product or service** as being free from any liability to capital	Ch.7, par.33			

(Continued)

Query	Source	Yes	No	N/A
taxation unless equal prominence is given to a statement, where applicable, that the value of the **advertised product or service** is linked to a product which is liable to capital taxation?				
(182) If the regulated entity is publishing an **advertisement** and the product that is the subject of **advertisement** can fluctuate in price or value, does the **advertisement** carry the following warning (in a box, in bold type and of a font size that is larger than the normal font size used throughout the **advertisement**): 'Warning: The value of your investment may go down as well as up.'	Ch.7, par.34			
(183) If the regulated entity is publishing an **advertisement** and the return on an **advertised product or service** is not set until a particular date (e.g. the maturity date of the **advertised product or service**), is this clearly stated?	Ch.7, par.35			
(184) If the regulated entity is publishing an **advertisement** and the product that is the subject of **advertisement** is described as being likely to yield income or as being suitable for a **consumer** particularly seeking income and the income from such product can fluctuate, does the **advertisement** carry the following warning (in a box, in bold type and of a font size that is larger than the normal font size used throughout the **advertisement**): 'Warning: The income you get from this investment may go down as well as up.'	Ch.7, par.36			
(185) If the regulated entity is publishing an **advertisement**, and a product the subject of an **advertisement** offers the facility of a planned withdrawal from capital as an income equivalent, has the regulated entity ensured that the effect of such a withdrawal upon such product is clearly explained in the **advertisement**?	Ch.7, par.37			
(186) If the regulated entity is publishing an **advertisement** and the **advertised product or service** is denominated or priced in a foreign currency or the value of an **advertised product or service** may be directly affected by changes in foreign exchange rates, does the **advertisement** carry the following warning (in a box, in bold type and of a font size that is larger than the normal font size used throughout the **advertisement**): 'Warning: This [product/service] may be affected by changes in currency exchange rates.'	Ch.7, par.38			

(*Continued*)

Query	Source	Yes	No	N/A
(187) If the regulated entity is publishing an **advertisement** and the **advertisement** is for a product that is not readily realisable, does the **advertisement** state that it may be difficult for **consumers** to sell or exit the product and/or obtain reliable information about its value or extent of the risks to which it is exposed?	Ch.7, par.39			
(188) If the regulated entity is publishing an **advertisement** and the **advertisement** is for a product that cannot be encashed prior to maturity or which incurs an early redemption charge, does the **advertisement** state clearly that this is the case?	Ch.7, par.40			
(189) If the regulated entity is publishing an **advertisement** and the **advertisement** is for a product subject to front-end loading, (i) does the **advertisement** state that deductions for **charges** and expenses are not made uniformly throughout the life of the product, but are loaded disproportionately onto the very early period; (ii) does the **advertisement** warn the **consumer** that if the **consumer** withdraws from the product in the early period, the practice of front-end loading will impact on the amount of money which the **consumer** receives; and (iii) if applicable, does the **advertisement** state that a **consumer** may not get back the amount they invest?	Ch.7, par.41			

DEFINITIONS OF TERMS EMPLOYED IN CONSUMER PROTECTION CODE CHECKLIST

In the Consumer Protection Code, and hence in the preceding checklist, the following terms bear the following meanings[1]:

- **advertisement** means any commercial communication usually paid for by a **regulated entity**, which is addressed to the **consumer** public or a section of it, the purpose being to advertise a product, service or regulated entity the subject of the Code, excluding name plaques, sponsorship material and a prospectus drawn up in accordance with the Prospectus Directive (2003/71/EC);
- **advertised product or service** means the product or service that is the subject of an **advertisement**;
- **associate** in relation to a **person** means: (a) an undertaking in the same **group** as that **person**; (b) any other **person** whose business, private or familial relationship with the first person or its **associate** might reasonably be expected to give rise to a community of interest between them which may involve a conflict of interest in

[1] *Cf.* Consumer Protection Code, Definitions Chapter, 3-6 (inclusive) and Addendum to Consumer Protection Code, 5.

dealings with third parties; or (c) any other **person** whose business, private or familial relationship (other than as arises solely because that **person** is a **client** of the firm) with the first person is such that he or she has influence over that **person's** judgment as to how to invest his property or exercise any rights attaching to his investments;

– **associated undertaking** means an associated undertaking within the meaning of Regulation 34 of the European Communities (Companies Group Accounts) Regulations 1992;

– **basic banking product or service** means a current account, overdraft, ordinary deposit account or a term deposit account with a term of less than one year;

– **business day** means any day except Saturday, Sunday, bank holidays and public holidays;

– **certified person** has the meaning assigned to it by s 55 of the Investment Intermediaries Act, 1995;

– **charges** means any cost or fee which a **consumer** must pay in connection with a product or service provided by a regulated entity;

– **Chinese walls** means an arrangement within the organisation of the regulated entity (or between the-regulated entity and any **associate** of that regulated entity) which requires information held by the regulated entity (or as the case may be, **associate** or a particular operating unit within the regulated entity or **associate** in the course of carrying on one part of its business of any kind) to be withheld in certain circumstances from other operating units or from persons with whom it deals in the course of carrying on another part of its business of any kind;

– **claimant** means a person making a claim under an insurance policy entered into by a **consumer**;

– **client premium account** means the account required under Requirement 24 of Chapter 5 of the Code (and referred to in Q.127 of the checklist);

– **complaint** refers to an expression of grievance or dissatisfaction by a **consumer**, either verbally or in writing, in connection with: (a) the provision of a product or service to a **consumer** by a regulated entity, or (b) the failure of a **regulated entity** to provide a service to a **consumer**.

– **compound annual rate** means the equivalent annual rate of interest, payable at the end of the year, on a deposit;

– **connected party**, except where otherwise stated, includes a partner, **officer**, controller, **associated undertaking**, **related undertaking** or subsidiary undertaking or **employee** of the regulated entity, including any **associate** of the **person** concerned;

– **consumer** means any of the following: (a) a natural **person** acting outside their business, trade or profession; (b) a **person** or **group** of **persons**, but not an incorporated body with an annual turnover in excess of €3 million (for the avoidance of doubt a **group** of **persons** includes partnerships and other unincorporated bodies such as clubs, charities and trusts, not consisting entirely of bodies corporate); (c) incorporated bodies having an annual turnover of €3 million or less in the previous financial year (provided that such body shall not be a member of a **group** of companies having a combined turnover greater than the said €3 million); or (d) a member of a credit union; and includes where appropriate, a potential '**consumer**' (within the meaning above);

– **credit institution** means the holder of an authorisation issued by the Financial Regulator or by a competent authority of another **Member State** for the purposes of EU Directive 2000/12/EC relating to the taking up and pursuit of the business of credit institutions;

– **customer** means any **person** to whom a regulated entity provides or offers to provide a service the subject of this Code, and any **person** who requests such a service;

– **default investment strategy** has the meaning in Part X of the Pensions Act 1990;

– **deposit agent** means any **person** who holds an appointment in writing from a single **credit institution** enabling him to receive deposits on behalf of that institution and prohibiting him from acting in a similar capacity on behalf of another **credit institution**;

– **deposit broker** means any **person** who brings together with **credit institutions persons** seeking to make deposits in return for a fee, commission or other reward;

– **equity release product** means a **lifetime mortgage** or a **home reversion agreement**;

– **employee** means a **person** employed under a contract of service or a **person** otherwise employed by a regulated entity;

– **group** includes a company, its parent and its subsidiaries and any **associated undertaking** or **related undertakings**;

– **home reversion agreement** has the meaning given that term in Part V of the Central Bank Act 1997;

– **inducement** means any gifts or rewards (monetary or otherwise) provided to a regulated entity but does not include: (a) disclosable commission; or (b) goods or services which can reasonably be expected to assist in the provision of services to **consumers** and which are provided or are to be provided under a **soft commission agreement**;

– **insurance intermediary** has the meaning in the European Communities (Insurance Mediation) Regulations 2005;

– **insurance undertaking** has the meaning in the Insurance Act 1989;

– **investment product** means: (a) a deposit with a term equal to or greater than one year; or (b) an investment instrument" within the meaning of s 2 of the Investment Intermediaries Act, 1995 but does not include: (i) insurance policies; and (ii) instruments listed in s C of Annex I of EU Directive 2004/39/EC;

– **investment product transaction** means: (a) the purchase or sale by a firm of an **investment product**; (b) the subscription for an **investment product**; (c) the underwriting of an **investment product**; (d) the placing or withdrawal of a deposit in relation to a), b), or c) above;

– **"lifetime mortgage"** means a loan secured on a borrower's home where: (a) interest payments are rolled up on top of the capital throughout the term of the loan; (b) the loan is repaid from the proceeds of the sale of the property; and (c) the borrower retains ownership of their home whilst living in it;

– **Member State** means a Member State of the European Economic Area;

– **mortgage intermediary** has the meaning specified in s 2 of the Consumer Credit Act, 1995;

– **MiFID Service** means any service or activity set out in Annex I of EU Directive 2004/39/EC, but not including any service or activity of a person to whom such Directive does not apply by virtue of Article 3 of such Directive;

- **officer** in relation to a regulated entity, means a director, chief executive, manager or secretary, by whatever name called;
- **outsourced activity** is where a regulated entity employs another **person** (other than a natural person who is an **employee** of the regulated entity under a contract of service) to carry out the activity on its behalf;
- **person** means a natural person or a legal person;
- **Personal Injuries Assessment Board** means the board known as such established under the Personal Injuries Assessment Board Act 2003, or any successor thereto;
- **protection policies** for the purposes of the Code include the following: (a) insurances of a class falling within the European Communities (Non-Life Insurance) Framework Regulations 1994; and (b) insurances of classes I, III and IV as set out in Annex I of the European Communities (Life Assurance) Framework Regulations 1994 where the purpose and intention of the policy is solely to provide protection;
- **PRSA** has the meaning in Part X of the Pensions Act 1990;
- **record** means any document, file or information (whether stored electronically or otherwise) and which is capable of being reproduced in a legible form;
- **regulated activities** means services of a financial or investment nature that are subject to the regulation of the Financial Regulator;
- **regulated entity** means a person who carries on a business of providing one or more regulated activities;
- **related undertaking** means: (a) companies related within the meaning of s 140(5) of the Companies Act 1990; (b) undertakings where the business of those undertakings has been so carried on that the separate business of each undertaking, or a substantial part thereof, is not readily identifiable; or (c) undertakings where the decision as to how and by whom each shall be managed can be made either by the same **person** or by the same **group** of **persons** acting in concert;
- **soft commission agreement** means any agreement under which a regulated entity receives goods or services, in return for which it agrees to direct business through or in the way of another **person**;
- **standard PRSA** has the meaning in Part X of the Pensions Act 1990;
- **terms of business** means the document in which a regulated entity sets out the basis on which it will conduct business with **consumers**;
- **tracker bond** means a deposit or life assurance policy which contains the following features: (a) a minimum payment, at the expiration of a specified period of time, of a specified percentage of the amount of capital invested by the **consumer** in the product; and (b) a potential cash bonus payable after a specified period of time, which is linked to, or determined by, changes over the period of investment in the level of one or more recognised stock market indices, commodity prices, any other recognised financial indices or the price of one or more securities specified at the outset or from time to time.

Appendix D

ASAI CODE OF STANDARDS CHECKLIST

The checklist that appears in this Appendix, as compiled by the author of this book, seeks to reduce the ASAI Code of Standards, insofar as it is relevant to financial advertisements generally, to a series of questions. The questions have been drafted so that a 'Yes' answer suggests compliance with the ASAI Code of Standards and a 'No' answer suggests non-compliance. Certain terms used in the checklist are terms that bear a defined meaning when used in the ASAI Code of Standards and when used in this checklist. Where a term used in the checklist is a defined term, it appears in **Bold** format, with the definition appearing in the appendix to this checklist.

Before proceeding to the detail of the checklist it is prudent to consider whether the Code of Standards applies at all.

The Code of Standards applies to "(a) **marketing communications** in newspapers, magazines and other printed publications, including 'free sheets'; (b) **marketing communications** in posters and other promotional media in public places, including moving images; (c) **marketing communications** in brochures, leaflets, circulars, mailings, fax transmissions, e-mails and text transmissions; (d) **marketing communications** broadcast on television or radio or screened in cinemas; (e) **marketing communications** carried on electronic storage materials and all other electronic media and computer systems; (f) promotional marketing and communications[1]; (g) **advertisement** features."[2]

The Code of Standards does not apply to "(a) statutory, public, Garda and other official notices; (b) material published as a matter of record only; (c) flyposting; (d) packages, wrappers, labels, tickets, timetables and menus, unless they advertise another product or a sales promotion or are recognisable in a **marketing communication**; (e) point-of-sale displays, except those covered by the promotional marketing rules or when part of a wider advertising campaign; (f) **marketing communications** whose principal purpose is to express the **advertiser's** position on a political, religious, industrial relations, social or aesthetic matter or on an issue of public interest or concern; (g) classified private **advertisements**, including those on-line; (h) press releases

---

[1] The phrase "promotional marketing and sales promotions" is not defined in the ASAI Code of Standards. However the phrase "promotional marketing practices, including sales promotions" is defined (at 9, para 1.3) as "those marketing techniques which involve the provision of direct or indirect additional benefits, usually on a temporary basis, designed to make goods or services more attractive to purchasers".

[2] Code of Standards, 9 et seq., par. 1.4.

and other public relations material; (i) the content of books and editorial material in media; (j) oral communications, including telephone calls; (k) works of art; (l) specialised **marketing communications** addressed to the medical, veterinary and allied professions; (m) the content of premium rate services; (n) **marketing communications** in foreign media...(o) website content, other than sales promotions and **marketing communications** in paid-for space; (p) sponsorship (**marketing communications** that refer to a sponsorship are covered by the **Code**."[3]

This checklist is structured as if a **marketing communication** has been or is about to be issued. Given that certain promotions by financial product or service providers may involve the distribution of goods, certain questions related to the distribution of goods (as opposed to financial products or services) have been included.

Query	Source	Yes	No	N/A
Chapter 2, General Rules				
Principles				
(1) Is the **marketing communication** legal, decent, honest and truthful?	Par.2.1			
(2) Is the **marketing communication** prepared with a sense of responsibility to **consumers** and to society?	Par.2.2			
(3) Does the **marketing communication** respect the principles of fair competition generally accepted in business?	Par.2.3			
(4) Has the **Code** been applied in the spirit and in the letter?	Par.2.4			
(5) Is the **marketing communication** such that it would not bring **advertising** into disrepute?	Par.2.5			
(6) Has the **advertiser/promoter** responded (without undue delay) to any contact from the **Authority**?	Par.2.7			
Substantiation				
(7) Before offering the **marketing communication** for publication, has the **advertiser** satisfied itself that it will be able to provide documentary evidence to substantiate all **claims**, whether direct or indirect, expressed or implied, that are capable of objective assessment?	Par.2.9			
(8) Has relevant evidence been sent without delay to the **Authority** (if requested) and is such evidence adequate to support both detailed **claims** and the overall impression created by the **marketing communication**?	Par.2.9			
(9) Has the full name and geographical business address of **advertisers** been provided without delay, where requested by the **Authority** from an agency or relevant third party?	Par.2.9			

(*Continued*)

---

[3] Code of Standards, 10 *et seq.*, para 1.5

Query	Source	Yes	No	N/A
(10) Are any statistics presented in such a way so as not to exaggerate the validity of an **advertising claim**, or give the unjustified impression that there is validity to the **claim**?	Par.2.10			
(11) Does the **marketing communication** avoid: (a) misusing, mis-characterising, or misleadingly citing, any technical data, e.g. research results or quotations from technical and scientific publications; and (b) using scientific terminology or vocabulary in such a way as to falsely or misleadingly suggest that an advertising **claim** has scientific validity?	Par.2.11			
(12) If there is a **claim** in the **marketing communication** about which there is a significant division of informed opinion, does the **marketing communication** avoid portraying the **claim** as universally accepted?	Par.2.12			
(13) Does the **marketing communication** avoid exaggerating the value, accuracy or usefulness of **claims** contained in books, tapes, videos, DVDs and the like that have not been independently substantiated?	Par.2.13			
Legality (14) Does the **marketing communication** avoid containing anything that breaks the law or incites anyone to break it, and avoid omitting anything that the law requires?	Par.2.14			
Decency and Propriety (15) Does the **marketing communication** avoid containing anything that is likely to cause grave or widespread offence?	Par.2.15			
(16) Does the **marketing communication** respect the dignity of all **persons** and avoid causing offence on grounds of gender, marital status, family status, sexual orientation, religion, age, disability, race or membership of the Traveller community?	Par.2.16			
(17) Does the **marketing communication** respect the principle of equality of men and women, avoid sex stereotyping and exploitation or demeaning of men and women, and (where appropriate) use generic terms that include both the masculine and feminine gender?	Par.2.17			
(18) Is the **marketing communication** responsive to the diversity in Irish society and when portraying or referring to people within the groups referred to in par.2.16 of the Code (see Q.16 above), does it (a) respect the principle of equality in any depiction of these groups, (b) fully respect their dignity and not subject them to ridicule or offensive humour, (c) avoid stereotyping and negative or hurtful images, (d) avoid exploiting them for unrelated marketing purposes, and (e) avoid ridiculing or exploiting religious beliefs, symbols, rites or practices?	Par.2.18			

(*Continued*)

213

Query	Source	Yes	No	N/A
(19) Has the **advertiser** taken account of public sensitivities in the preparation and publication of the **marketing communication** and avoided (a) the exploitation of sexuality and the use of coarseness and undesirable innuendo and (b) the use of offensive or provocative copy or images merely to attract attention?	Par.2.19			
(20) Has the **advertiser** considered public sensitivity before using potentially offensive material?	Par.2.19			
Honesty				
(21) Has the **advertiser** avoided exploiting the credulity, inexperience or lack of knowledge of **consumers**?	Par.2.22			
(22) Does the design and presentation of the **marketing communication** allow it to be easily and clearly understood and where footnotes or 'small print' are used, are they (a) of sufficient size and prominence and easily legible, and (b) where appropriate, linked to the relevant part of the main copy?	Par.2.23			
Truthfulness				
(23) Does the **marketing communication** avoid misleading (and being likely to mislead) by inaccuracy, ambiguity, exaggeration, omission or otherwise?	Par.2.24			
(24) If, in the **marketing communication**, there are any obvious untruths or deliberate hyperbole that are unlikely to mislead, or any incidental minor inaccuracies or unortho-dox spellings, do these avoid affecting the accuracy or perception of the **marketing communication** in any material way?	Par.2.25			
(25) If the **marketing communication** contains a **claim** such as 'up to' or 'from', does the **marketing communication** nonetheless avoid exaggerating the value or range of benefits likely to be achieved in practice by **consumers**?	Par.2.26			
Matters of opinion				
(26) If the **advertiser** states an opinion about the quality or desirability of a **product**, is it clear that what the **advertiser** is expressing is its own opinion rather than a matter of fact, is there no likelihood of **consumers** being misled about any matter that is capable of subjective assessment, and is any assertion or comparison that goes beyond subjective opinion capable of substantiation?	Par.2.27			

(Continued)

Query	Source	Yes	No	N/A
Fear and Distress (27) Does the **marketing communication** avoid causing fear or distress without good reason (such as the encouragement of prudent behaviour or the discouragement of dangerous or ill-advised actions) and, where there is good reason for causing fear or distress, is the fear aroused proportionate to the risk?	Par.2.28			
Safety (28) Save where the **marketing communication** is concerned with promoting safety, does the **marketing communication** avoid encouraging or condoning dangerous behaviour and unsafe practices?	Par.2.29			
Violence and Anti-Social Behaviour (29) Does the **marketing communication** avoid containing anything that condones or is likely to provoke: violence or anti-social behaviour; nuisance; personal injury or damage to property?	Par.2.30			
Portrayal of Persons or Property (30) Where a **person** is portrayed in the **marketing communication**, has written permission from such person to this portrayal been obtained in advance of the said **marketing communication**? (Exceptions to the requirement imposed by the Code of Standards in this regard include "(a) the use of crowd scenes or property depicted in general outdoor locations, or where the purpose of the **marketing communication** is to promote a **product** such as a book, newspaper article, broadcast programme or film of which the **person** concerned is a subject; (b) in the case of people with a public profile, references that accurately reflect the contents of books, newspaper articles, broadcast programmes, films or other electronic communications *etc.* may be acceptable without permission." (Code of Standards, par.2.33)).	Par.2.32			
(31) Where a **person's** house or other possessions is featured in the **marketing communication** in a manner which identifies the owner to the public, has written permission from such **person** been obtained in advance of the said feature? (The same exceptions as stated beneath the previous question apply).	Par.2.32			

(Continued)

215

Query	Source	Yes	No	N/A
(32) Does the **marketing communication** avoid exploiting the public reputation of **persons** in a manner which is humiliating or offensive, and does it avoid claiming (note: '**claim**' is a defined term) or implying an endorsement where none exists?	Par.2.34			
(33) Where the **marketing communication** makes reference to a deceased **person**, has such reference been handled with particular care to avoid causing offence or distress?	Par.2.35			

Testimonials and Endorsements

Query	Source	Yes	No	N/A
(34) If the **advertiser** is using a testimonial: is the **advertiser** able to provide relevant supporting documentation; does the **advertiser** hold signed and dated proof for any testimonial used; if the **Authority** has requested the aforementioned information, has it been provided immediately to the **Authority**; is there prior and continuing permission to the use of such testimonial by the person named or depicted in the relevant **marketing communication**?	Par.2.36			
(35) If a testimonial is being relied upon, does it relate to a **product** as currently offered, bearing in mind that testimonials may be misleading if the formulation of such product or its market environment changes significantly?	Par.2.37			
(36) If a testimonial is being relied upon, can the opinions expressed in them be supported, where necessary, with independent evidence of their accuracy, and do any **claims** based on such testimonial conform to the Code of Standards?	Par.2.38			
(37) If the **marketing communication** contains an endorsement by a fictitious or historical character, does the **marketing communication** avoid presenting such endorsement as though it is a genuine testimonial?	Par.2.39			
(38) If the **marketing communication** makes reference to research tests, trials, professional endorsements, research facilities or professional journals: have such references been used only with the permission of those concerned; are such references relevant and current; are all such tests, trials and endorsements as are referred to, signed and dated; and is any establishment referred to under appropriate professional supervision?	Par.2.40			

Prices

Query	Source	Yes	No	N/A
(39) If a price is stated in the **marketing communication**: does it relate to the **product** depicted or specified in the marketing communication; and has care been taken to ensure that prices and illustrated **products** match?	Par.2.41			

(Continued)

Query	Source	Yes	No	N/A
(40) If the **marketing communication** is not addressed primarily to the trade: does any price quoted include VAT and other taxes, duties and inescapable costs to the **consumer**; where applicable, are the amounts of any other charges, such as those arising from the method of payment/ purchase stated?	Par.2.42			
(41) If the **marketing communication** is addressed to the trade and quotes a VAT-exclusive price, is it clear that the price is VAT-exclusive?	Par.2.42			
(42) If the price of one **product** is dependent on the purchase of another, is the extent of any commitment required of **consumers** made clear?	Par.2.43			
(43) If the cost of accessing a message or service, or of communicating with an advertiser is greater than the standard rate, has this been made clear in the **marketing communication**?	Par.2.44			
Availability of Products				
(44) Is the **advertiser** in a position to meet any reasonable demand created by its **advertising**?	Par.2.45			
(45) If a **product** proves to be available in insufficient quantity, will the **advertiser** take immediate action to ensure that any further **marketing communications** are amended or withdrawn?	Par.2.45			
(46) Where there is limited availability of some or all of the **products** advertised, apart from indicating that there may be other terms and conditions which apply: has the **advertiser** avoided exaggerating the availability of any of those **products**; and is the **advertiser** able to demonstrate that there is a reasonable supply or proportion of each of the various **products** available?	Par.2.46			
(47) If a **product** is being advertised as a way of gauging possible demand, does the **marketing communication** make this clear?	Par.2.47			
(48) Has the **advertiser** avoided using the technique of switch selling (i.e. where sales staff criticise the advertised **product** or suggest that it is not available and recommend purchase of a more expensive alternative); and has the **advertiser** avoided placing obstacles in the way of purchasing the advertised **product** or delivering it promptly?	Par.2.48			

(Continued)

Query	Source	Yes	No	N/A
Comparisons				
(49) If the **marketing communication** contains a comparison: is it fair and so designed that there is no likelihood of a **consumer** being misled; and is the basis of selection clear and the elements of comparison not unfairly selected in a way that gives the advertisers an unfair advantage?	Par.2.50			
(50) If there is any claim that a **product** is superior to others, is there clear evidence to support the claim (if wording such as 'number one', 'leading', 'largest', and the like is used, is this capable of substantiation with market share data or similar proof?	Par.2.51			
(51) Has the **advertiser** avoided unfairly attacking or discrediting other businesses or their profits?	Par.2.52			
Guarantees				
(52) Where the **marketing communication** refers to a guarantee: are the full terms of the guarantee available for **consumers** to inspect before they are committed to purchase; are any substantial limitations clearly indicated in the **marketing communication**; and does the term 'guarantee', if used in a colloquial sense, avoid causing confusion about **consumers'** statutory rights?	Pars. 2.53 and 2.54			
Exploitation of Goodwill				
(53) Has the **advertiser** avoided exploiting or making unfair use of the goodwill attached to the name, trademark, brand, slogan or **marketing communications** campaign of any other **person**?	Par.2.55			
Imitation				
(54) Has the **marketing communication** avoided so closely resembling another as to be likely to mislead or cause confusion?	Par.2.56			
Recognisability				
(55) Is the **marketing communication** designed and presented in such a way that it is clear that it is a **marketing communication**?	Par.2.57			
(56) If the **advertisement** feature, announcement or promotion is published or electronically broadcast in exchange for a payment or other reciprocal arrangement and the content is controlled by the **advertiser** does it comply with the Code of Standards and is it clearly identified and distinguished from editorial matter?	Par.2.58			

(Continued)

Query	Source	Yes	No	N/A
(57) Unless the **marketing communication** is a 'teaser **advertisement'**, the sole purpose of which is to attract attention to communication activities to follow, is the identity of the **advertiser**, product or service apparent?	Par.2.59			
(58) If appropriate, does the **marketing communication** include contact information to enable the **consumer** to get in touch with the **advertiser** without difficulty?	Par.2.60			
(59) Does the **marketing communication**: avoid misrepresenting its true purpose; and avoid being presented as, for example, market research or a consumer survey where its true purpose is marketing, i.e. the promotion of a **product**?	Par.2.61			
(60) If the **marketing communication** solicits a response constituting an order for which payment will be required (e.g. entry in a publication), does it make this clear?	Par.2.62			
(61) If the **marketing communication** solicits an order, is it presented in a form that avoids being mistaken for an invoice or otherwise falsely suggesting that payment is due?	Par.2.63			

Promotional Marketing Practices

Recognisability

(62) Is the **sales promotion** conducted equitably, promptly and efficiently, is it seen to deal fairly and honourably with **consumers**, and will the **promoter** avoid causing unnecessary disappointment?	Par.3.3			

Protection of consumers

(63) Does the **promoter** have proper regard for normal safety precautions; are promotional **products** and samples distributed in such a way as to avoid the risk of harm to **consumers**; has special care been taken where a sales promotion is addressed to children or where **products** intended for adults may fall into the hands of children; and does literature accompanying promotional items contain any necessary safety warnings?	Par.3.4			
(64) Is the **sales promotion** designed and conducted in a way that respects the right of **consumers** to a reasonable degree of privacy and freedom from annoyance?	Par.3.5			
(65) Are **consumers** to be told before entry if participants may be required to become involved in any of the **promoters'** publicity or **advertising**, whether it is connected with the **sales promotion** or not and has the compromising of prizewinners' interests through the publication of excessively detailed information been avoided?	Par.3.6			

(Continued)

Query	Source	Yes	No	N/A
Suitability (66) Is the **promoter** offering promotional **products** of a nature that are not likely to cause offence or **products** which, in the context of the promotion, will not reasonably be considered to be socially undesirable?	Par.3.7			
Availability (67) Is the **promoter** able to demonstrate that it has made a reasonable estimate of the likely response and that it is capable of meeting the response; and, in the case of prize promotions, is the number of prizes to be awarded made clear to participants?	Par.3.8			
(68) If the **promoter** is unable to meet demand for a promotional offer because of an unexpectedly high response or some other unanticipated factor outside the **promoter's** control, will **products** of a similar or greater quality and value or a cash payment be substituted?	Par.3.10			
Quality (69) Has the **promoter** ensured that promotional **products** meet satisfactory standards of safety, durability and performance in use and, where appropriate, are matters such as guarantees and after-sales service clearly explained?	Par.3.11			
Presentation (70) Does the presentation of the **sales promotion** and associated publicity avoid misleading **consumers**?	Par.3.12			
(71) Does all supporting **advertising** material conform to the law and to the general and sectoral rules of the Code of Standards, as appropriate; and, in particular, do descriptions of promotional **products** avoid overstating their quality, availability, uses or value?	Par.3.13			
Terms of the Promotion (72) Are the terms in which a promotion is presented clear, complete and easy for the **consumer** to understand and are the following points clearly explained: (a) how to participate, including any conditions and costs; (b) the **promoter's** full name and business address in a form that can be retained by **consumers**; (c) the closing date prominently displayed (with it being made clear to participants where the final date for the purchase of the promoted **product** differs from the closing date for the submission of claims or entries); (d) any proof-of-purchase requirements (emphasised, for example, by using bold type, separating same from other text or using a different colour), with any requirement to purchase more than one unit of a **product** to participate in	Par.3.15			

(Continued)

Query	Source	Yes	No	N/A
a promotion being stated on the front of any label or material carrying details of the promotion; (e) any geographical or personal restrictions; (f) any necessary permissions (e.g. those of parents or guardians); (g) any limit on the number of applications permitted; (h) any limit on the number of promotional **products** or prizes that an individual consumer or household may claim to win; (i) any other factor likely to influence **consumers'** decisions or understanding about the promotion?				
(73) Are any terms of the **promotion**, the effect of which is either (1) to exclude some **consumers** from the opportunity to participate or (2) to impose requirements that are likely to affect a **consumer's** decision whether or not to participate, clearly and prominently stated so as to be clear to the **consumer** before any commitment is made?	Par.3.16			
Administration				
(74) Is the **sales promotion** conducted under proper super-vision and with adequate resources, with the **promoter** and any **intermediary** avoiding giving justifiable grounds for complaint to **consumers**?	Par.3.17			
(75) Is the **promoter** allowing ample time for each phase of the promotion, notifying the trade, distributing the goods, issuing rules where appropriate, collecting wrappers and the like, and judging and announcing the results?	Par.3.18			
(76) Will the **promoter** fulfil applications within 30 days and, if not, have participants (a) been told in advance that it is impractical to do so, (b) been informed promptly of unforeseen delays and been offered another delivery date or an opportunity to recover any money paid for the offer?	Par.3.19			
(77) If damaged or faulty goods are received by **consumers**, will the **promoter** ensure either that they are replaced without delay or send a refund immediately, with the full cost of replacing damaged goods falling on **promoters** and with any applicant who does not receive goods having them replaced free of charge?	Par.3.20			
Free offers				
(78) If an offer is described as free: do **consumers** pay no more than: (a) the minimum unavoidable cost of responding to the promotion (*e.g.* the current public rate of postage, the cost of telephoning up to and including the national rate or the minimum, unavoidable cost of sending an e-mail or SMS text message), (b) the actual cost of freight or delivery, and	Par.3.21			

(*Continued*)

221

Query	Source	Yes	No	N/A
(c) the cost, including any incidental expenses, of any travel involved if **consumers** collect the offer; and is the **consumer's** liability for such costs made clear, with no additional charges for packaging or handling?				
(79) Has the marketer avoided attempting to recover its costs by reducing the quality or composition of a product, by imposing additional charges or inflating incidental expenses, or by increasing the price of any other **product** that must be purchased as a pre-condition of obtaining a free item?	Par.3.22			
(80) If a trial is described as free, has it been made clear, if so, to the **consumer** when the offer is made, that the **consumer** is expected to pay the cost of returning any goods?	Par.3.23			
(81) If an offer appears on a **product** and, to benefit from that offer, requires that several purchases of that **product** be made, has the need to make additional purchases been clearly indicated?	Par.3.24			
(82) If an offer covers two or more items, of which only one is free, is it made clear what is offered free and what they must pay for?	Par.3.25			
(83) If unsolicited samples of gifts are distributed through a promotion, is it clear to the consumer that the consumer is under no obligation to buy or return items?	Par.3.26			

Promotions with prizes

Query	Source	Yes	No	N/A
(84) Are entry conditions clearly worded and do they set out the following details: (a) the closing date; (b) any age, eligibility or geographical restrictions; (c) any restrictions on the number of entries or prizes; (d) any requirements for proof of purchase; (e) any permissions required (e.g. from parent or employer); (f) the criteria for judging prizes; (g) a full and accurate description of the prizes; (h) any limitations imposed on acceptance of the prizes and any duties or obligations on the part of winners (e.g. in regard to post-event publicity); (i) whether a cash alternative can be substituted for any prize; (j) how and when winners will be notified of results; (k) how and when results will be published; (l) where appropriate, who owns the copyright of entries; (m) whether and how entries will be returned?	Par.3.28			
(85) Has the **promoter** avoided complex rules and the need to supplement conditions of entry with additional rules and, if further rules cannot be avoided: have participants been informed how to obtain these further rules; do the rules contain nothing that would have influenced a **consumer** against making a purchase or participating; and are participants able to retain the entry instructions and rules?	Par.3.29			

(Continued)

Query	Source	Yes	No	N/A
(86) Is the closing date clearly stated in each **advertisement**, on each entry form and on the outer surface of any relevant pack, wrapper or label (with this date not changing unless circumstances outside the control of the **promoters** make this unavoidable)?	Par.3.30			
(87) If a poor response or low level of entries prompts a **promoter** to extend the duration of a promotion or withhold prizes, has the **promoter** expressly reserved the right to do this at the outset and, if the **promoter** has not so reserved this right, and is minded to extend, for a reasonable duration, a promotion involving a collection or redemption mechanic, has there been a poor response to the promotion that is to be so extended?	Par.3.31			
(88) Will the **promoter** either publish or make available on request details of the name and country of residence of major prizewinners (bearing in mind the risk of theft or harassment that may arise if the details given are sufficient to allow the address of a winner of a prize of substantial value to be pinpointed)?	Par.3.32			
(89) Unless otherwise stated in advance, are prizewinners to receive (or have prizewinners received) their prizes no more than six weeks after a promotion ends?	Par.3.33			
(90) If the selection of winning entries is open to subjective interpretation: has an independent judge, or a panel including one member who is independent of the competition's **promoters** and **intermediaries**, been appointed; are those appointed to act as judges competent to judge the subject-matter of the competition; and has (or will) the identity of the judges be made available to the Advertising Standards Authority of Ireland on request?	Par.3.34			
(91) If a prize promotion involves any form of draw, has the **promoter** ensured that tokens, tickets or numbers are or will be allocated on a fair and random basis, with an independent observer supervising the draw to ensure that individual entries enjoy equal chances?	Par.3.35			
(92) If the prize promotion has been or is to be widely advertised, has the **promoter** ensured that entry forms and any goods needed to establish proofs of purchase are widely available?	Par.3.36			
(93) Is the distinction between a prize/gift being properly maintained; is it the case that a gift offered to all or most participants in a promotion is not described as a prize; if the **promoter** is offering a gift to all entrants in addition to giving a prize to those who win, has particular care been taken to avoid confusing the two?	Par.3.37			

(Continued)

Query	Source	Yes	No	N/A
(94) Has the **promoter** avoided exaggerating the likelihood of **consumers** winning a prize?	Par.3.38			

Advertisement promotion

Query	Source	Yes	No	N/A
(95) Is the **advertisement** promotion designed and presented in such a way that it can easily be distinguished from editorial material?	Par.3.39			
(96) If a feature, announcement or promotion is published in exchange for a payment or other reciprocal arrangement where content is controlled by the **promoter**, is the said feature, announcement or promotion in compliance with the Code of Standards?	Par.3.40			
(97) If a publisher is announcing a reader promotion on the front page or cover, has the publisher ensured that **consumers** know whether they will be expected to buy subsequent issues of the publication or if any financial contribution is required, and do any major qualifications that may significantly influence **consumers** in their decision to purchase the publication appearing on the front page or cover?	Par.3.41			
(98) If a promotion claims that participation will benefit a charity or good cause, does the promotion: (a) name the charity or good cause that will benefit and can it be demonstrated that those benefiting consent to the **advertising** or promotion; (b) define the nature and objectives of the charity or cause unless that information is widely available; (c) specify the extent and the nature of the advantage to be gained by the charity or cause; (d) state if the **promoters** have imposed any limitations on the contribution they will make; (e) not limit **consumers'** contributions (with any extra money collected being given to the named charity or cause on the same basis as contributions below that level); (f) not exaggerate the benefit to the charity or cause derived from individual purchases of the promoted **product**; (g) make available on request a current or final total of the contributions made?	Par.3.42			

Promotions and the Trade

Query	Source	Yes	No	N/A
(99) Is the promotion/incentive scheme designed and implemented to take account of the interests of everyone involved and does it avoid conflict with the duty of employees to their employer or their obligation to give honest advice to **consumers**?	Par.3.43			

(Continued)

Query	Source	Yes	No	N/A
(100) Has the promoter secured the prior agreement of employers or of the manager responsible if the promoter intends to ask for assistance from, or offer incentives to, any other company's employees; has the promoter observed any procedures established by companies for their employees, including any rules for participating in promotions; in the case of a trade incentive scheme that has been advertised rather than individually targeted, have employees been advised to obtain their employer's permission before participating?	Par.3.44			
(101) Has it been made clear to those benefiting from an incentive scheme that they may be liable for tax?	Par.3.45			

Distance Selling (Mail Order and Direct Response)

Promotions with prizes

Query	Source	Yes	No	N/A
(102) In the case of a mail order or direct **marketing communication**: is the name and full address of the **advertiser** stated in the **marketing communication** (in the case of a print **marketing communication** separate from any response coupon); have arrangements been made for enquirers to be informed by media of the name and full address of the advertiser?	Par.4.1			
(103) Does the distance selling **market communication**: (a) include the main characteristics of the **product**; (b) include the price, including any VAT, taxes payable, and other inescapable costs to the **consumer**, and payment arrangements; (c) provide information on how to access the **advertiser's** details if the offer is sent by Short Message Service (SMS) or Wireless Application Protocol (WAP) and all details cannot be included in the communication?	Par.4.2			
(104) Except (a) where security is provided for purchaser's money through an independent scheme, (b) for goods such as plants and made-to-measure **products** where the estimated time of delivery should be made clear, (c) where a series of goods is to be dispatched in sequence, has any order been (or will any order be) fulfilled within 30 days (in the case of (c) only the first delivery need be made within 30 days but has the period within which subsequent deliveries will be made been stated)?	Par.4.3			
(105) Do goods supplied conform to any relevant and accepted standard and to the description given in the **marketing communication**?	Par.4.4			

(Continued)

Query	Source	Yes	No	N/A
(106) Except in the case of (i) perishable, personalised or made-to-measure goods, provided all contractual and statutory obligations to the **consumer** are met; and (ii) goods that can be copied, unless they fall under category (a), (b) or (c) hereafter, with the exception of audio or video recordings or computer software if unsealed by the **consumer**, has the **advertiser** refunded (or will the advertiser refund) all money promptly, and at the latest within 30 days of notice of cancellation being given when: (a) **consumers** have not received their goods or services (alternatively, **advertisers** may, if asked, provide a replacement); (b) goods are returned because they are damaged or faulty or are not as described, in which case the **advertisers** should bear the cost of their return, provided that the **consumer** gives notice within a reasonable period of time; (c) **consumers** cancel within seven clear working days after delivery (**consumers** may assume that they can try out goods unless the **marketing communication** says otherwise, though such goods should nevertheless be returned undamaged); (d) an unconditional money-back guarantee is given and the goods are returned within a reasonable period; (e) goods that have been returned are not received back, provided **consumers** can produce proof of posting?	Pars. 4.5 and 4.6			
(107) Is the **advertiser** in a position to meet any reasonable demand created by its **advertising** and, if a **product** proves to be available in insufficient quantity, will the **advertiser** take immediate action to ensure that any further **marketing communications** are amended or withdrawn?	Par.4.8			
(108) If the **advertiser** intends to call on respondents personally, has this been made clear in the **marketing communication** or in a follow-up letter, and has the **advertiser** provided a reply-paid postcard or telephone contact to allow **consumers** an adequate opportunity to refuse a home visit?	Par.4.9			
(109) If the **advertiser** is using media primarily targeted at children, has it avoided promoting **products** that are unsuitable for children?	Par.4.10			
(110) Are goods and, where applicable, samples packaged in such a way as to be suitable for delivery to a customer, with particular care being taken when packaging **products** that may fall into the hands of children?	Par.4.11			

(Continued)

Query	Source	Yes	No	N/A
Children (111) If the **marketing communication** is addressed directly or indirectly to children or likely to be seen by a significant proportion of **children**, does it have regard to the special characteristics of **children** and the ways in which they perceive and react to **marketing communications**?	Par. 5.3			
(112) Does the **marketing communication** contain nothing that is likely to result in physical, mental or moral harm to children or that is likely to frighten them, except to promote safety or in the public interest?	Par.5.5			
(113) Does the **marketing communication**: (i) avoid portraying **children** in a manner that offends against accepted standards of good taste and decency; (ii) avoid encouraging **children** to enter into unsafe situations or strange places or talk to strangers (e.g. for the purpose of making collections or accumulating labels, wrappers or coupons); (iii) avoid showing **children** in morally or physically dangerous situations or behaving dangerously in the home or outside and avoid showing children unattended in street scenes unless they are old enough to take responsibility for their own safety; (iv) avoid encouraging children to engage in, or be portrayed engaging in, anti-social behaviour; (v) show **children** observing the Rules of the Road where they appear as pedestrians or cyclists; (vi) pay special attention, where relevant, to the use of **child** car seats and the wearing of car seat-belts and safety helmets; (vii) avoid showing younger **children** in particular using or in close proximity to dangerous substances or equipment without direct adult supervision (examples include matches, petrol, gas, medicines and certain household substances, as well as certain electrical appliances and machinery, including agricultural equipment); (viii) in instances where an open fire is included in a scene with a young **child**, also show a clearly visible fireguard; (ix) avoid encouraging **children** to copy any practice that might be unsafe?	Par.5.5			
(114) Does the **marketing communication**, if addressed to **children**, avoid exploiting the loyalty, credulity, vulnerability or lack of experience of **children**, for example (a) not make them feel inferior or unpopular for not buying an advertised **product**, (b) not make them feel lacking in courage, duty or loyalty if they do not buy or do not encourage others to buy a particular **product**, (c) not undermine the authority, responsibility or judgment of parents, guardians, or other appropriate authority figures, (d) not include any appeal to	Par.5.6			

(Continued)

Query	Source	Yes	No	N/A
children to persuade their parents or other adults to buy advertised **products** for them, and (e) clearly indicate a **product** is part of a series (where so) and include the method of acquiring such product series?				
(115) Does the **marketing communication**, if addressed to **children**, (a) avoid featuring **products** that are unsuitable for **children**, (b) avoid exaggerating what is attainable by an ordinary **child** using the **product**, (c) avoid making it difficult to judge the actual size, characteristics and performance of any **product** advertised, (d) avoid asking **children** to disclose personal information about themselves or their families without first having obtained permission from their parents or guardians, (e) avoid minimising the price of **products** by the use of such words as 'only' or 'just'?	Par.5.7			
(116) Has the **advertiser** taken particular care when packaging a **product** that may fall into the hands of younger **children**?	Par.5.8			
Promotions				
(117) In addition to complying with the provisions set out under the heading 'Promotional Marketing Practices' above, if a promotion is addressed to or likely to attract **children**, (i) does the promotion avoid offering promotional **products** that are unsuitable for distribution to **children**; (ii) is it carried (or to be carried) out responsibly, taking into account the location in which the promotion is conducted; (iii) does it make clear that parental permission is required if prizes and incentives might cause conflict between children and their parents (examples include animals, bicycles, outings, concerts and holidays); (iv) does it allow a sufficient timeframe for participation in a manner that will reflect moderate consumption of a **product**; (v) does it clearly explain the number and type of any additional proofs of purchase needed to participate; (vi) does it contain a prominent closing date; (vii) does it avoid exaggerating the value of prizes or the chances of winning them; (viii) does it avoid exploiting children's susceptibility to charitable appeals?	Par.5.11			
Financial Services and Products				
(118) If the **marketing communication** is for a financial service or **product**, has it been prepared with care and with the conscious aim of ensuring that members of the public fully grasp the nature of any commitment into which they may enter as a result of responding to the **marketing communication** and does it avoid taking advantage of people's inexperience or gullibility?	Par.10.1			

(Continued)

Query	Source	Yes	No	N/A
(119) If the **marketing communication** invites a response by mail, does it contain the full address of the **advertiser** separate from any response coupon?	Par.10.2			
(120) Does the **marketing communication** indicate the nature of the contract being offered and provide information on any limitations on eligibility, any charges, expenses or penalties attached and the terms on which withdrawal may be arranged?	Par.10.3			
(121) If the **marketing communication** is short or general in its content, will free explanatory material giving full details of the offer be made available before a binding contract is entered into?	Par.10.3			
(122) If the **marketing communication** contains any forecast or projection, does it make clear the basis on which the forecast or projection is made, explaining for, example, whether (i) reinvestment of income is assumed; (ii) account has been taken of any applicable taxes; (iii) any penalties or deductions will arise on premature realisation or otherwise?	Par.10,4			
(123) Does the **marketing communication** make clear that the value of investments is variable, and unless guaranteed, can go down as well as up and, if the value of the investment is guaranteed, have details been included in the **marketing communication**?	Par.10.5			
(124) Does the **marketing communication** specify that past performance or experience does not necessarily give a guide for the future, and are any examples used representative?	Par.10.6			

APPENDIX TO ASAI CODE OF STANDARDS CHECKLIST

In the ASAI Code of Standards, and hence in the preceding checklist, the following terms bear the following meanings:

— **advertiser** "includes anyone disseminating marketing communications, including promoters and direct marketers; references to advertisers should be interpreted as including intermediaries and agencies unless the context indicates otherwise"[4]

— **advertising** or **advertisement** "includes but is not limited to a form of marketing communication carried by the media, usually in return for payment or other valuable consideration"[5]

---

[4] Code of Standards, 9, par.1.3.
[5] *ibid.*

— **Authority** "means the Advertising Standards Authority for Ireland"[6]
— **child** "is anyone under 18 years of age"[7]
— **claim** "can be direct or implied, written, verbal or visual"[8]
— **consumer** "is anyone who is likely to see or hear a particular marketing communication"[9]
— **intermediary** "is any person or body, other than the promoter, responsible for the implementation of any form of sales promotional activity"[10]
— **marketing communication** "includes but is not limited to advertising, as well as other techniques such as promotions, sponsorships and direct marketing, and should be interpreted broadly to mean any form of communication produced directly by or on behalf of advertisers intended primarily to promote products, to influence the behaviour of and/or to inform those to whom it is addressed"[11]
— **person** "should be construed as including legal persons and groups, as appropriate"[12]
— **product** "can encompass goods, services, facilities, opportunities, fundraising, prizes and gifts"[13]
— **promoter** "is any person or body by whom a sales promotion is initiated or commissioned"[14]
— **promotional marketing practices, including sales promotions** "are those marketing techniques which involve the provision of direct or indirect additional benefits, usually on a temporary basis, designed to make goods or services more attractive to purchasers".[15]

Note: Singular words used in the above definitions also import the plural and vice versa.[16] Moreover, words importing the masculine gender also import the feminine gender and vice versa.[17]

---

[7] Code of Standards, 9, par.1.3.
[8] *ibid.*
[9] *ibid.*
[10] *ibid.*
[11] Code of Standards, 8, par.1.3.
[12] Code of Standards, 8, par.1.2.
[13] Code of Standards, 9, par.1.3.
[14] *ibid.*
[15] *ibid.*
[16] Code of Standards, 8, par.1.2.
[17] *ibid.*

Appendix E

BCI GENERAL ADVERTISING CODE CHECKLIST

The checklist that appears in this Appendix, as compiled by the author of this book, seeks to reduce the BCI General Advertising Code, insofar as it is relevant to financial advertisements generally, to a series of questions. The questions have been drafted so that a 'Yes' answer suggests compliance with the BCI General Advertising Code and a 'No' answer suggests non-compliance. Certain terms used in the checklist are terms that bear a defined meaning when used in the BCI General Advertising Code and when used in this checklist. Where a term used in the checklist is a defined term, it appears in **Bold** format, with the definition appearing in the appendix to the checklist that follows. As discussed in the main text above, the BCI General Advertising Code is intended to govern the behaviour of broadcasters and not financial product or service providers (who would not necessarily be able to answer all of the questions in the attached). Even so, it is worth including the attached checklist in this book as a financial advertisement which, when reviewed in light of the attached checklist, appears not to be in compliance with the BCI General Advertising Code, will most likely not be broadcast by a broadcaster subject to that Code. This checklist is structured as if a **commercial communication** has been or is about to be issued. Given that certain promotions by financial product or service providers may involve the distribution of goods, certain questions related to the distribution of goods (as opposed to financial products or services) have been included.

Query	Source	Yes	No	N/A
Section 3 - General principles and rules applying to all commercial communications				
Protecting the Individual and Society				
(1) Has the **commercial communication** been prepared with a sense of responsibility both to the individual and to society and does it avoid prejudicing the interests of either and is the **commercial communication** legal, honest, decent and truthful?	Par.3.1			
(2) Does the **commercial communication** comply with applicable Irish and European legislation?	Par.3.1.1			

(Continued)

231

Query	Source	Yes	No	N/A
(3) Does the **commercial communication** avoid containing any element of spoken or visual presentation which misleads or is likely to mislead, either directly or by implication, by act or omission, with regard to the merits of the product or service being promoted or its suitability for the purpose recommended?	Par.3.1.2			
(4) Does the **commercial communication** avoid containing inaccurate or misleading claims, statements, illustrations or representations either direct or implied?	Par.3.1.3			
(5) Does the **commercial communication** avoid omitting relevant information in a manner that, in the result, is misleading or is likely to mislead and are all pertinent details of an offer stated in a clear and understandable manner?	Par.3.1.4			
(6) Is it the case that disclaimers and asterisked or footnoted information: do not contradict more prominent aspects of the message; and are located and presented in such a manner as to be clearly visible and/or audible?	Par.3.1.5			
(7) If the **commercial communication** is required to carry a tagline or an on-screen message, does it do so in a way that is clearly visible and/or audible?	Par.3.1.6			
(8) Has the broadcaster been mindful of the potential for sound effects to distract and/or alarm viewers and listeners; has particular care been taken when including in any **commercial communication** sound effects such as sirens, horns, ringing phones and screeching tyres; and are there no such sound effects at the beginning of a **commercial communication**?	Par.3.1.7			
(9) If the **commercial communication** contains direct or implied comparisons with other products or services; does it objectively compare products or services meeting the same needs or intended for the same purpose; are points of comparison based on facts that can be substantiated; and is it the case that the subject-matter of the comparison has not been chosen in such a way as to confer an artificial or unfair advantage to a promoter of a product or service?	Par.3.1.8			
Offence, Harm and Human Dignity (10) Does the **commercial communication** avoid prejudicing human dignity, causing harm or serious or widespread offence?	Par.3.2.1			

(Continued)

Query	Source	Yes	No	N/A
(11) Does the **commercial communication** avoid supporting or condoning discrimination against any person or section of the community, in particular on the basis of age, gender, marital status, membership of the Traveller community, family status, sexual orientation, disability, race or religion?	Par.3.2.2			
(12) Does the **commercial communication** avoid being offensive to religious or political beliefs and avoid encouraging behaviour prejudicial to the protection of the environment or to health or safety?	Par.3.2.2			
(13) Will the **commercial communication** be appropriately scheduled with regard to the time of broadcast, type of programme, channel/service type, nature of the product or service being promoted and the likely composition of the audience?	Par.3.2.3			
(14) Assuming the **commercial communication** is not a **commercial communication** governed by the BCI Children's Advertising Code, does it avoid causing moral or physical detriment to **children** and, in particular, does it comply with the following criteria for the protection of **children**: (i) it does not directly exhort **children** to buy a product or a service by exploiting their inexperience or incredulity; (ii) it does not directly encourage **children** to persuade their parents or others to purchase the goods or services being advertised; (iii) it does not exploit the special trust **children** place in parents, teachers or other persons; (iv) it does not unreasonably show **children** in dangerous situations?	Par.3.2.4			
(15) Does the **commercial communication** avoid portraying or referring to individual living persons without their permission (with the exception of inoffensive and accurate references to living persons in circumstances where the **commercial communication** is for a book, film, radio or television programme, newspaper, magazine, etc. which features the person referred to in the **commercial communication**)?	Par.3.2.5			
(16) Is it the case that the **commercial communication** is not calculated to induce unwarranted fear on the part of the viewer or listener?	Par.3.2.6			
Transparency (17) Is any commercial arrangement within programming identifiable as such and shall the listener/viewer be made aware of such an arrangement?	Par.3.3			

(Continued)

Query	Source	Yes	No	N/A
(18) Do presenters and other on-air personnel avoid advertising or endorsing products or services during editorial content?	Par.3.3.1			
(19) Is it the case that advertisers and sponsors do not exercise any editorial influence over the content of programmes?	Par.3.3.2			
(20) If the **commercial communication** includes one or more of the words 'guarantee', 'guaranteed', 'warranty', or 'warranted', is it the case that a legal guarantee/warranty is available to the broadcaster and the purchaser?	Par.3.3.3			
(21) Does the **commercial communication** avoid containing a direct or implied reference which purports to take away or diminish the statutory or common law rights of the purchaser?	Par.3.3.3			
(22) If the **commercial communication** makes use of a testimonial, is such testimonial genuine, relevant and contemporary, does it relate to the person giving the testimonial and is documentary evidence of the testimonial available to the broadcaster?	Par.3.3.4			
(23) If the **commercial communication** describes a product or service as 'free', is it the case that the said product or service is supplied at no cost or at no extra cost (other than post or carriage) to the recipient?	Par.3.3.5			
(24) If the **commercial communication** features a person who regularly presents a news programme, is the **commercial communication** promoting an appeal by a registered charity or public service campaign for safety, health, education, etc?	Par.3.3.6			
(25) Does the **commercial communication** involve any **product placement**? (Note: Under the BCI Code, incidental references to products or services in a programme are legitimate where their inclusion is editorially justified and their inclusion does not result in undue prominence being given to the product or service during the programme. Moreover, for television, the inclusion of products or services in a programme acquired from outside Ireland and films made for cinema are not considered **product placement**, provided no broadcaster regulated in Ireland and involved in the broadcast of that programme or film directly benefits from the arrangement).	Par.3.3.7			
(26) Has the Code been applied in the spirit as well as in the letter?	Par.3.4.2			

(*Continued*)

Query	Source	Yes	No	N/A
Section 3 - General rules pertaining to all advertising				
(27) Does all **advertising** observe the principle of separation whereby commercial content in advertising breaks between and within programmes is separate from programme content?	Par.4.1			
(28) Does the insertion of **advertising** avoid affecting the editorial integrity and value of programming and is **advertising** inserted into programmes in such a way that takes into account the natural breaks in, and the duration and nature of, the programme, while ensuring that the rights of the rights holders are not prejudiced?	Par.4.2			
(29) In the case of feature films and films made for television, where their duration is more than 45 minutes, is there no more than one interruption per 45-minute period, and where their scheduled duration is at least 20 minutes longer than two or more complete periods of 45 minutes, is there no more than one further interruption?	Par.4.3			
(30) Except as regards television programmes referred to in the preceding question, is it the case that a period of at least 20 minutes elapses between each successive break within a programme?	Par.4.4			
(31) Is it the case that no **advertising** has been or is to be inserted into a broadcast of a religious service?	Par.4.5			
(32) Is it the case that no **advertising** has been or is to be inserted into any television broadcast of news and current affairs programmes, documentaries or religious programmes where their scheduled duration is less than 30 minutes?	Par.4.6			
(33) Is it the case that in an intended television broadcast, isolated **advertising** will remain the exception?	Par.4.7			
(34) Is any **advertising** break signalled by visual or audio means and that such means do not contain any **commercial communication**?	Par.4.8			
(35) Does a broadcast or **commercial communication** involve any of the following (prohibited) practices: **surreptitious advertising, subliminal advertising** or **misleading advertising**?	Par.4.9			
(36) Has a broadcaster taken all reasonable measures to ensure that an advertisement does not sound louder than adjacent programming and has that broadcaster established clear limits on the use of compression, limiting and equalisation as these apply to advertisements provided to broadcasters by third parties?	Par.4.10			

(Continued)

235

Query	Source	Yes	No	N/A
Section 5 - Rules pertaining to specific advertising techniques				
Split-screen advertising				
(37) Does any **split-screen advertising** comply with all the various general principles and rules applying to all **commercial communications** and, where relevant, the general rules pertaining to all **advertising**?	Par.5.1.1			
(38) Where **split-screen advertising** is employed, does it appear during natural breaks and during end credits, and if it appears in a programme, is that programme a long-form sports programme which does not have a natural break (e.g. Formula One racing)	Par.5.1.2			
(39) Does any **split-screen advertising** avoid exceeding 50 percent of screen space, with only one split-screen advertisement appearing at a given time?	Par.5.1.3			
(40) Is it the case that any **split-screen advertising** does not appear in news or current affairs programmes, feature films or broadcasts of religious services?	Par.5.1.4			
Virtual advertising				
(41) Does any **virtual advertising** comply with all the various general principles and rules applying to all **commercial communications** and, where relevant, the general rules pertaining to all **advertising**?	Par.5.2			
Interactive advertising				
(42) Does any **interactive advertising** comply with all the various general principles and rules applying to all **commercial communications** and, where relevant, the general rules pertaining to all **advertising**?	Par.5.3.1			
(43) Is it the case that: any **interactive advertising** does not bring the viewer immediately/directly to products or services that are advertised; viewers are warned by appropriate optical and acoustical methods that they are about to enter a commercial interactive environment not governed by the BCI General Advertising Code (done by way of an intermediate screen which appears at the first click, with the viewer being able to access interactive content only after a second click)?	Par.5.3.2			
(44) Is it the case that **interactive advertising** does not bring the viewer immediately/directly to **commercial communications** for products or services prohibited under the BCI General Advertising Code?	Par.5.3.3			

(Continued)

Query	Source	Yes	No	N/A
Section 7 - Rules pertaining to Sponsorship				
(45) Does any **sponsorship** announcement avoid making promotional references to the products and/or services of the sponsor which contain advertising copy, product descriptions, endorsements, attributes or a call to action (apart from generic branding slogans), and are the only prices quoted required by statute to be included?	Par.7.2			
(46) Is it the case that programme material is not sponsored by one or more sponsors involved in the manufacture, supply or provision of a product or service that is not permitted to be advertised under the BCI General Advertising Code?	Par.7.3			
(47) Is it the case that a programme is not sponsored by one or more sponsors whose products or services are not permitted to appeal to the typical audience for that programme or during which it would not be permitted to advertise?	Par.7.4			
(48) Is it the case that a news, current affairs or religious affairs programme is not sponsored on television?	Par.7.5			
(49) Is it the case that a radio news programme is not sponsored?	Par.7.6			
Competitions				
(50) Does any competition comply with the sponsorship rules of the BCI General Advertising Code (considered at Questions 45 to 49 above)?	Par.7.7			
(51) Does any competition announcement avoid containing advertising copy, endorsements attributes or a call to action? (Note: A competition announcement may contain a short factual description of a prize)	Par.7.7			
(52) Is it the case that the mechanism used to participate in a competition (i.e. information concerning what the viewer or listener must do to enter and/or win the prize) does not contain **advertising** content?	Par.7.7			
(53) Where a prize is of a monetary value (e.g. vouchers), are the only prices quoted required by statute to be included? (Note: The value may be stated).	Par.7.7			
Section 8 – Rules pertaining to specific products and services				
Financial services and products				
(54) Is the **commercial communication**, if for financial services and products, presented in terms which do not mislead, whether by exaggeration, omission or in any other way?	Par.8.7.1			

(*Continued*)

Query	Source	Yes	No	N/A
(55) Does the **commercial communication**, if for financial services and products, comply with relevant Irish and European legislation and with the rules, regulations and codes of practice issued from time to time by the competent authorities responsible for the implementation of this legislation, in particular the Irish Financial Services Regulatory Authority and the "Director of Consumer Affairs" (now the National Consumer Agency)?	Par.8.7.2			
Betting Services (56) If the **commercial communication** seeks to promote services to those who want to bet, does it contain the address of the service provider and factual descriptions of services available, does it avoid containing anything which could be deemed to be an encouragement to bet, and does it contain no information detailing special offers, discounts, inducements to visit any betting establishment (including on-line), references to betting odds available or any promotional offer intended to encourage the use of services of this nature?	Par.8.8.2			
Premium-rate telecommunications services (57) If the **commercial communication** is for premium-rate telecommunication services, does it state clearly all charges for accessing those services in terms which do not mislead, whether by exaggeration, omission or in any other way?	Par.8.9.1			
(58) Does the **commercial communication** comply with the Code of Practice issued by the Regulator of Premium Rate Telecommunication Services (Regtel) as set down from time to time? (Note: Although the General Advertising Code refers to "all **commercial communications**" in this regard, it presumably intends only to refer to all **commercial communications** concerning, or concerned in part with, premium-rate telecommunications services).	Par.8.9.2			
Section 9 - Prohibited communications (59) Is it the case that the **commercial communication** is not either within the recognised character of, or concerned with the following: an advertisement directed towards a political end or which may have any relation to an industrial dispute?	Par.9			

Appendix E

BCI GENERAL ADVERTISING CODE CHECKLIST DEFINITIONS

In the BCI General Advertising Code, and hence in the preceding checklist, the following terms bear the following meanings:

— **"Advertising"** means "[a]ny form of announcement broadcast in return for payment or for similar consideration or broadcast for self-promotional purposes by a public or private undertaking in accordance with a trade, business, craft or profession in order to promote the supply of products or services, including immovable property, activities, rights and obligations, in return for payment".[1]
(Note: The following announcements do not constitute advertising, namely: "[i] informational announcements about upcoming programmes on broadcast services[2]....[ii] free-of-charge air time given to any registered charity for it to make an appeal....[iii] public service announcements (such as public safety and health announcements) that are not broadcast for payment or similar consideration....[iv] certain information announcements of forthcoming concerts, recitals or performances[3]....[v] announcements of outside broadcasting events or of non-

broadcast events organised in whole or in part by the broadcaster if the public are

---

[1] BCI General Advertising Code, 3.

[2] Such informational announcements may include the date and time of transmission of the named programmes and include 'trailers' and/or a brief description of the content of such programmes. However, they may not contain advertising content; if they do, they will constitute advertising and, depending on the context, may constitute one of the various specific forms of advertising mentioned in the main text above. (BCI General Advertising Code, 5).

[3] I.e. " forthcoming concerts, recitals or performances, whether intended for broadcast or not, given by the National Symphony Orchestra, the RTÉ Concert Orchestra, and other RTÉ performing groups or of any other comparable groups which are employed by or under contract to RTÉ or employed by or under contract to a sound broadcasting contractor or a television broadcasting contractor licensed in the State." (BCI General Advertising Code, 5). The BCI Guidance Notes indicate that the exclusion, from the definition of "advertising", of announcements concerned with the foregoing, applies whether the public is granted free entry, or is required to pay a fee, to view the performance. (BCI Guidance Notes, 7).

[4] BCI General Advertising Code, 5. The BCI General Advertising Code further provides in respect of such announcements that "[i] The broadcaster may credit the sponsor providing the facilities, for example the commercial outlet providing the facilities for the outside broadcast, at the beginning and/or end of the programme and at prudent intervals during the programme on an informational basis....[ii] In the case of non-broadcast events jointly sponsored by the broadcaster and one or more commercial concern, the broadcaster may credit the joint sponsor(s) in broadcast announcements.....[iii] In both of these cases, sponsorship acknowledgements shall comply with the sponsorship rules contained in this code." (BCI General Advertising Code, 5). The BCI Guidance Notes confirm that the exclusion from the definition of "'advertising" of announcements coming within category [v], as referred to in the main text above, only applies where the public are admitted to the relevant event free of charge and does not "extend to paid events including those where the broadcaster has made a contra deal for tickets or other similar commercial promotional arrangements". (BCI Guidance Notes, 8).

[5] BCI General Advertising Code, 3.

allowed entry free of charge)[4];
— the terms "**child**" and "**children**" mean persons under 18 years of age[5];
— "**Commercial communication**" means "[a]ny form of announcement on radio and television coming within the recognised character [presumably the popularly recognised character] of advertising, sponsorship and teleshopping and any other form of commercial communication".[6]
— "**Comparative advertising**" means "[a]dvertising that contains explicit or implicit identification of a competitor or products or services offered by a competitor"[7];
— "**Interactive advertising**" means "[a]n advertising technique which allows the viewer to interact with television by actively choosing the advertising content to which s/he wishes to be exposed for so long as s/he wants. Interactive advertising allows the viewer to provide information directly to the broadcaster/advertiser by means of a return path, and/or participate in an interactive environment which is separate from the broadcast content"[8];
— "**Misleading advertising**" means "[a]dvertising which contains any element of spoken or visual presentation which misleads or is likely to mislead, either directly or by implication, by act or omission, with regard to the merits of the product or service advertised or its suitability for the purpose recommended and which, by reason of its misleading nature, is likely to prejudice the interests of individuals or a competitor"[9];
— "**product placement**" is defined as "[t]he inclusion of, or a reference to, a product or service within a programme in return for payment or similar consideration to the programme maker or broadcaster for the specific purpose of promoting that product or service".[10]
— "**Split-screen advertising**" means "[a]n advertising technique which allows the simultaneous presentation of editorial content and commercial information on the same screen, divided into two or more parts"[11];
— "**Sponsorship**" is defined as "[a]ny contribution made by a public or private undertaking not engaged in television and/or radio broadcasting activities or in the production of audio visual works, to the financing of television and/or radio programmes with a view to promoting its name, its trademark, its image, its activities, its products or its services".[12]
— "**Subliminal advertising**" means "[a]dvertising that includes any technical device which, by using images of very brief duration or by any other means, exploits the possibility of conveying a message to, or otherwise influencing the minds of,

---

[6] *ibid.*
[7] BCI General Advertising Code, 4.
[8] *ibid.*
[9] *ibid.*
[10] *ibid.*
[11] *ibid.*
[12] *ibid.*
[13] *ibid.*

members of an audience without their being aware or fully aware of what has been done"[13];

— **"Surreptitious advertising"** means "[t]he representation in words or pictures of products, services, the name, the trade mark or the activities of a producer of products or a provider of services in programmes when such representation is intended to serve advertising and might mislead the public as to its nature, Such representation is deemed to be intentional if it is done in return for payment or similar consideration"[14];

— **"Teleshopping"** is defined as "[a] direct offer broadcast to the public with a view to the sale, purchase, rental or supply of products or the provision of services, including immovable property, rights and obligations, in return for payment"[15];

— **"Virtual advertising"** means "[a]n advertising technique which allows broadcasters to electronically insert virtual advertising messages or sponsorship announcements into a television programme by altering the broadcast signal itself."[16]

---

[14] *ibid.*
[15] BCI General Advertising Code, 3.
[16] BCI General Advertising Code, 4.

Appendix F

BCI CHILDREN'S ADVERTISING CODE CHECKLIST

The checklist in this Appendix, as compiled by the author of this book, seeks to reduce the BCI Children's Advertising Code, insofar as it is relevant to financial advertisements generally, to a series of questions. The questions have been drafted so that a 'Yes' answer suggests compliance with the BCI Children's Advertising Code and a 'No' answer suggests non-compliance. Certain terms used in the checklist are terms that bear a defined meaning when used in the BCI Children's Advertising Code and when used in this checklist. Where a term used in the checklist is a defined term, it appears in **Bold** format, with the definition appearing in the appendix to the checklist that follows. As discussed in the main text above, the BCI Children's Advertising Code is intended to govern the behaviour of broadcasters and not financial product or service providers (who would not necessarily be able to answer all of the questions in the attached). Even so, it is worth including the attached checklist in this book as a financial advertisement which, when reviewed in light of the attached checklist, appears not to be in compliance with the BCI Children's Advertising Code will most likely not be broadcast by a broadcaster subject to that Code. The checklist is structured as if a **commercial communication** has been or is about to be issued. Given that certain promotions by financial product or service providers may involve the distribution of goods, certain questions related to the distribution of goods (as opposed to financial products or services) have been included.

Query	Source	Yes	No	N/A
1. Social Values				
(1) Does the **children's advertising**: avoid reflecting a range of values which are inconsistent with the moral or ethical standards or diversity of contemporary Irish society; respect human dignity and not discriminate on grounds of gender, marital status, family status, sexual orientation, religion, age, disability, race or membership of the Traveller community; avoid being offensive to religious or political beliefs or encouraging behaviour which is damaging to the environment; and respect the principle of equality and avoid sex stereotyping and any exploitation or the demeaning of men, women or children? ('U/18')	Par.1.1			

(*Continued*)

Query	Source	Yes	No	N/A
2. Inexperience and incredulity (2) Does the **children's advertising** avoid: taking advantage of the natural credulity and sense of loyalty of children; misleading or deceiving or being likely to mislead or deceive children, abuse their trust or exploit their lack of knowledge, whether by implication, omission, ambiguity or exaggerated claim; exploiting or (without justifiable reason) playing on fear? ('U/18')	Par.2.1			
Factual Presentation (3) Does the **children's advertising**: clearly indicate what parts, elements or accessories are included as part of the normal purchase of a product or service and differentiate between those which are only available at extra cost ('U/18'); where it contains on-screen messages and/or 'small print', have on-screen messages and/or 'small print' that are clear, simple and legible and remain on-screen for a sufficient length of time to enable a **child** to read it ('U/15'); give children an indication of the actual size of a product ('U/15'); clearly indicate when a product has to be assembled and what age level is generally required to assemble the product ('U/15'); avoid the use of language, special effects or imaginative scenes which could confuse a **child** or have them believe that a product or service has capabilities or characteristics which it does not have in reality ('U/15'); in the case of toys or children's possessions, not make direct comparisons between existing and 'improved' versions/models of the product that under-15-year-olds could ordinarily be expected to possess, even when the statements or claims are valid ('U/15'); and state orally any on-screen messages or small print in order to ensure that under-six-year-olds understand the message ('U/6')?	Par.2.2			
Price of product/service (4) With regard to how the price of a product or service is presented, are the following rules observed by the **children's advertising**: the price, when given, is in euro and inclusive of VAT or any other extra or related charges ('U/18'); if the price is dependent on the purchase of another item, this is made clear in the advertisement ('U/18'); if there are a number of products in the advertisement and the price of an item or items is highlighted, it is made clear that the price refers to the said item/s only ('U/18'); if the **children's advertising** refers to 'free gifts' or offers, any and all qualifying conditions	Par.2.3			

(Continued)

Query	Source	Yes	No	N/A
are specified ('U/18'); the **children's advertising** does not offer any prizes or rewards to children for attracting new purchasers for the product or service ('U/18'); the price is presented in clear, simple and legible font and, where appropriate, voiced as part of the audio ('U/15'); the language used in presenting the price does not minimise its cost, e.g. through the use of words such as 'only' or 'just' ('U/15')?				
3. Undue Pressure				
(5) Does the **children's advertising** avoid directly encouraging or exhorting children to ask adults to buy them the products or services being advertised ('U/18')?	Par.3.1			
(6) Does the **children's advertising** avoid implying that possession or use of the product or service will make the child or his/her family superior, either physically, socially or psychologically ('U/18')?	Par.3.2			
(7) Does the **children's advertising** avoid implying that the child or his/her family will be inferior or open to ridicule or contempt if they do not possess a particular product/ service and avoid implying also that the product is affordable to all families ('U/18')?	Par.3.3.			
(8) Is the **children's advertising** particularly careful to avoid the implication that possession of a product or service will contribute to or detract from the child's popularity or acquisition of friends ('U/18')?	Par.3.4			
(9) Does the **children's advertising** avoid making a child feel inferior, disloyal, or doubtful about their self-image ('U/18')?	Par.3.5			
4. Special Protection for Children in Advertising				
Children Endorsing Products				
(10) If a **child** is being used to comment on or endorse a product in **children's advertising**, could the products/ services being advertised reasonably be expected to be used by such **child** and would the **child** usually be interested in such products/services themselves ('U/18')?	Par.4.1			
(11) If a **child** appears in **children's advertising** for adult products is the child's appearance a natural element in the depicted environment or necessary to explain or demonstrate the use of the product or services ('U/18')?	Par.4.1			

(Continued)

Query	Source	Yes	No	N/A
Sexualisation of children (12) Does the **children's advertising** avoid portraying a **child** in a sexually provocative manner and avoid provoking bodily anxiety in children over their bodily appearance ('U/18')	Par.4.2			
Privacy and provision of information (13) Does the **children's advertising**: avoid asking children to submit private information or details regarding themselves, their family or friends; or, assuming the advertising is part of a campaign which relates to the safety, health or well-being of children, state, where reasonable, that children must seek adult approval before sending the requested information ('U/18')?	Par.4.3			
Adults pretending to be children (14) If an adult is pretending to be a child in **children's advertising**, does the use of such adult avoid being offensive to the dignity of children ('U/18')?	Par.4.4			
5. General Safety (15) Does the **children's advertising** avoid encouraging children to enter into unsafe situations or strange places or to talk to strangers ('U/18')?	Par.5.1			
(16) Does the **children's advertising** avoid showing children in morally or physically dangerous situations or behaving dangerously in the home or outside, including street and road scenes, except when the sole purpose of the advertisement is to promote safety ('U/18')	Par. 5.2			
(17) Does the **children's advertising** show children using appropriate safety equipment and respecting all applicable safety rules, when engaged in activities that require such and with adult supervision where appropriate, for example, as passengers in vehicles, pedestrians, cyclists, when rollerblading, skateboarding, swimming, watersports or horse riding ('U/18')?	Par.5.3			
(18) Does the **children's advertising** avoid showing children using the internet without appropriate adult supervision ('U/18')	Par.5.4			
(19) Does the **children's advertising** avoid unreasonably showing children using or close to dangerous substances or dangerous equipment (for example, matches, gas appliances, petrol, certain household substances or in possession of, or administering, medicines unless under appropriate supervision) ('U/15')?	Par.5.5			

(Continued)

Query	Source	Yes	No	N/A
Behaviour (20) Does the **children's advertising** avoid encouraging children to engage in, or being portrayed engaging in, anti-social behaviour (in particular, bullying, taunting or teasing other children) unless the sole purpose of the advertisement is to discourage such behaviour ('U/18')	Par.5.6			
(21) Does the **children's advertising** avoid disparaging education or condoning aggression or greed as admirable qualities ('U/18')?	Par.5.7			
6. Violence (22) Does the **children's advertising** avoid including violence or scenes that will cause distress to children ('U/18')?	Par.5.8			
(23) In instances where the inclusion in the **children's advertising** of violent scenes may be necessary as part of a public service message or in order to demonstrate the product, has the broadcaster scheduled responsibly so as to avoid causing distress to under-six year old children ('U/6')?	Par.5.9			
7. Diet and nutrition (24) Is the **children's advertising** responsible in the manner in which food and drink are portrayed and does it avoid encouraging an unhealthy lifestyle or unhealthy eating or drinking habits such as immoderate consumption, excessive or compulsive eating ('U/18')?	Par.7.1			
(25) If the **children's advertising** represents mealtime, does it clearly and adequately depict the role of the product within the framework of a balanced diet ('U/18')?	Par.7.2			
8. Parental Responsibility (26) Does the advertiser support the parent/guardian relationship by scheduling responsibly and by not undermining the authority, responsibility or judgment of parents or guardians in the content of the advertisement (this includes the use of plot lines which encourage children to deceive or manipulate adults into purchasing or providing the product or service advertised), and does the **children's advertising** avoid suggesting that a parent or adult who purchases or provides a product or service for the child is better, more intelligent or more generous than one who does not ('U/18')?	Par.7.3			

(Continued)

Query	Source	Yes	No	N/A
9. Programme characters (27) Is it the case that: in the **children's advertising**, no characters or personalities from children's programmes which are currently broadcast on indigenous services are being used to endorse or advertise products or services (the term 'currently' includes regular programming due for return in the next broadcast season); or, if such characters or personalities are included for such purpose, that the said **children's advertising** is for products, events or services directly associated with programmes in which the characters or personalities normally appear and the advertising is not broadcast for two hours prior to the beginning and following the end of the relevant children's programme ('U/18')?	Par.9.1			
10. Product prohibitions and restrictions ('U/18') (28) Are the prohibitions and restrictions imposed by the BCI General Advertising Code in respect of financial and legal products also observed in respect to the **children's advertising** and are the following additional matters also not advertised in the **children's advertising**: betting and gaming services (apart from the National Lottery) ('U/18')?	Par.10.1			
11. Identification and separation (29) Is the children's advertising clearly distinguishable from programme content with respect to image, text and sound, and does it avoid including excerpts from children's programming which might blur the distinction between advertising and programme content ('U/18')?	Par.11.1			
(30) Is the **children's advertising** clearly separated from programming content and does any broadcaster of same provide a visual or acoustic cue to children during and around children's programming to denote when a commercial break is starting/ending and is such cue not itself sponsored and devoid of advertising material?	Par.11.2			
12. Insertion of Advertising (31) If the **children's advertising** is 'Christmas-themed', is it the case that it will not be broadcast before 1 November of the year of broadcast? ('U/18') ('Christmas-themed' meaning advertising that contains references, either visual or acoustic, to Christmas).	Par.12.1			
(32) If a children's programme is less than 30 minutes scheduled duration, is it the case that it will not be interrupted by advertising?	Par.12.2			

BCI CHILDREN'S ADVERTISING CODE CHECKLIST
DEFINITIONS

In the BCI Children's Advertising Code, and hence in the preceding checklist, the following terms bear the following meanings:

— **"child"** means anyone under 18 years of age[1];
— **"children's advertising"** means "advertising that promotes products, services or activities that are deemed to be of particular interest to children and/or are broadcast during and between children's programmes"[2];
— **"children's programmes"** means "programmes that are commonly referred to as such and/or have an audience profile of which 50 percent are under 18 years of age.[3]

---

[1] BCI Children's Advertising Code, 4.
[2] *ibid.*
[3] *ibid.*

INDEX

non-realisable product, 4–50
'officer', 4–35n
'passporting' institutions and, 4–03
past performance, 4–44, 4–52
'person', 4–35n
position or holding in product, 4–45
prospectuses, 4–18
recognisability, 4–30, 9–51n
recommendations and commendations, 4–34, 4–35
'record', 4–12
'regulated activity', 4–03
'regulated entity', 4–03
regulatory disclosure statement, *see* regulatory disclosure statement
reinsurance, 4–05
reinsurance mediation, 4–05
restriction of duties/liabilities, 4–08
sanctions régime and, 4–01
savings and investments warnings, 4–52
scale and resources of regulated entity, 4–32
scarcity of product/service, 4–32
services, alteration or amendment of, 4–13
simulated performance, 4–46, 4–52
soft commission agreements, 4–13
statutory basis, 4–01
supplementary letters of Financial Regulator, 1–15, 1–15n, 4–01, 4–07, 4–08n, 4–09, 4–24, 4–25
taxation, 4–48
term loans, 4–39
termination of deposit agency, 4–14
terms of business, 4–13, 4–13n
unavailable interest rates, 4–25
voluntary codes and, 4–01
warnings, position and size, *see* Font and footnotes
withdrawal from capital (in lieu of income equivalent), 4–50

Consumer Protection Code Clarifications, 4–01
duplication of warnings, 4–02n
internet address of on-line text, 4–01n
non-binding interpretation of Code, 4–01n

Copyright, 8–05, 8–05n

Credit
advertisement for provision of, 1–07, 1–08
credit advertisement provision and housing loans, *see* Housing loans
definition in Consumer Credit Act, 1–02, 1–05

free credit, *see* Free credit
provision at lower rate than advertised, 1–11
requirement for statement of restrictions on, 1–11

Credit agreement
applicability of Consumer Credit Act, 1–01n

Credit intermediary, *see also* Insurance intermediary, Intermediary
Consumer Protection Code and, 4–25
definition in Consumer Credit Act, 1–24n
liability as regards advertisements, 1–24

Credit union
applicability of Consumer Credit Act, 1–01n, 1–07n
applicability of Consumer Protection Code, 4–05
Credit union legislation, 8–06

Customer, *see* Consumer Protection Code

Data protection, 8–07

Debt consolidation housing loan
interest-only housing loans and, 1–27

Deceit, *see* Tortious liability

Defamation, *see* Tortious liability

Discrimination, *see* Equality
BCI Children's Advertising Code and, 7–09
BCI General Advertising Code and, 6–20

Distance marketing and selling, 8–08
ASAI Code of Standards and, 9–73 to 9–74

Drink driving, 6–24

EAR (equivalent annual rate), *see* AER

EASA, *see* European Advertising Standards Alliance

Endorsements
ASAI Code of Standards and, 9–43
BCI Children's Advertising Code and, 7–14, 7–23

credit and, 1–01, 7–01
definition in BCI General Advertising Code, 6–10
exhortation to purchase, 2–16, *see also* Prohibited commercial practices
sponsorship, 6–40

Misleading advertising, *see also* Misleading and Comparative Marketing Communications, Misleading Commercial Practices
ASAI Code of Standards and, *see* ASAI Code of Standards
BCI Children's Advertising Code and, *see* BCI Children's Advertising Code
BCI General Advertising Code and, *see* BCI General Advertising Code

Misleading and Comparative Marketing Communications, 3–01 to 3–07
comparative advertising, *see* Comparative advertising
'comparative marketing communication', 3–05
deception as to goods, product, trader, 3–04n
code of practice, *see* Codes of practice
confusion among traders, 3–05
definition of 'advertising' in Misleading and Comparative Advertising Directive, *see* Advertisement
'goods', 3–03n
internet address of on-line text, 3–01n
'marketing communication', 3–01, 3–03
'misleading marketing communication', 3–04, 3–04n
misleading advertising, 3–01, 6–07
misleading and comparative advertising, 3–01
Misleading and Comparative Marketing Communications Directive, 3–01
overlap with Consumer Protection Act, 3–07
'product', 3–03
prohibited 'comparative marketing communication', 3–05
prohibited misleading commercial practice, *see* Misleading commercial practices
remedies, 3–06
'representation', 3–03
'services', 3–05
trade marks, trade names and other marks, 3–05
'trader' 3–02

Misleading commercial practices
advertising as, advertising as, 2–08 to 2–09

concealment or omission of 'material information', 2–11
Consumer Protection Act, 2–06 to 2–14
elements of, 2–06, 2–07, 2–07n
invitations to purchase, 2–12, 2–16
'material information', 2–12, 2–12n, 2–13
ministerial regulations, 2–14
Misleading and Comparative Marketing Communications Regulations, 3–05

Misrepresentation, 8–12

Mortgage
fixed and floating-rate mortgage loan warnings, 4–41
increased repayments warning, 4–41
interest-only mortgage warning, 4–41
lifetime mortgage, 4–15n
lifetime mortgage warnings, 4–15, 4–16

Mortgage agent, 1–17
definition in Consumer Credit Act, 1–17n
direction under s 135 of Consumer Credit Act, *see* Section 135 Directions
endowment loan warning, *see* Endowment loans
housing loan warnings, *see* Housing loans

Mortgage intermediary
definition in Consumer Credit Act, 1–17n

Mortgage lender, 1–01
definition in Consumer Credit Act, 1–17n

Multiplexes, 5–02n

National Consumer Agency, 5–17
application in respect of prohibited act or practice, 2–18
review of industry codes of practice, 2–10n
undertakings as to future behaviour, 2–18

National Lottery, *see* Betting

Parental responsibility, 7–04, 7–22, 9–75, 9–76

Passing off, *see* Tortious liability
ASAI Code of Standards and imitation, 9–50

Politics, *see also* Religion, politics and industrial disputes
prohibited communications, 6–46, 6–46n

Index

consultation regarding legislation a political matter, 5–17
religious ceremony, 5–16
religious newspaper/magazine/periodical, 5–16

Residential mortgage credit, *see* Section 135 directions

RTÉ
establishment of, 5–02
maximum advertising time, 5–04
multiplexes, *see* Multiplexes
'programme material', *see* Broadcasting legislation

Safety
ASAI Code of Standards and, 9–40, 9–58
BCI Children's Advertising Code and, 7–18, 7–18n
BCI General Advertising Code and health and safety, 6–20
Personal security, 2–16n

Sale of goods and supply of services, 8–13

Scheduling
BCI Children's Advertising Code and, 7–05, 7–22
BCI General Advertising Code and, 6–20, 6–21

Section 135 directions, 1–25 to 1–27
Direction effective 24 March 1997, 1–26
Direction effective 1 January 2007, 1–27
meaning of 'residential mortgage credit', 1–26n
meaning of 'debt consolidation housing loans' 1–27n
text required in billboard, radio and television advertisements, 1–26

Security
statement that security required, 1–11

Social values
ASAI Code of Standards and, 9–33, 9–34
BCI Children's Advertising Code and, 7–09, 7–19, 7–22

Sound effects
BCI General Advertising Code and, 6–15, 6–15n

Split-screen advertising
BCI General Advertising Code and, 6–07, 6–07n, 6–36, 6–36n

Sponsorship
BCI General Advertising Code and, 6–39
competitions and, *see* Competitions
definition in BCI General Advertising Code, 6–10, 6–39, 6–40
editorial influence of sponsors, 6–26, 6–26n
endorsements and, *see* Endorsements
entertainment programmes and, 6–40
minors and, *see* Minors
news programmes and, 6–40
politics programmes and, 6–40
prohibited products and, 6–40
regulatory disclosure statement and, 4–09
religious programmes and, 6–40
religious service and, 6–40
traffic news and, 6–40
weather programmes and, 6–40

Spread-betting, *see* Betting

Statutory rights
BCI General Advertising Code and, 6–26

Subliminal advertising
BCI General Advertising Code and, 6–07, 6–07n, 6–35

Surreptitious advertising, *see also* Product placement
BCI General Advertising Code and, 6–07, 6–07n, 6–35
product placement as, 6–32

Teilifís na Gaeilge, 5–08
advertising on, 5–09
maximum advertising time, 5–04
religion, politics and industrial disputes, 5–09, 5–16 to 5–22

Teleshopping, 5–03, 5–08, 5–11
BCI General Advertising Code and, 6–38
definition in BCI General Advertising Code, 6–10

Television advertisements
lifetime mortgages warnings, 4–15, 4–16
sponsorship, *see* Sponsorship